The Hessian mercenary state

Hesse-Cassel under Frederick II.

The Hessian mercenary state

Ideas, institutions, and reform under Frederick II, 1760–1785

Charles W. Ingrao

Purdue University

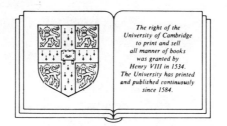

The right of the
University of Cambridge
to print and sell
all manner of books
was granted by
Henry VIII in 1534.
The University has printed
and published continuously
since 1584.

Cambridge University Press

Cambridge

London   New York   New Rochelle
Melbourne   Sydney

Published by the Press Syndicate of the University of Cambridge
The Pitt Building, Trumpington Street, Cambridge CB2 1RP
32 East 57th Street, New York, NY 10022, USA
10 Stamford Road, Oakleigh, Melbourne 3166, Australia

First published 1987

Printed in the United States of America

Library of Congress Cataloging-in-Publication Data
Ingrao, Charles W.
The Hessian mercenary state.
Bibliography: p.
Includes index.
1. Hesse (Germany) – History – Landgraviate, 1567–1806.
2. Frederick II, Landgrave of Hesse-Kassel, 1720–1785.
I. Title.
DD801.H57I54   1987   943'.41053   86–8274

British Library Cataloguing in Publication Data
Ingrao, Charles W.
The Hessian mercenary state: ideas,
institutions, and reform under Frederick II,
1760–1785.
1. Hesse-Kassel (Germany) – History
I. Title
943'.41053   DD801.H57

ISBN 0 521 32756 3

To my wife
Kathleen Beloin Ingrao

Contents

Tables and figures

Acknowledgments

The last task in writing a book is to acknowledge the help of those individuals and institutions who assisted in the project. It is impossible to research and write a scholarly work without incurring such debts, both to those individuals and institutions whose publications appear in the notes and bibliography and to those whose names do not. It is, however, one chore that I have looked forward to during each of these last seven years.

I received considerable financial support from a number of sources. A grant from the Deutsche Akademische Austauschdienst (DAAD) enabled me to begin the project during the summer of 1979. A fellowship from the Alexander von Humboldt Foundation funded three subsequent research trips during 1980, 1982, and 1985. In the end its assistance extended far beyond monetary support to virtually every consideration one could imagine of a funding institution. The American Philosophical Society provided travel funds for the summers of 1979 and 1982. Finally, a Purdue University XL grant allowed me to devote the summer of 1983 to the project.

No less important were the great number of individuals who offered me their help at various stages of the research. As my sponsor for both the DAAD and Humboldt Foundation, Karl Otmar Freiherr von Aretin gave me much valuable advice, not the least of which was his suggestion that I focus my study on Frederician Hesse-Cassel. The staff of the Hessisches Staatsarchiv in Marburg reminded me in a multitude of ways of my good fortune in doing research at Germany's main archive school; in their readiness to answer my questions, Drs. Gerhard Menk and Fritz Wolff were especially helpful. Through the outstanding hospitality and facilities it offered my family, the *Universitätsgästehaus* of the University of Marburg was also instrumental in providing an ideal research environment. In Vienna, the director of the Haus- Hof- und Staatsarchiv, Dr.

Anna Hedwig Benna, was every bit as forthcoming as she had been ten years earlier when I first approached her as a graduate student working on Emperor Joseph I. Nor will I soon forget my guided tour of Cassel's *Stadtmuseum*, during which Manfred Söder supplemented my research with several bits of information that are unavailable in the published literature.

Ruth Rothenberg and her colleagues at Purdue's Interlibrary Loan Department were persistent and usually successful in obtaining titles from other American libraries. My colleague Richard Haywood complemented their work by ordering the microfilming of scores of rare books for the Purdue University Library, requisitions that were filled with unfailing regularity by Annemarie Mauersberger and her staff at the *Mikrostelle* of the University of Marburg Library. Gregory Pedlow and Gerald Soliday were generous in filling in gaps in my statistical data. Graduate students Scott Meiller and Paul Lockhart spent many hours entering and correlating the data in the random sample of Hessian desertions mentioned in Chapter 5, note 136.

Barbara Tuchman is doubtless correct in stating that research is endlessly enticing but writing is hard work. My colleague Mark Edwards helped reduce that burden by introducing me to the world of computers and word processing. Without his help I would have begun writing this book a year earlier – but doubtless finished it much later than I did. Once the manuscript was completed it benefited from the criticism of several of my colleagues, all of whom volunteered (at least in the Hessian sense of the word) to read it. Donald Berthrong, G. Thomas Fox, Paul Lockhart, Karl Roider, Gerald Soliday, Garry Stice, and the late James Vann read parts or all of the manuscript.

To all these people and the many others who assisted me I express my sincere appreciation. Finally, I would like to reserve a special word of thanks to my wife, Kathleen, and my two children, Kate and Chris. If they ever read this book, which I daresay is unlikely, they will doubtless see certain parallels between these last six years and the cameralist *Polizeistaat* that I describe. After having dragged them across the Atlantic three times in five years and subjected them all to the demands and discipline that were necessary to complete this project, I can only express my gratitude that not one of them ever considered deserting.

CHARLES W. INGRAO

West Lafayette, Indiana

Abbreviations of source names

Journals

AHR	*The American Historical Review*
HB	*Hessische Beiträge*
HJLG	*Hessisches Jahrbuch für Landesgeschichte*
HLO	*Sammlung fürstlich hessischer Landesordnungen*
HZ	*Historische Zeitschrift*
JMH	*The Journal of Modern History*
Mitt	*Mitteilungen an die Mitglieder des Vereins für hessische Geschichte und Landeskunde*
SAK	*Fürstlich hessen-casselscher Staats- und Adresskalender*
ZHG	*Zeitschrift des Vereins für hessiche Geschichte und Landeskunde*

Archives

AAE	Archives des Affaires Etrangères, Paris
CP	Correspondance Politique
HC	Hesse-Cassel
HHStA	Haus- Hof- und Staatsarchiv, Vienna
PRO	Public Record Office, London
RK	Reichskanzlei
StAMg	Hessisches Staatsarchiv, Marburg

Government bureaus

AW	Armen- und Waisenhaus Direktion
GD	General Direktorium
GR	Geheime Rat
KDK	Kriegs- und Domänenkammer
Reg	Regierung (Cassel)
SK	Steuerkolleg

Hesse-Cassel and the problem of enlightened absolutism

And you betrayed people, oppressed, sold, humiliated by your fate: open your eyes, quit this country sullied by despotism, cross the ocean, flee to America. Embrace your brothers, defend that noble nation against the arrogant greed of its oppressors!'

With these words Gabriele Riquetti, comte de Mirabeau, appealed to the Hessian people and their American expeditionary force to abandon the petty despotism of Landgrave Frederick II (1760–85). In the two centuries since, Hesse-Cassel and its ruler have retained a certain notoriety that has become a part of the popular mythology of the American Revolution. In the United States, historians have moved little from the image first projected by Mercy Otis Warren of the Hessians as "barbarous strangers" who committed atrocities against the American freedom fighters but were themselves the "slaves" of a typically greedy and corrupt European despot. Recent American scholars have been somewhat more sympathetic to the mercenaries themselves, portraying them as naive and oppressed peasants, "simple farming people" who were either unwilling or unknowing pawns of their sovereign.[2] There has, however, been no revision in their view of the regime that first dispatched them to America. Until this century the landgrave's reputation has suffered from the Uriasbrief that he purportedly wrote to his field commander Baron Hohendorff, decrying the death of "only" 1,465 of his subjects at Trenton because the British paid him appreciably more for soldiers killed in action than for those who were merely wounded or captured, and suggesting that in

---

'Gabriele Riquetti, comte de Mirabeau, *Avis aux Hessois et autres peuples de l'Allemagne vendus par leurs Princes à l'Angleterre* (Cleves, 1777), 15.
[2]Mercy Otis Warren, *History of the Rise, Progress and Termination of the American Revolution*, 1 (Boston, 1805), 278, 283; Don Higginbotham, *The War of American Independence* (New York, 1971), 131; John R. Alden, *The American Revolution, 1775–1783* (New York, 1954), 67.

the future his soldiers emulate the heroism of the Spartans who fought at Thermopylae.[3] Today American historians still portray him as a greedy "petty despot" who sought British subsidies in order to finance a decadent court life and the needs of his one hundred bastard offspring.[4]

If the Frederician legend has prospered in the New World, it survived until recently in the Old, nourished as it was by a separate cultural and political agenda. British scholars have been scarcely more charitable in their portrayal of the landgrave, having taken their cue from the reports of royal ministers and diplomats who had turned against him after his conversion to Catholicism and the resulting breakup of his marriage to George II's daughter Mary. Until recently the numerous slanders they spread about him have been generally accepted as fact and have helped to perpetuate his unsavory image among some British historians. Indeed, Frederick's Catholicism and preference for French culture also made him a pariah among nineteenth-century German historians who, as liberals and nationalists, were especially eager to discredit the Hessian dynasty's later opposition to constitutional government and German unification. To prepare the way for Bismarck's annexation of Hesse-Cassel they resurrected the *Uriasbrief* and publicized Frederick's use of a "chattel fund" (*Schattulkasse*) in which he deposited his enormous earnings from the mercenary trade for his own personal use.[5]

Only within this century has Frederick been rehabilitated within Germany as well as among British and American scholars acquainted with the German sources. There is, in fact, a consensus among modern Hessian scholars that the mercenaries were not the downtrodden and reluctant warriors or the monarch who dispatched them the oppressive despot we had supposed. Frederick never wrote a *Uriasbrief*, although there were

[3]Philipp Losch, *Soldatenhandel* (Kassel, 1974), 37–55, and "Der Uriasbrief des Grafen von Schaumburg. Zur Geschichte der öffentlichen Meinung über den sogenannten Soldatenhandel," *Hessische Chronik*, 2 (1913), 37–40, 83–8, 99–105; W. Grotefend, "Ein gefälschter Brief," *Hessenland*, 14 (1900), 70–1.
[4]Higginbotham, *The War of American Independence*, 130–1; Alden, *The American Revolution*, 66-7; Edward Jackson Lowell, *The Hessians and the Other German Auxiliaries of Great Britain in the Revolutionary War* (New York, 1884), 5; James Kirby Martin and Mark Edward Lender, *A Respectable Army: The Military Origins of the Republic, 1763–1789* (Arlington Heights, Ill., 1982), 50.
[5]Franz Piderit, *Geschichte der Grafschaft Schaumburg* (Rinteln, 1831), 159; Friedrich Kapp, *Der Soldatenhandel deutscher Fürsten nach Amerika* (Berlin, 1874), 50; Heinrich von Treitschke, *Das neunzehnte Jahrhundert*, 3 (Leipzig, 1889), 520–1; Robert Friderici, "'Juchheisa nach Amerika.' Haben die hessischen Landgrafen ihre Truppen verkauft?" *Kasseler Post*, 22, 23, 29, 30 December 1951; Karl E. Demandt, *Geschichte des Landes Hessen* (Cassel, 1972), 279.

several copies of the infamous letter – all of them penned and distributed by Benjamin Franklin from his post in Paris. There was never a "Baron Hohendorff," a "blood money" clause in the Anglo-Hessian subsidy treaty, or 1,465 Hessian dead at Trenton (where only about twenty were killed). The landgrave also had few, if any, bastards and no separate treasury from which to support them. In short, the Frederician legend arose and has survived this long principally because it conformed comfortably to the cultural prejudices and mythologies of those who accepted and perpetuated it as fact.[6]

This book will present a more complex and balanced, though not altogether positive, view of the Frederician regime that dispatched 19,000 of its soldiers to America. By itself the need to revise the standard American interpretation might justify such an undertaking, especially given the unfamiliarity of native historians of the American Revolution with the German-language scholarship. This book is, however, aimed primarily at European historians and a second issue that, much like the Anglo-American acceptance of the Frederician legend, involves the interplay of historical analysis with deeply ingrained cultural prejudices.

Among early modern historians few controversies have endured so long and resolved so little as the ongoing debate over what has come to be known as enlightened absolutism. In examining and analyzing the judgments of those scholars who have engaged in it, it is difficult to avoid the conclusion that the task of reaching a consensus has been complicated by an underlying clash of national cultural and historical perspectives, a cleavage that has pitted German historians against the majority of their

---

[6]This century's revision of Frederician legend can be traced through the works of Carl Preser, *Der Soldatenhandel in Hessen. Versuch einer Abrechnung* (Marburg, 1900), 1–8; Hugo Brunner, *Geschichte der Residenzstadt Cassel* (Cassel, 1913), 301; Leo Just, "Der aufgeklärte Absolutismus," in *Handbuch der deutschen Geschichte*, 2 (Stuttgart, 1938), 98; Ernst Kipping, *Die Truppen von Hessen-Kassel im amerikanischen Unabhängigkeitskrieg 1776–1783* (Darmstadt, 1965), and *The Hessian View of America* (Monmouth Beach, N.J., 1971); Wolf von Both and Hans Vogel, *Landgraf Friedrich II. von Hessen-Kassel. Ein Fürst der Zopfzeit* (Munich, 1973); Max von Eelking, *Die deutschen Hülfstruppen im nordamerikanischen Befreiungskriege 1776 bis 1783* (Cassel, 1976), 21; Staatliche Kunstsammlungen Kassel, *Aufklärung & Klassizismus in Hessen-Kassel unter Landgraf Friedrich II. 1760–1785* (Kassel, 1979). Modern German criticism of Frederick has been limited to Karl Demandt's more muted observation that Frederick's reign marks the beginning of the "degeneration" of the Hessian dynasty; *Geschichte des Landes Hessen*, 279. For Anglo-American revisions see Rodney Atwood, *The Hessians: Mercenaries from Hessen-Kassel in the American Revolution* (Cambridge, 1980); Charles Ingrao, "'Barbarous Strangers': Hessian State and Society during the American Revolution," *AHR*, 87 (1982), 954-76, from which a few brief passages have been employed in this volume.

colleagues from France, Great Britain, and the United States.[7] On the one hand German historians, from Wilhelm Roscher and Fritz Hartung to such leading contemporary scholars as Karl Otmar von Aretin, Rudolf Vierhaus, and Eberhard Weis, have generally embraced the notion of *aufgeklärter Absolutismus* by arguing that most rulers were both benevolent and influenced to varying degrees by Enlightenment ideas.[8] Yet, in their haste to endorse the record and utterances of Frederick the Great, they have never attempted to reconcile the blatant militarism and cynical foreign policy of this paradigm of enlightened absolutism with the humanitarian ethos of the Enlightenment.

At the same time, the rest of the Western community has exhibited its own cultural biases in rejecting the concept of enlightened absolutism. In a modern age of brutal authoritarian regimes we have been inclined to argue the incompatibility of humanitarian motives and Enlightenment notions of human freedom with absolute rule, even though most of the philosophes themselves readily embraced the utility of having strong monarchs.[9] We have also tended to judge their rule by standards that even our own presumably more benevolent regimes cannot meet. Hence, in an age that has witnessed the steady growth of government, we have dismissed even the most humanitarian domestic reforms with the rejoinder that they were merely by-products of the state-building process. We

[7]This is not the place for a full-length review or analysis of the enlightened despotism debate. I have attempted to present a more comprehensive treatment in "Enlightened Absolutism and the German States," *JMH*, 58 (1986), from which a small portion of this text has been taken.

[8]For the most notable German proponents, see Wilhelm Roscher, *Geschichte der National-Oekonomik in Deutschland* (Munich, 1874), 380–1; Fritz Hartung, "Die Epochen der absoluten Monarchie in der neueren Geschichte," *HZ*, 145 (1932), 46–52, and *Enlightened Despotism* (London, 1957); Leo Just, "Der aufgeklärte Absolutismus," 1–126; Ernst Walder, "Zwei Studien über den aufgeklärten Absolutismus," *Schweizer Beiträge zur allgemeinen Geschichte*, 15 (1957), 136; Karl Otmar Freiherr von Aretin, ed., *Der aufgeklärte Absolutismus* (Cologne, 1974), 14; Eberhard Weis, "Absolute Monarchie und Reform im Deutschland des späten 18. und des frühen 19. Jahrhunderts," in *Geschichte in der Gesellschaft. Festschrift für Karl Bosl* (Stuttgart, 1974), 438–43; Rudolf Vierhaus, "Deutschland im 18. Jahrhundert," in Franklin Kopitsch, ed., *Aufklärung, Absolutismus, und Bürgertum in Deutschland* (Munich, 1976), 182–3.

[9]See Georges Lefebvre, "Enlightened Despotism," in Heinz Lubasz, ed., *The Development of the Modern State* (New York, 1964), 53; Alfred Cobban, *In Search of Humanity* (New York, 1960), 161-7; Robert Darnton, "In Search of Enlightenment: Recent Attempts to Create a Social History of Ideas," *JMH*, 43 (1971), 122; Peter Gay, *The Enlightenment: An Interpretation* (New York, 1967–9), 2: 494–6; Helen P. Liebel, "Enlightened Despotism and the Crisis of Society in Germany," *Enlightenment Essays*, 1 (1970), 168; Leonard Krieger, *An Essay on the Theory of Enlightened Despotism* (Chicago, 1975), 20–3, 42–3, and *Kings and Philosophers 1689–1789* (New York, 1970), 253–4.

have also criticized the primary importance the monarchs attached to the military and to foreign policy as evidence of their lack of commitment to the public welfare – forgetting, it would seem, that ours, like all modern societies, has usually established the same priorities.[10] Finally, in a world in which the dramatic restructuring of institutions usually comes only with war or revolution, we have stressed nonetheless that the monarchs' domestic reforms were often little more than cosmetic.[11]

In recent years increasing numbers of American and British historians have begun to accept the notion of enlightened absolutism and to attribute Enlightenment ideas and benevolent motives to the princes. They have also begun to identify the presence of strong internal opposition to change from various groups such as the church, nobility, bureaucracy, or even the general population that limited the princes' ability to initiate sweeping reform and to tear down the anachronistic structures of the Old Regime.[12] Under the impact of this research it has become more evident that the philosophes' (and especially the Physiocrats') vision of an all-powerful *despote juste et éclairé* was a utopian one that in all probability had been hewn from the Ludovican paradigm of absolutism of which all Frenchmen were aware but which was no longer a reality anywhere in Europe during

[10]Liebel, "Enlightened Despotism," 164; John Gagliardo, *Enlightened Despotism* (New York, 1967), 66–8, 81, 83, 86-7; Reinhold Dorwart, *The Prussian Welfare State before 1740* (Cambridge, Mass., 1971), 19–20; Isser Woloch, *Eighteenth-Century Europe. Tradition and Progress, 1715–1789* (New York, 1982), 250; Paul Hazard, *European Thought in the Eighteenth Century* (New York, 1963), 329–30; Roland Mousnier, *Histoire générale des civilisations*, 5: *Le xviiie siècle* (Paris, 1953), 173; François Bluche, *Le Despotisme éclairé* (Saint Amand, 1968), 331–3. Led by a number of French historians, several scholars have explained the monarchs' policies solely as a remedial attempt to emulate and compete with Ludovican France. Lefebvre, "Enlightened Despotism," 58; Charles Morazé, "Finance et despotisme, essai sur les despotes éclairés," *Annales Économies, Sociétés, Civilisations*, 3 (1948), 279–82, 293–6; Michel L'Héritier, "Le role historique du despotisme éclairé, particulièrement au 18e siècle," in *Bulletin of the International Committee of Historical Sciences*, 1 (1928), 601–12; Mousnier, "Quelques problèmes concernant le monarchie absolue," in *Relazioni del X° congresso internazionale di scienze storiche*, 4: *Storia moderna* (Florence, 1955), 17; Bluche, *Despotisme eclairé*, 354; George Matthew Dutcher, "The Enlightened Despotism," *The Annual Report of the AHA for the Year 1920*, 189–98, and "Further Considerations on the Origins and Nature of Enlightened Despotism," in *Persecution and Liberty. Essays in Honor of George Lincoln Burr*, 375–403; M. S. Anderson, *Europe in the Eighteenth Century* (London, 1961), 122–3; Ernst Wangermann, *From Joseph II to the Jacobin Trials* (Oxford, 1969), 2–3.
[11]Gagliardo, *Enlightened Despotism*, 65; Raymond Birn, *Crisis, Absolutism, Revolution: Europe 1648–1789/91* (Hinsdale, Ill., 1977), 240. Helen Liebel goes even further by arguing that the rulers actually went out of their way to perpetuate the old system and that "the effect of their work was to impede the modernization of their societies." "Enlightened Despotism," 168.
[12]See Hamish M. Scott, "Whatever [*sic*] Happened to the Enlightened Despots?" *History*, 68 (1983), 245–57.

the remainder of the prerevolutionary era. Enlightened absolutism as the philosophes envisioned it could never exist, even if the rulers were enlightened, because they were simply not "absolute."

Of course, the question remains exactly how "enlightened" these rulers would have been had they not been constrained by the competing priorities of foreign policy and the opposition of entrenched or broadly based popular forces. The German states provide us with an ideal opportunity to answer that question. Until recently one of the regrettable oversights in the debate over enlightened absolutism has been the almost total neglect of the smaller European states, and especially the German principalities, in favor of the "big three" of Austria, Prussia, and Russia. This is particularly unfortunate since both advocates and critics of enlightened absolutism – though often dismissing the principalities either because they were too small to indicate feasibility or because they never faced the same problems as larger states – have conceded that it was precisely there that enlightened government functioned best. This neglect is especially ironic because such philosophes as Montesquieu, Voltaire, and Rousseau specifically expressed a preference for smaller states as more efficient and responsive to the popular welfare.[13]

In several respects the German states offered a more favorable environment for enlightened absolutism than the great powers. Above all they were rarely distracted by foreign-policy considerations. Indeed, the concept of the "incubator," so profitably employed by Mack Walker as a metaphor for the insularity of German community life within the empire,[14] can also help us to comprehend the insulation of the German principalities from the dynamics of power politics. The empire not only provided military security for the smaller states (thereby solving what the philosophes foresaw as the primary disadvantage of small states) and predisposed them toward a working interstate community that opposed aggression; more important, it permitted them to concentrate on domestic policy – without eliciting the rejoinder of modern-day skeptics that these monarchs were also impelled by foreign-policy considerations. The pro-

---

[13]Eduard Sieber, *Die Idee des Kleinstaates bei den Denkern des 18. Jahrhunderts in Frankreich und Deutschland* (Freiburg, 1920), 7–10, 15, 25–6. The Physiocrats, however, felt that larger states could promote economic prosperity more effectively; see Sieber, 39–40.
[14]Walker, *German Home Towns. Community, State, and General Estate, 1648–1871* (Ithaca, 1971), 11–13.

- tection afforded by the empire also permitted the princely regimes to
- eschew centralization to the extent that it was pursued by the great
powers, thereby sparing them the otherwise inevitable clash with the
estates that generally characterized crown-country relations elsewhere.

If the dynamics of the German "incubator" are useful to the historian
of enlightened absolutism, so is the smaller size of the principalities.
Whereas the larger states were generally oblivious of conditions in the
smaller European states, the German principalities constantly examined
and readily emulated their neighbors, both large and small. As a result
they served as fertile ground for transplanting the ideas and reform projects of other regimes, providing the opportunity for numerous pilot projects, the results of which could be made known to neighboring states
through the medium of Germany's extensive list of political and public
affairs journals. Because of their smaller size, the principalities were also
subject to fewer intermediary levels of provincial estates or administrative
offices that might defuse, dilute, or divert the primary reform objectives
of the sovereign authority. Similarly, the petty princes could devote
greater attention to the local application of their initiatives without the
resulting loss of overall perspective or effectiveness that afflicted their
Prussian and Austrian counterparts. They could afford their subjects
greater sensitivity and closer contact, an ideal envisioned by the philosophes, and one that made for closer, more amicable cooperation with
the existing corporate bodies in the execution of government programs.[5]
Finally, the existence of Germany's *Kleinstaaterei* was also responsible
for another indispensable component of enlightened government within
the empire, namely the great proliferation of universities and their close
association with their governments and the reforms they initiated.

In view of the reputed advantages that the German states enjoyed over
the major powers, Hesse-Cassel would appear an unlikely choice for a
study of enlightened absolutism. Although there is no such thing as a
typical German state, it was clearly *atypical* in its maintenance of a large
standing army and involvement in the European mercenary trade. Nevertheless, even if the heavy emphasis it placed on the military hardly cor-

---

[5]Charles Ingrao, "Barbarous Strangers," 960–7; Marc Raeff, "The Well-Ordered Police
State and the Development of Modernity in Seventeenth- and Eighteenth-Century Europe:
An Attempt at a Comparative Approach," *AHR*, 80 (1975), 1227–8, and *The Well-
Ordered Police State. Social and Institutional Change through Law in the Germanies and
Russia 1600–1800* (New Haven and London, 1983), 46.

responds to our ideal perception of enlightened government, it is at worst a mixed blessing that offers tangible advantages for the study of domestic policy within Germany. Choosing the German principalities as a model for the study of enlightened absolutism is not wholly without its drawbacks. Given their smaller size, their financial resources were usually barely enough to provide for a separate court, administration, university, and modest military establishment, thereby limiting their ability to pursue expensive domestic programs. Furthermore, because they did not maintain standing armies, most of the German dynasties had never been pressed to eliminate the corporate constitutional privileges that obtained in the typical *Ständestaat*. Indeed, their reliance on the estates to fund existing expenditures afforded the estates the leverage they needed to preserve their often formidable position within the state. Thus, unlike many of their larger neighbors, the princes were obliged to work with their territorial estates and were generally more vulnerable to corporate opposition to controversial domestic reforms.

Yet this was not the case in Hesse-Cassel. Though it did maintain a large army for its size, Hesse-Cassel – like the other principalities – did not entertain an independent foreign policy that could compete against or influence the thrust of domestic policy. At the same time, however, the highly profitable *Soldatenhandel* afforded the Hessian landgraves both the financial and constitutional resources to launch domestic programs of their own choosing, regardless of expense or the opposition of the estates. In fact, the crown was actually able to use the money earned from its trade in mercenaries to seduce the estates into actively cooperating with its military and domestic policies. Thus, Hesse-Cassel presents us with the opportunity to study the path of princely reform in a setting free of the complications posed by foreign-policy influences, yet without sacrificing the financial and constitutional leverage of a more powerful monarch. Its unique circumstances permit us to discard the formula to which critics of the notion of enlightened absolutism have sometimes attributed progressive reform:

Reforms → Economic → Increased → Larger → Achievement
                 growth   revenue   army   of foreign-
                                                                          policy
                                                                          objectives[16]

[16]Such as Roland Mousnier, who states flatly that "the sovereign's goal was simply [to increase] state power in order to dominate, invade and dismember" neighboring countries

Indeed, for such a sequence to have any utility it becomes necessary to reverse it. In Hesse-Cassel diplomacy was essentially a first step toward enlarging the army, in order to attract subsidies that would increase both state and private revenue, thus providing the government with funds that could be invested either in economic growth or in reform programs.

Of course, Hesse-Cassel was not without its own peculiar circumstances that limited what government could undertake or accomplish. The Seven Years' War devastated the country and preoccupied the Hessian regime for a decade. Though initially created for national defense and expanded for economic reasons, the large Hessian army – like all established institutions – enjoyed a life and ethic of its own that helped shape the thrust of government policy in many areas. The repercussions of Frederick II's ill-fated conversion to Roman Catholicism limited his flexibility, especially in religious matters. Finally, like all but the largest German states, Hesse-Cassel was obliged to contend with the problems posed by the Holy Roman Empire, which may have served as an "incubator" in a cultural and political sense, but which proved to be an economic straitjacket whose trade barriers stymied commercial and industrial growth.

Nor was it immune from more serious limitations that were endemic to reforming governments throughout the Continent. Indeed, exposing the cultural prejudices of those who have condemned both enlightened absolutism and the Frederician regime does not, by itself, justify an apology for either. The generally positive portrait of the Hessian landgrave and his government that emerges from this study is not altogether unqualified. Rather, the findings are mixed. Yes, it is possible to identify Enlightenment influences in domestic policymaking, especially in the fields of education and justice, as well as in the government's support for the maintenance of at least limited intellectual, religious, and economic freedom. It is also true that all levels of the regime from the prince down to the lowest levels of the bureaucracy saw themselves as the agents of a new age of Enlightenment and were sincerely motivated by the desire to serve what they saw as the popular welfare. Nevertheless, it is equally

(*Histoire générale des civilisations*, 173); or Helen Liebel, who writes that "The ruler himself ... would personally have to ... see to the encouragement of industry and agriculture, promotion of the general welfare, and ... prosperity of his lands. In this way he would be assured a steady revenue, a full war chest. Thus enabled to maintain a substantial army, he would be assured of his absolute power and then, by using it, lead his nation to glory." "Enlightened Despotism," 164.

clear that the Physiocrats' vision of *despotisme légal* as the ideal tool for a radical transformation of society was a utopian one, that government was far more limited than they imagined, that the regimes themselves were hampered by more than just the competing demands of national security, or by constitutional and fiscal restraints on their authority.

Above all, the society itself was simply less dissatisfied and desperate for change than it was in France. Within Hesse, as in most of Europe, the institutions of the Old Regime had not discredited themselves to the extent that they had in France, where under Louis XIV the monarchy had become tainted by despotism, the military by senseless wars of aggression, the church by obscurantism and intolerance, and the nobility by the loss of any meaningful role in society. Even within the ranks of the intelligentsia there was a basic complacency and acceptance of the status quo, together with confidence that progress could be effected by working within the existing system. Largely as a result the Enlightenment constructs of the philosophes had to compete with preexisting ideas and values, as well as entrenched institutions and vested interests that reshaped and frequently defused their abstract notions of social and economic reform. It is worth mentioning at the outset that no single component in the mind-set of the Hessian ruling elite was more pervasive than its commitment to cameralism and the social benefits of a thoroughly integrated system of *Polizei.* Although cameralism was by no means wholly incompatible with Enlightenment currents, it selectively co-opted those of its ideas that it found most useful, much as it had done with the underlying Protestant values and militarist ethos it encountered in Hessian society. In fact, it is clear that if absolutism in Hesse-Cassel was "enlightened" it was so principally in a broadly utilitarian way that embraced a host of ethical philosophies of which the Enlightenment was only one. It is in this broader sense only that it is possible to speak meaningfully of "enlightened" government in Hesse-Cassel, and it is in this sense that I will employ the term in this book.

It will, then, be a principal goal of this study to profile the mind-set of the government as it formulated and implemented policies that reflected the interplay of different cultural parameters and institutions that predetermined both the extent and limits of reform. It will also attempt to trace the formulation of individual initiatives to their sources. Notwithstanding the original conceptualization of the philosophes and the perception of many historians, enlightened government was rarely the work of a single man. Domestic reform in Hesse-Cassel was clearly the creation of all components of the ruling elite, including the social groups represented in the Hessian diet. Finally, this book will study the relative effectiveness of government policy in attaining the goals it sought to achieve through its domestic initiatives. It will, in fact, do more than demonstrate the difficulties in integrating new currents of thought, such as Enlightenment constructs, with existing values and institutions. To an even greater extent it will lay bare the profound obstacles involved in the implementation of cameralist *Polizei*.

Such an analysis will, I hope, succeed in shedding light on more than just the problems of the "enlightened" governments of the closing decades of the Old Regime and also will help to sharpen our understanding of the difficulties that reforming regimes face in all societies and ages. One of the unfortunate effects of the skepticism among Western historians is that, by maintaining the incompatibility of enlightened and absolutist government and by tying enlightened absolutism to the endless debate between authoritarianism and democracy, they have emphasized the distinctiveness of these regimes. Such a focus has come, however, at the expense of overlooking the far more significant and numerous similarities between them and the modern centralized bureaucratic welfare state.[17]

Like modern-day governments, the Frederician regime was obliged to contend with preexisting structures that were essentially inimical to the thrust of its programs: unfavorable demographic and economic circumstances, entrenched institutions that enjoyed lives and constituencies of their own, and existing philosophies of government not wholly compatible with the new ideas of government reformers. It was further compelled to deal with the stress between its desire for rational, equitable reform and vested interests whose welfare it also respected; between the desire to provide poor relief and the responsibility to maintain fiscal integrity; and, above all, between its own conviction of the effectiveness of government assistance and growing popular frustration over the unexpected ill effects of its programs. Far more important than allowing us to affirm or reject the notion of enlightened absolutism, its record underscores the pitfalls of executing effective, orderly change in any society.

[17]For two American scholars who have directed our focus on the cameralist *Polizeistaat* as a protomodern social welfare state, see Reinhold Dorwart, "The Theory of the Welfare State," chapter 1 of *The Prussian Welfare State before 1740*, 1–29; and Raeff, "The Well-Ordered Police State," 1242.

Policymaking

For most of the last century the stress on the authoritarian nature of enlightened absolutism has led us to underemphasize the degree to which government functioned by consensus. Rather we have tended to credit the prince with taking the initiative and shaping the course of enlightened government. Over the last two decades historians have come to appreciate the bureaucracy's role as an agent for progressive change. Thus, while the character and philosophical stance of the prince was clearly the single most important factor in determining government policy, most scholars would agree today that it was the bureaucracy that provided the greatest common denominator in developing a uniform view toward the role of governments throughout the German states. Of late historians have also come to realize that the German regimes cooperated with the corporate bodies and the nobility that controlled them — whether out of choice or necessity — and have stressed their willingness to preserve and work with existing social and political institutions. At no point, however, have historians indicated that these corporate bodies actively participated in the making of policy or themselves helped develop the kinds of reform programs that we have come to associate with the legacy of Enlightenment politics. It is possible that further research will show that this was the case in some of the German states. Whatever the findings, they did play an active and positive role in Hesse-Cassel.

Enlightened government in Hesse-Cassel was, in fact, not the work of one man or executive authority operating from the residence, but rather the contribution of three separate forces that made a conscientious attempt to represent what they perceived as the needs and wishes of all segments of the population. Each component — prince, bureaucracy, and diet — was essentially distinct and capable of a certain degree of independent initiative, but each was also inclined to respect the prerogatives, interests, and sensibilities of the others, and to cooperate through twenty-five years of policymaking. A mix of old and new ideas is evident in all three elements of the Hessian power structure, with new currents tending to coexist with or reinforce existing values and institutions that functioned as best they could to serve the public welfare.

The landgrave

Nowhere was this coexistence of cultural values more evident than in Landgrave Frederick II. Born in 1720, Frederick was first exposed to Enlightenment philosophy by his childhood tutor, Jean Pierre de Crousaz, a professor of philosophy and mathematics at Lausanne. That exposure intensified in 1732 when Crousaz brought him to Geneva, where he began five years' study at the university under the leading figures of the Swiss Enlightenment. In addition to studying law under Charles Fréderic Necker (father of the French financier) and mathematics under the preeminent philosopher Jean-Louis Calandrini, the young prince was instructed in theology by Jean-Alphonse Turrettini, Geneva's leading champion of religious toleration, who was instrumental in the secularization of all public and university offices. Clearly the most influential figure was Jean-Jacques Burlamaqui, who had only recently gained notoriety in Geneva by revamping the university's curriculum to permit his teaching of natural law.[1] Following the outbreak of a bourgeois revolt against the Genevan patriciate in 1735 Burlamaqui accompanied Frederick to Cassel, where he stayed eight months as the prince's guest and private teacher. The prince was unquestionably fascinated with natural law philosophy. At one point when he was bedridden he persuaded Burlamaqui to continue his lessons by correspondence. Following their return to Geneva at the end of the year, his father wrote Burlamaqui in the most glowing terms about the influence he had had on his son.[2]

It is possible to glean evidence on the nature of that influence from the principally philosophical content of Frederick's letters to Burlamaqui as well as to Crousaz, with whom he maintained a fourteen-year correspondence until the tutor's death in 1748. His lifelong faith in education and human reason surfaces in his letters to both men.[3] We also learn of

[1] Charles Borgeaud, *Histoire de l'université de Genève* (Geneva, 1900), 510–18; Bernard Gagnebin, *Burlamaqui et le droit naturel* (Geneva, 1944), 199.
[2] StAMg, 4a)90,15: Burlamaqui to Frederick, 19 Dec. 1735; Gagnebin, *Burlamaqui et le droit naturel*, 61.
[3] StAMg, 4a)90,13 and 15.

the fifteen-year-old prince's conviction that a prince "is naturally obliged to adopt as his main goal the good of his subjects" and of his impatience with the leisure life of many aristocrats, since "work is an obligation that natural law imposes on all men, without exception."[4] Frederick retained his fascination with philosophy after the conclusion of his formal education. Though he was especially interested in Voltaire's work, he appears to have read widely in the literature of the English and French Enlightenment.[5] Moreover, during his mid-thirties he practiced his English by writing a lengthy volume of reflections on Senecan philosophy in that language. Though obviously intended for his eyes only, these "English exercises," with their apotheoses to natural philosophy and basic human equality, help establish the philosophical continuity of the mature Frederick with the teenaged student of Burlamaqui.[6]

There were, however, other pieces to the intellectual mosaic that composed Frederick's worldview, through which the light of the new philosophy had to be filtered. Burlamaqui was himself instrumental in teaching his charge respect for the corporate institutions of the Old Regime. Historians have long recognized Burlamaqui's role as the great popularizer of eighteenth-century political thought and especially of Montesquieu's work. In championing Montesquieu's call for government by the consent of the governed, with tangible safeguards against the executive authority's potential for despotism, Burlamaqui has been hailed as "a primary source" for the U.S. Constitution.[7] Yet, whereas the American and French revolutions eventually utilized Montesquieu in the creation of "democratic" institutions, the notion of checks and balances had far more utility in eighteenth-century Geneva or Germany in justifying the maintenance of a tightly structured and privileged corporate society. Indeed, though Burlamaqui, like Montesquieu, only published at midcentury, his ideas were already formed in the early 1730s, when he was tutoring the young Hessian prince. Himself the member of a

[4]StAMg, 4a)90,15: Frederick to Burlamaqui [Dec. 1735].
[5]Peter Brockmeier, Roland Desné, and Jürgen Voss, eds., *Voltaire und Deutschland* (Stuttgart, 1979), 9; Both and Vogel, *Landgraf Friedrich II.*, 12.
[6]Among his more notable reflections: #16 ("Mankind must be guided by philosophy"); #44 (endorsing the Senecan concept that "the nobility and the poor have the same origins," with the claim that true nobility comes from the heart rather than from bloodright); #122 ("Let us live as Nature has taught us"). StAMg, 4a)90,17: Englische Übungen.
[7]Ray F. Harvey, *Jean Jacques Burlamaqui. A Liberal Tradition in American Constitutionalism* (Chapel Hill, N.C., 1937), vii, 36–9, 49, 79–140; Cobban, *In Search of Humanity*, 162–3.

prominent patrician family, Burlamaqui played a major role in the Genevan conflict as a determined advocate for the inviolability of the city's existing corporate structure that had excluded the bourgeoisie from all political participation. In a 1734 report to the Genevan magistracy refuting the demands of the bourgeoisie, he was already claiming that each society had a unique constitutional structure that corresponded to its own separate traditions and was promoting the notion of an inviolable "reciprocal contract" obligating both government and the governed.[8] It is difficult to imagine how Burlamaqui's corporatism could have been lost on Frederick, especially during their eight months of self-imposed exile in Cassel in 1735, or in the prince's second flight alone at the beginning of 1737 when his personal baggage was unceremoniously searched by bourgeois guards.[9]

Notwithstanding everything that he imbibed from the Enlightenment's teaching of natural law, it was inevitable that Frederick would derive a more sanguine attitude toward the military and warfare. As a German and Hessian, contact with the martial life and its values was inevitable. His governor and constant companion, August Moritz von Donop, was an army officer from a Hessian military family. Like all Hessian princes he was trained to be a soldier. During the War of the Austrian Succession he served with the Hessian forces, first under Emperor Charles VII fighting the Austrians and then under Austria's British allies against both the French and the Scottish rebels. He then spent most of the Seven Years' War as commandant of the Prussian fortresses at Wesel and Magdeburg.

Frederick's exposure to Prussia reinforced not only his ties to the martial life and its values but also his admiration for Frederick the Great and virtually everything Prussian. It also facilitated the marriage of Enlightenment and militarism so effortlessly affected by the prince's Prussian namesake and idol. It was, in fact, in wartime Berlin in 1743 that he began his lifelong relationship with Voltaire. And it was off to Prussian East Frisia that he repaired in the opening months of the Seven Years' War "for rest and philosophy" – although the only reading he describes

---

[8]Gagnebin, *Burlamaqui et le droit naturel*, 53.
[9]Ibid., 61–3. Burlamaqui's belief in distinctive national traditions was certainly digested by Frederick, who wrote to his mentor that "diversity of sentiment can come from different sources: temperament, age, the air, the food, education, the government, the passions . . . and all contribute more or less to their use of reason." StAMg, 4a)90,15: Frederick to Burlamaqui, 2 Jan. 1736.

in detail during his stay is Vauban's *Mémoire pour servir d'instruction dans la conduite de siège et dans la défense de place.*[10] Given his environment it is altogether likely that Frederick visualized warfare as an element of human nature, at least within its German setting.

Yet another distinctive feature of Frederick's outlook that stemmed from his cultural environment was his acceptance of Christianity. Like most educated German Protestants, Frederick accepted the legacy of early *Aufklärer* like Leibniz and Wolff who merged revealed with natural religion. He was being true to this synthesis when at age fifteen he qualified Burlamaqui's claim that "natural law is nothing other than the principles that reason presents us" with the rejoinder that the "law of God is natural law" and "religion is an essential part of natural law."[11] It was also in this vein that he completed his religious instruction following his return from Geneva with two thick volumes written by the same author, one entitled *La Religion naturelle*, the other *La Religion révélée.*[12] Though he retained his faith in the afterlife and in the efficacy of prayer, Frederick never lost either his view of "nature" and "God" as one and the same or his Wolffian confidence in the equal justification of all faiths. Moreover, Frederick's religious relativism sparked a certain fascination with the world's religions, especially Roman Catholicism and the Protestant denominations. As the Huguenot preacher De la Porte told Boswell during a visit to Cassel in 1764, Frederick "has studied thoroughly the controversy between the Catholics and Protestants. He knows the history of the Church well and one must be well equipped by special study to be able to dispute with him."[13]

Frederick's cultural orientation was rather typical for the elite of his generation. Yet the combination of his martial life and fascination with religious study nearly cost him his throne. The young prince's problems began with his marriage to Princess Mary in May 1740. The marriage had been in the works for over a decade and was part of a subsidy treaty that sent 6,000 Hessian auxiliaries to fight for the British in the War of the Austrian Succession. Yet, although the match somehow produced

[10]StAMg, 4a)91,16: Cappelmann to Frederick, 5 Nov. 1756, Frederick to Cappelmann, 15 Nov. 1756.
[11]StAMg, 4a)90,15: Burlamaqui to Frederick, 2 Jan. 1736, Frederick to Burlamaqui [early 1736].
[12]StAMg, Handschriften, 91–3. The author, Jean Bolacre, was a Genevan pastor.
[13]StAMg, 4a)90,17: Englische Übungen, #65, 110; Frederick A. Pottle, *Boswell on the Grand Tour. Germany and Switzerland 1764* (New York, 1953), 155–6.

three sons over the next four years, it suffered from Frederick's almost continuous absence at the front. By 1746 the couple was quite estranged, both because of Frederick's prolonged absences and the sexual peccadilloes that were fast becoming his favorite form of recreation.[14] *jerk*

In the end it was Frederick's secret conversion to Catholicism in 1749 that doomed the marriage. The conversion was largely the work of advisers to Archbishop-Elector Clement August of Cologne, who had stressed the political advantages of such a conversion during their wartime meetings at the court of Clement August's brother, Charles VII.[15] Frederick's decision hinged, however, on the small importance he ascribed to doctrine itself. He shared the Enlightenment's skepticism about human beings' ability to comprehend the religious metaphysics of the different Christian faiths, complaining at one point that "the Protestants have erred to say that the Holy Scripture is so easy to understand and that human reason permits even the common man to study it. These matters will always remain a mystery for all those who engage in reason and who do not wish to believe blindly."[16] Given these doubts and the religious relativism that his religious studies had inspired, Frederick saw no reason not to indulge his own preference for the more elaborate ceremony of the Roman church.[17] The discovery of his conversion five years later caused a sensation throughout Protestant Germany. The possibility that the first Calvinist prince to convert since 1612 had done so for want of more ceremony left Protestant observers searching for more sinister explanations, the most popular being that Frederick had been seduced by a Catholic lover who promised that, if he were to "surrender his soul to her, she would give him up her body."[18]

Far worse than such slanders were the countermeasures taken by the prince's father, Landgrave William VIII. At first the landgrave was determined to exclude his son from the succession but soon dropped the idea when he realized that he would never be able to secure the necessary ratification from the Catholic emperor. Instead he subjected his heir to

[14]G. Eisentraut, "Über das Leben Friedrichs II.," *Mitt* (1913–14), 88–9; Wilhelm Rogge-Ludwig, "Langräfin Maria von Hessen," *Hessenland*, 4 (1890), 297.
[15]Ferdinand von Pfister, *Landgraf Friedrich II. und sein Hessen* (Cassel, 1879), 25; Achatz Ferdinand von der Asseburg, *Denkwürdigkeiten* (Berlin 1842), 352–6.
[16]Gräflich von Bocholtz-Asseburg'sches Archiv, A Akte 668: Frederick to Asseburg, 8 Mar. 1761.
[17]Both and Vogel, *Landgraf Wilhelm VIII. von Hessen-Kassel. Ein Fürst der Rokokozeit* (Munich, 1964), 98–100, and *Landgraf Friedrich II.*, 15; Pottle, *Boswell on the Grand Tour*, 155; Leopold M. E. Stoff, *Die Katholiken in Kassel* (Cassel, 1899), 10.
[18]Pottle, *Boswell on the Grand Tour*, 154; PRO, SP 87/45: 19 May 1763 Clavering report.

the *Assekurationsakte*, a succession document far more restrictive than the oaths sworn to by the Catholic princes of Saxony or Württemberg. The law not only removed all confessional matters from Frederick's hands and restricted his right to appoint Catholics to the bureaucracy, army, or diet but also guaranteed that he would have no religious influence or leverage over his wife and children by compelling him to separate from them and cede them full possession of the Hessian county of Hanau. Frederick's request for a formal divorce was denied since that would have permitted him to remarry and have Catholic children. As a final precaution William obliged the bureaucracy, diet, and eventually all his subjects to swear to the *Assekurationsakte* and secured guarantees from every Protestant European state and the *Corpus Evangelicorum*.[19]

While the *Assekurationsakte* may have reassured William, it did not prevent Frederick's situation from deteriorating. Part of the prince's continuing problems stemmed from the vindictiveness of his father, who discontinued their correspondence, totally excluded him from all state affairs, and initially even denied him his own priest, obliging him to summon one from Mainz's enclave of Fritzlar, twenty miles to the south.[20] Yet, in seeking assistance from sympathetic Catholic rulers – first the Wittelsbach electors and then Empress Maria Theresa – Frederick further endangered his chances of succeeding his father.[21] In fact, Frederick's greatest crisis broke at the beginning of 1756, after Maria Theresa had become convinced that he would be eventually disinherited and possibly executed. Working closely with Landgrave Constantin, head of the Catholic cadet line of Hesse-Rotenburg, and his Austrian wife, the empress authorized Frederick's flight to Vienna, where he would receive a military commission in the imperial army. The attempt was betrayed, however, and Frederick was exiled to Hersfeld, where he was placed under house arrest and denied all contact with Roman Catholics and even with his father, who never saw him again.[22] In order to frustrate continuing Aus-

[19]C. W. Ledderhose, *Kleine Schriften*, 1 (Marburg, 1787), 30; Heinrich Heppe, *Kirchengeschichte beider Hessen* (Marburg, 1876), 262; G. Eisentraut, "Hessen zur Zeit des Regierungsantritts Friedrich II.," *Mitt* (1924–6), 38.

[20]StAMg, 4a)91,1; [Hardenberg], *Ein kleinstaatlicher Minister des achtzehnten Jahrhunderts. Leben und Wirken Friedrich August's Freiherrn von Hardenberg* (Leizpig, 1877), 223; Stoff, *Katholiken in Kassel*, 11.

[21]Asseburg'sches Archiv, A Akte 668: Frederick to Asseburg, 29 Jan., 14 Feb. 1755; HHStA, RK, Kleinere Reichsstände 162: Frederick to Maria Theresa, 29 Apr. 1755.

[22]Karl Scherer, "Erbprinz Friedrich von Hessen-Kassel und Pfarrer Valentin Fuchs von Rasdorf," *Fuldaer Geschichtsblätter*, 7 (1908), 4, 52; Pfister, *Landgraf Friedrich II. und sein Hessen*, 54.

trian meddling,[23] William finally dispatched Frederick to Berlin, where he was immediately given a commission in the Prussian army.

Frederick the Great's invasion of Saxony afforded the Hessian heir a most welcome opportunity to forsake his family problems for a resumption of military service. Yet he soon discovered that his Protestant allies trusted him no more than his father had. Fear that he would desert to the Austrians led the Prussian king to assign him to garrisons far from the front. Once he had succeeded to the throne and to the command of the Hessian forces operating under the duke of Brunswick, he was shadowed by the British envoy Clavering, who watched closely for any contact between him and Landgrave Constantin, whose sister had just married the French marshal Soubise. Even the allied garrison in Cassel was heavily reinforced with Hanoverian units to deter Frederick from turning it over to the French.[24] Nor did his succession bring any thaw in his relationship with Mary, who resisted all attempts at rapprochement, fearing he would try to turn their sons against her. Indeed, Mary received considerable support in her resistance from her British countryman Clavering, who demonstrated his loyalty by slandering her estranged husband in his reports to London.[25] Frederick was no more trusted within Hesse-Cassel, where the diet betrayed the widespread fear that he might promote Catholicism by asking him to reaffirm his oath to abide by the *Assekurationsakte*.[26] From the countryside came a steady stream of insulting letters from Calvinist clergymen, and at court he found himself surrounded by men who had assisted in his downfall and who now tensely awaited any sign of princely retribution.[27]

In several respects Frederick's difficulties resemble the crisis that his great Prussian namesake confronted in the last decade of his own father's reign. The parallels are obvious. Both were rejected by disillusioned fathers,

[23]HHStA, RK, Kleinere Reichsstände 162: William to Francis I, 16 Mar. 1756, 24 Mar., 28 Apr. 1756 rescripts.

[24]Reginald Savory, *His Britannic Majesty's Army in Germany during the Seven Years War* (Oxford, 1966), 360–1; Brunner, *Geschichte der Residenzstadt Cassel*, 273–4.

[25]Such as in his ludicrous assertion that Frederick hoped for the return of Hanau in order to have a base for renewing liaisons with Catholic lovers living in Frankfurt and the Rhenish principalities. PRO, 30/8/91: 18 Nov. 1760 Clavering report; PRO, SP 87/45: 19 May 1763 Clavering report.

[26]HHStA, RK, Berichte aus dem Reich 81: 9 Feb. 1765 Pergen report; Heppe, *Kirchengeschichte beider Hessen*, 261.

[27]Jonas Apelblad, *Beschreibung seiner Reise durch Ober- und Niedersachsen und Hessen* (Berlin and Leipzig, 1785), 281; Pottle, *Boswell on the Grand Tour*, 155.

betrayed when they tried to flee, and subsequently disciplined with confinement and the threat of disinheritance or execution. In her ill-fated attempt to help Frederick, Maria Theresa even retraced Charles VI's efforts to save the life of the young prince of Prussia. That, however, is where the comparison ends. Although the Hohenzollern heir regained his father's favor through a successful apprenticeship in the Prussian administration and army, his Hessian counterpart was totally excluded from the government and his father's presence until his tense succession as landgrave. Furthermore, whereas biographers have found little psychological or other "baggage" encumbering King Frederick in 1740, Landgrave Frederick's nightmare was decisive in determining not only his authority in confessional affairs but also his character and, by extension, the substance of his leadership.

The "English exercises" that Frederick wrote immediately after the confessional crisis portray a melancholy figure shorn of self-confidence and optimism, a man grievously wounded by his loneliness and the loss of his children. Exactly one decade later the French envoy Hennenberg drew much the same picture.[28] Indeed, the reports of foreign observers sketch an unmistakable profile of psychological insecurity – of a shy person who nonetheless felt the need to talk once he was in the presence of others, an indecisive individual who was afraid of what people thought of him and, hence, was easily swayed by both the arguments and blandishments of stronger personalities.[29]

Frederick's need for approval assumed other forms as well. Upon succeeding to the throne he made a conscious attempt to regulate his sex life, effecting a change that drew favorable comment from some foreign observers, though not from the British, who continued to vilify him with increasingly outlandish slanders.[30] He also strengthened his resolve to

[28]StAMg, 4a)90,17: Englische Übungen, #3, 5, 104; AAE, CP, HC 12: 3 June 1766 Hennenberg mémoire.

[29]HHStA, RK, Kleinere Reichsstände 163: [1766] Moser report, Berichte aus dem Reich 81: 9 Feb. 1765 Pergen report, 106: 1 Nov. 1771 Neipperg report; AAE, CP, HC 12: 3 June 1766 Hennenberg mémoire; HC 13: D'Auguillon to Verac, 13 July 1773; Forster to Sömmerring, 4 May 1779, in Hermann Hettner, ed., *Georg Forster's Briefwechsel mit S. Th. Sömmerring* (Brunswick, 1877), 2; Robert Uhland, ed., *Herzog Carl Eugen von Württemberg: Tagebücher seiner Rayssen* (Tübingen, 1968), 133.

[30]AAE, CP, HC 12: 3 June 1766 Hennenberg mémoire; Both and Vogel, *Friedrich II.*, 24; PRO, SP 87/45: 19 May 1763 Clavering report; Eduard Vehse, *Geschichte der deutschen Höfe*, 27 (Hamburg, 1853), 185–6, and *Badische und hessische Hofgeschichten* (Munich, 1922), 208–9.

rule benevolently, modeling himself after the example of Frederick the Great. This determination is evident in a personal memoir entitled *Pensées sur les princes et les ministres* that he appears to have written shortly after his succession, somewhat in the fashion of his namesake's *Anti-Machiavel*. As a declaration of principles and intentions in such fields as education, public welfare, criminal jurisprudence, and religious toleration, the memoir represents an enthusiastic endorsement of the Enlightenment creed that is consistent both with his earlier writings and with his subsequent record as landgrave.[31] Yet, if Frederick was determined to rule wisely, he was also motivated by the need to win acclaim for his accomplishments as landgrave. His sensitivity to the interplay of vanity and altruism surfaces in the "English exercises," in which he confesses, "I question whether the marvelous love of mankind does not derive more from vanity than good nature. I suspect the desire of being applauded and admired has a great share in it." It also emerges from one passage of the *Pensées* in which he enumerates "leaving a name to posterity" among the justifications for being a great ruler.[32]

Frederick definitely worked toward that goal, not only by following what he thought was right but by remaining sensitive to the need to posture for the benefit of audiences in places like Paris and Berlin. It is evident in the lengthy, fawning correspondence he sustained with both Voltaire and the famed philosophe's confidante Madame Gallatin, whom he had first met in Geneva in 1732.[33] It is also apparent in the reports of his ministers, who occasionally reminded him of the likely reaction of the outside world to various government programs and actions. Of course the princely capacity for self-promotion was not limited to Frederick, though his own needs for both self-esteem and outside recognition were doubtless greater than most. Nor does it refute his sincerity. That princes such as Frederick even took the trouble to cater to the philosophes' expectations constitutes by itself evidence of the value they attached to Enlightenment principles. Nevertheless, a comprehensive understanding

---

[31]StAMg, 4a)90,21: "Pensées sur les princes et les ministres," published in *Hessische Blätter*, Nr. 856-7 (1882).

[32]StAMg, 4a)90,17: Englische Übungen, #6, 4a)90,21: "Pensées."

[33]Marc Peter, *Une Amie de Voltaire. Madame Gallatin* (Lausanne, 1925), 36; Brockmeier et al., eds., *Voltaire und Deutschland*, 10, 23; Edmund Stengel, "Ungedruckte Briefe Voltaire's an ... den Landgrafen von Hessen-Kassel nebst Auszügen aus dem Briefwechsel der Madame de Gallatin an den Landgrafen," *Zeitschrift für neufranzösische Sprache und Literatur*, 7 (1885). Both correspondences are extant in StAMg: 4a)91,44–5.

of the dynamics of enlightened absolutism in Hesse-Cassel, as elsewhere, compels us to recognize that the princes were motivated not only by the determination to do good but also by the desire to *appear* to do so.

The bureaucracy

Regardless of their overall evaluation of Frederick, scholars have generally agreed that the Frederician ministry and civil service were among the best in the Holy Roman Empire.[34] Moreover, throughout the reign every level of the administration proved an important instrument of state policy, not only by faithfully carrying out the landgrave's programs but also by actively participating in their formulation. Frederick benefited from its diligence and loyalty largely because he remembered to extend to his officials the rights and privileges afforded them by past landgraves, while forgetting their association with the mistreatment he had received at the hands of his father. Frederick came to the throne with a clear vision of the importance of the ministry and of the need to enlist its support. Both the title and content of the *Pensées* reflect the instruction he had received since early childhood to appoint competent ministers and to consult them regularly.[35] His tentative nature only served to reinforce this teaching. Though he always retained the final say on all substantive decisions and often personally pursued matters that interested him, Frederick nevertheless delegated power well, consulting with and frequently deferring to his ministers.[36]

Like most new rulers the landgrave was initially most intimate with those men who had been especially close to him during his "apprentice" years. Given his exclusion from power during the last six years of his father's reign, Frederick's closest advisers were not members of the previous regime or even Hessian subjects but rather three Prussian army officers with whom he had served during the Seven Years' War: Martin Ernst von Schlieffen, Dietrich-Wilhelm von Wackenitz, and Friedrich

[34]Treitschke, *Das neunzehnte Jahrhundert*, 519; Friedrich Kapp, "Friedrich II. von Hessen und die neuere Geschichtsschreibung," review in *HZ*, 42 (1879), 329; Albert Lotz, *Geschichte des deutschen Beamtentums* (Berlin, 1909), 302–4; Josef Sauer, *Finanzgeschäfte der Landgrafen von Hessen-Kassel* (Fulda, 1930), 10; HHStA, RK, Kleinere Reichsstände, 163: Moser report [1766].
[35]Theodor Hartwig, "Instruktion für die Erziehung des Landgrafen Friedrich II.," *ZHG*, 43 (1909), 78; "Pensées," #7–10, 13, 22.
[36]StAMg, 5)8703: "Instruktionen und Vollmacht" 26 May 1769, 5, 29. Nov 1776, 8 June 1781, 4 June 1784; HHStA, RK, Kleinere Reichsstände, 163: Moser report [1766]; Staatliche Kunstsammlungen Kassel, *Aufklärung & Klassizismus*, 10.

Christian Arnold von Jungkenn. Although the landgrave did not entrust his "Prussian junta" with any specific ministerial posts until the second half of the reign, they maintained their dominant influence throughout.

Frederick's reliance on his Prussian advisers occasioned a good deal of personal animosity and factionalism within the ministry, especially during the first half of the reign.[37] These conflicts do not appear, however, to have prevented the two groups of ministers from agreeing or cooperating with each other when it came to making policy. Much of the credit for this belongs to the Prussians themselves, who helped smooth over relations by earning the respect of their Hessian counterparts with their diligence and competence. Frederick's chief minister, Count Schliefen, earned truly extraordinary and unanimous praise from contemporaries for his intellect and his talents as a statesman.[38] Frederick himself also played a role. He made no attempt to punish or replace his father's ministers for whatever role they might have played in his earlier disgrace. Nor did he attempt to rule exclusively through the "kitchen cabinet" of his closest associates, as did Duke Charles Eugene of Württemberg. Despite the almost total lack of camaraderie and his own personal dislike for some of the chief Wilhelmine incumbents, Frederick continued to involve his Hessian ministers in all major policy matters and entrusted them with the running of the major government departments to the point of naming the most talented among them to numerous positions.

The trust was well placed. Thuringian-born Jacob Sigmund Waitz, Freiherr von Eschen, had served the Hessian landgraves since 1723 and enjoyed a superb reputation throughout the *Reich* for his mastery of economic and fiscal affairs.[39] Notwithstanding his own dislike for Waitz,

[37]PRO, SP 87/45: 19 May 1763 Clavering report; AAE, CP, HC 12: 3 June 1766 Hennenberg mémoire; HC 13: 9 Mar. 1773 Aigremont report; HHStA, RK, Kleinere Reichsstände, 163: Moser report [1766]. Even one of Frederick's later Prussian appointments, Heinrich Christian Bopp, criticized the landgrave's reliance on non-Hessians, if only because of their questionable loyalty to the state. Murhard'sche Bibliothek, Kassel, 8° Ms. Hass. 16a: Bopp, "Fehler, Missbräuche, und Verbesserungen in Hessen!," n.d. [1773–6] 181.
[38]HHStA, RK, Berichte as dem Reich 106: 1 Nov 1771 Neipperg report; AAE, CP, HC 13: 1 June, 11 Dec. 1773 Verac report; PRO, SP 81/182: 25 Feb. 1776 Faucitt report; Forster to his father, 13 Feb. 1783, in Hermann Hettner, ed., *Briefwechsel*, 321; Friedrich Justinian Freiherr von Günderode, *Briefe eines Reisenden über den gegenwärtigen Zustand von Cassel mit aller Freiheit geschildert* (Frankfurt and Leipzig, 1781), 206.
[39]Among Waitz's many admirers were Friedrich Karl von Moser, who rated him with Necker and Silva-Tarouca as a financial genius; Frederick the Great, who sought his advice and actively tried to lure him away from Cassel; and Marshal de Broglie, who once exclaimed, "Oh, if my kingdom had only a couple of such financiers France would be in a totally different position." AAE, CP, HC 13: 20 May 1772 Aigremont report;

Frederick ennobled him in 1764 and subsequently named him to direct seven major departments before he finally resigned a decade later. No one at court seems to have liked the humorless Leonhard Heinrich Ludwig Georg von Canngiesser. Yet Frederick appreciated the distinguished reputation the Prussian-born minister had built as an eminent jurist and administrator over a quarter century at Wetzlar, Darmstadt, and Cassel. When he died in 1772 he directed eight separate departments in addition to his original post as president of the Hessian Supreme Court (*Oberappellationsgericht*).[40]

Frederick also put professional considerations ahead of personality preferences when the time came to replace Canngiesser and Waitz with two transitional figures, the like-named Heinrich Christian Ernst Bopp and Carl Philipp Kopp. Though Kopp was the only Hessian native to attain a major ministerial position, he was just one more personality to whom the landgrave took an instant dislike. Nevertheless, Frederick championed the career civil servant as one of the finest minds in the regime, naming him to replace Canngiesser in a position Kopp would hold until his death in 1777.[41] Meanwhile, Bopp owed his rise and fall to his reputation as a fiscal expert who might adequately replace Waitz, a reputation he had built up in the Prussian service – and which he destroyed in his disappointing and correspondingly brief three-year tenure as director of Hessian finances. For the last decade of Frederick's reign the Prussian junta was complemented by two talented ministers who appear to have earned both the landgrave's confidence and affection: Julius Jürgen von Wittorf, a career Hessian army officer and lifelong acquaintance of the landgrave who was eventually named to direct seven departments, and Johann Philipp Franz von Fleckenbühl, a Wetzlar *Kammerassessor* who henceforth shared responsibility for state finances with the Prussian Wackenitz.

The deference Frederick displayed toward his ministers extended beyond professional ethics. By all accounts ministerial salaries were high.[42]

HHStA, RK, Berichte aus dem Reich 81: 9 Feb. 1765 Pergen report; PRO, SP 87/45: 19, 30 May 1763 Clavering reports; Friedrich Wilhelm Strieder et al., *Grundlage zu einer hessischen Gelehrten, Schriftsteller und Künstler Geschichte vom 16. Jahrhundert bis auf gegenwärtigen Zeiten*, 21 vols. (Cassel, 1781–1863), 16: 407; Vehse, *Geschichte der deutschen Höfe*, 194.
40 HHStA: RK, Kleinere Reichsstände, 163: Moser report [1766]; AAE, CP, HC 12: 3 June 1766 Hennenberg mémoire, 13: 20 May 1772 Aigremont report.
41 AAE, CP, HC 13: 13 Sept. 1774 Verac, 20 May 1772 Aigremont reports.
42 The Austrian envoy Pergen even reported that it was the high level of Hessian remuneration that was preventing Waitz from accepting Frederick the Great's offers of employment

Nor were they the only source of ministerial remuneration. Frederick often made special gifts and low-interest loans to his top ministers, even if they were only needed to pay off gambling debts. Later in the reign certain ministers could also count on receiving commissions from those foreign princes and governments to which the landgrave had granted loans.[43] Although they seldom benefited from the landgrave's personal largesse, the middle and lower ranks of the Hessian bureaucracy were also attractively remunerated. To be sure, civil servants were in a strong position throughout the *Reich.* Given the large number and expanding size of the German bureaucracies, civil officials enjoyed sufficient mobility with which to negotiate high salaries and satisfactory working conditions. Yet, if we are to believe contemporary observers, the Hessian bureaucracy compared favorably to the other German civil services in enjoying unusually high levels of satisfaction and confidence in its government's willingness to care for its needs.[44] Although entry-level salaries were no better than average, junior civil servants knew that high performance and seniority would lead to salaries well above those of most other German states.[45] They also drew comfort from a special widow's and orphan's fund that had been established for their families in 1750 and that Frederick expanded in 1769.[46] For commoners entering the bureaucracy there was also the prospect that long and distinguished service would bring ennoblement. A statistical analysis of 184 Hessian bureaucrats in key middle- and upper-level positions indicates that 32 (24.6 percent) of those 130 civil officers whose fathers were not born into the nobility became nobles either in recognition of their own work or through the ennoblement of a father who was himself a civil servant (Table 1).

As in other German bureaucracies, the satisfaction of Hessian civil servants was reinforced by their own strict professional standards and

in the Prussian service. HHStA, RK, Berichte aus dem Reich 81: 9 Feb. 1765 Pergen, 106: 1 Nov. 1771 Neipperg reports; AAE, CP, HC 13: 25 Sept. 1773 Verac report.
[43]S. L. Ruhl, *Einiges vom Hof Landgraf Friedrich's von Hessen* (Melsungen, 1884), 5; Sauer, *Finanzgeschäfte*, 35.
[44]Günderode, *Briefe eines Reisenden*, 208–9; Peter Gerret Thielen, *Karl August von Hardenberg, 1750–1822* (Cologne and Berlin, 1967), 26.
[45]Günderode, *Briefe eines Reisenden*, 210, 228; Gregory Wick Pedlow, "The Nobility of Hesse-Kassel: Family, Land, and Office, 1770–1870," Johns Hopkins University diss. (1979), 254.
[46]Friedrich Christoph Schmincke, *Versuch einer genauen und umständlichen Beschreibung der hochfürstlichen-hessischen Residenz- und Hauptstadt Cassel* (Cassel, 1767), 385; Friedrich Münscher, *Geschichte von Hessen* (Marburg, 1894), 426. Frederick also advanced loans to the widows of several civil officials. 12)Kriegszahlamtsrechnungen 1760–85.

Table 1. *Ennobled civil servants, 1760–85*

	Ennobled officials	Sons of ennobled officials	Total
Before 1760	2	6	8
By Frederick	17	7	24
Total	19	13	32

Principal sources: SAK; Franck, Standeserhebungen und Gnadenakte.

exclusivity. Under Frederick the last vestiges of venality were eliminated. Applicants were generally required to have university-level training and pass an entry examination, with promotion based on a combination of performance evaluations and seniority.[47] As was common elsewhere, marriage and career choices reflected a high persistence within the tight circle of non-noble bureaucratic families: Of the eighty Frederician officials for whom I was able to locate genealogical data, 89 percent of their fathers, 81 percent of their brothers, and 65 percent of their sons were also civil officials, as were 80 percent of their fathers-in-law. When they were not marrying into other Hessian bureaucratic families, the children of civil officials almost invariably intermarried with one of four other elite groups that coexisted and, to a great extent, merged with them to form a "governing elite" in Hesse's three administrative centers of Cassel, Marburg, and Rinteln.

—*Nobles.* The largest distinctive element within the bureaucracy was the nobility. The noble born had customarily accounted for about one-third of civil officials since the early seventeenth century.[48] Their numbers increased significantly during Frederick's reign, rising from 34 percent to 55 percent of the group of 184 officials in my survey. Such a development invites the hypothesis that the landgrave intentionally increased noble representation in the bureaucracy, perhaps in imitation of Frederick

[47]Pedlow, "Nobility of Hesse-Kassel," 251–2; Both and Vogel, *Friedrich II.*, 36; Otto Berge, "Die Innenpolitik des Landgrafen Friedrich II. von Hessen-Kassel," Mainz University diss. (1952), 36-7. Not all of the German university registers are published and those that are do not provide a complete list of all students, some of whom avoided registration in order to escape tuition payments. In addition, many wealthier noble and professional families retained tutors to provide equivalent training for their children. Hence, it was possible to identify only 114 civil officials (62 percent) of the total of group of 184 officials in my survey.

[48]Wolfgang Metz, "Zur Sozialgeschichte des Beamtentums in der Zentralverwaltung der Landgrafschaft Hessen-Kassel bis zum 18. Jahrhundert," *ZHG*, 67 (1956), 144.

Table 2. *Distribution of noble, ennobled, and non-noble bureaucrats,*
by year

	Noble born		Ennobled[a]		Total noble	Non-noble		Total
	#	%	#	%	%	#	%	#
1765	15	24	6	10	34	41	66	62
1770	23	32	7	10	42	42	58	72
1775	34	35	8	8	43	55	57	97
1780	30	33	13	14	47	47	52	90
1785	35	36	18	19	55	44	45	97

[a]First and second generation.
Principal sources: SAK; Franck, *Standeserhebungen und Gnadenakte.*

the Great. In fact, the increase is explained by three unrelated developments: the landgrave's gradual elevation of several junta members to
ministerial rank, his ennoblement of common-born bureaucrats, and his
creation in 1772 of ten provincial governors (*Landräte*), all of whom
were appointed jointly by the crown and *Ritterschaft* from whose ranks
they came (Table 2). Discounting the ten *Landräte* positions, noble-born
bureaucrats held only 29 percent of the upper- and middle-level positions
in 1785, the same percentage they occupied in the overall group of 184
officials surveyed:

98 non-noble	(53%)
32 ennobled	(17%)
54 noblemen	(29%)[49]

The noble born did, however, dominate the government's highest bodies,
in this case the Privy Council and General Directory, while remaining a
definite minority in the three next most important bodies that were entrusted with state finances (War and Domains Board), the judiciary (Su
preme Court), and the execution of day-to-day affairs (*Regierung Cassel*)
(Table 3).

As a well-established pattern of patronage, the appointment of nobles

[49]The term "ennobled" signifies first- or second-generation nobles. My findings are roughly
comparable to those of Gregory Pedlow, "Nobility of Hesse-Kassel," 248, whose com-
posite group of noble and ennobled officials rises from 29 percent to 51.6 percent of the
total surveyed for 1765–85.

Table 3. *Distribution of noble, ennobled, and non-noble bureaucrats,*
by office

Office	1765	1770	1775	1780	1785
Privy Council	—	5-0-0	5-0-0	5-0-0	5-1-0
General Directory	—	—	7-0-3	6-0-2	6-4-0
War & Domains Board	2-2-10	3-2-7	2-0-7	2-0-6	2-5-6
Supreme Court	2-1-3	1-1-4	1-1-3	1-1-2	2-2-1
Regierung (Cassel)	1-1-7	2-2-6	2-1-7	1-1-8	2-4-6

Principal sources: SAK; Franck, *Standeserhebungen und Gnadenakte.*

occasioned only minor friction within the civil administration.[50] Although they themselves benefited from the ennoblement of a quarter of their number, middle- and upper-level common-born bureaucrats found the crown willing to protect their own standards of professionalism against inroads by the nobility. The landgrave successfully resisted noble pressures directed against the merit system, generally ignoring family petitions for preference.[51] In 1762 he adopted a new *Rangordnung* with ten classifications that ranked court officials solely according to their civil service positions.[52] Although, in practice, only the noble-born were ever appointed to posts in the highest category, the *Rangordnung* represented the first time that the Hessian court protocol had not distinguished between noble and common-born officials. In addition, non-noble bureaucrats were afforded certain legal privileges previously reserved for noblemen, and those who enjoyed the title of privy councillor (*Geheimer Rat*) were even permitted to marry noblewomen without subjecting their wives or offspring to a loss of social status.[53]

Meanwhile, there is considerable evidence that noble-born civil servants readily assimilated themselves into the bureaucracy by adopting its professional standards and characteristics. Although noble-born civil officials tended to come from nonbureaucratic families in which about three-fourths of their fathers and brothers had military careers, their own sons now chose evenly between the civil and military service. Noble-born

[50]Hans Erich Bödeker has found some instances of rivalry between noble courtiers and upper-level bourgeois officials. "Strukturen der Aufklärungsgesellschaft in der Residenzstadt Kassel," in *Mentalitäten und Lebensverhältnisse: Beispiele aus der Sozialgeschichte der Neuzeit; Rudolf Vierhaus zum 60. Geburtstag* (Göttingen, 1982), 63, 69.
[51]Pedlow, "Nobility of Hesse-Kassel," 251.
[52]*HLO*, 42–4: 13 Mar. 1762.
[53]Pedlow, "Nobility of Hesse-Kassel," 206.

bureaucrats were also generally better educated than most members of their class, both because university training was a prerequisite for most government posts and because they tended to come from wealthier families that could afford the expense of advanced education. Moreover, many of those nobles who were without university training were concentrated in less sensitive posts such as forestry, which did not require advanced education.[54]

~ *Non-Hessians.* Non-Hessian Germans comprised the next largest group of Frederician bureaucrats. Official hiring policy did afford some preference to Hessian-born applicants.[55] Yet, although existing genealogical data will not support an exact figure, about a third of the 184 middle- and upper-level officials surveyed came from other German states, especially neighboring states like Hanover and Prussia.[56] Hesse-Cassel was not altogether unique in employing so many non-natives, although its merit-based system and good benefits made it an especially attractive opportunity. What is truly remarkable is the degree to which non-Hessians dominated the highest levels of the ministry. For the first two decades of the reign, there was never more than one native Hessian among Frederick's half-dozen or so top ministers. This situation persisted in the all-important Privy Council (*Geheime Kabinett*) and was only

[54]Pedlow, "Nobility of Hesse-Kassel," 213, 271–2. Although it is impossible to account for those noble officials who received private instruction, the admittedly incomplete *Universitätsmatrikel* turn up the names of thirty of the fifty-four noble-born civil officials in my survey (56 percent), roughly twice the Hessian noble average and not far removed from the 70 percent figure for non-noble-born bureaucrats.

[55]Günderode, *Briefe eines Reisenden*, 211–12.

[56]The sketchy genealogical evidence that is available is supported both by the remarks of Günderode, who found the number of non-native bureaucrats remarkable, and by the evidence from university registers listed below. Although many Hessian natives attended Göttingen, the large number of bureaucrats who received their education elsewhere in Germany suggests their non-Hessian origins. Many non-natives also entered the Hessian service after attending Marburg.

Universities attended by Hessian bureaucrats[a]

Marburg	68	Leipzig	6	Strasbourg	1
Göttingen	49	Helmstedt	2	Utrecht	1
Jena	23[b]	Königsberg	2	Frankfurt/O	1
Rinteln	12	Heidelberg	1	Erfurt	0
Halle	8[c]	Duisberg	1	Erlangen	0
Giessen	7	Leiden	1		

[a]Many officials attended more than one university.
[b]Published data are available only for the period 1723–64.
[c]Published data only go up to 1730.
Principal sources: University Matrikel (See *Published sources: Statistical and Prosopographical Material* in Bibliography.)

Table 4. *Natives and non-Hessians in ministerial positions, 1775–85*

	Privy Council			General Directory			
	Native	Prussian	Other	Native	Prussian	Other	Unknown
1775	1	2	2	4	4	2	
1780	1	3	1	2	3	1	2
1785	1	3	2	2	3	2	3

Principal sources: SAK; Buttlar-Elberberg, *Stammbuch;* Strieder, *Gelehrten, Schriftsteller und Künstler Geschichte.*

marginally different in the larger General Directory (*General Direktorium*) that oversaw all government operations (Table 4).

Nevertheless, aside from resentment against the Prussian "junta" the presence of so many non-Hessians generated no opposition from native bureaucrats, the *Landtag*, or the population as a whole. The recruitment of non-Hessians – especially top ministers like Canngiesser and Waitz – was, in any event, already accepted practice well before Frederick's succession.

Soldiers. One of the features of the Hessian government that distinguished it from the other principalities was the overwhelming presence of the military near the centers of power. The Hessian army was not only large but also so well represented in Cassel that the Austrian envoy claimed military officers outnumbered the civilian members of the court, giving it the appearance of a military headquarters.[57] If Frederick liked to surround himself with his soldiers, he also did not mind bringing them into the government, especially at the highest levels. Yet the number of soldiers actually admitted into the Hessian bureaucracy, although significant, was hardly exceptional. Military officers account for only 25 (13.5 percent) of the 184 civil officials in my group. Furthermore, except for five military men in ministerial positions, most served outside Cassel in positions that utilized their military experience, whether in a constabulary role as *Commissarius Loci* (eight) and *Polizeikommissar* (five) or in road construction commissions (two). Since only two of their number appear on any of the university registers, it is safe to assume that they were exempted from the civil service requirement of university training.

[57]HHStA, RK, Berichte aus dem Reich 81: 9 Feb. 1765 report.

Notwithstanding this special treatment, such a modest presence helped assure the absence of serious friction with professional bureaucrats. The integration of active or retired soldiers was, after all, not unusual in the German states, or even in the United States, where they comprised over a quarter of the new federal bureaucracy.[58] That non-noble civilian bureaucrats accepted the military presence per se is evident from the career choices of their own sons, 30 percent of whom were permitted to choose the army over a career in the civil service.

—*Academics.* In recent years historians have identified the German professoriate and the legions of bureaucrats it trained for public office as a primary force for innovation and change. With their twin advocacy of cameralism and natural law, the university faculties turned out civil officials who were equipped to serve as surrogates for a German bourgeoisie that was too small and provincial to perform its "historic" liberal function. Hesse-Cassel was certainly part of this process. Christian Wolff had personally brought the *Aufklärung* to Hesse in 1723 when, following his expulsion from Prussia by Frederick William I, he began a seventeen-year career at Marburg. Although he returned to his old post at Halle in 1740, following the accession of Frederick the Great, he left a lasting imprint on the Hessian university system. As in most of Germany's Protestant universities, the faculties at Marburg, its sister institution at Rinteln, and the *Collegium Carolinum* at Cassel came to be dominated by his former students or by other *Wolffianer.*[59] Although only a handful of academics actually held positions in the Hessian bureaucracy, the university training demanded of civil officials guaranteed that virtually all Hessian bureaucrats would be exposed to these ideas, whether at Marburg and Rinteln, or at other progressive universities such as Göttingen, Jena, and Halle that were a popular choice among aspiring bureaucrats. Once they had entered the civil service, Hessian bureaucrats

[58]Carl E. Prince, *The Federalists and the Origins of the U.S. Civil Service* (New York, 1977), 269–70.
[59]Wilhelm Dersch, "Beitrag zur Geschichte der Universität Marburg im Zeitalter der Aufklärung," *ZHG*, 54 (1924), 165; H. Hermelink and S. A. Kaehler, *Die Philipps-Universität zu Marburg 1527–1927* (Marburg, 1927), 387; Rudolf Schmitz, *Die Naturwissenschaften an der Philipps-Universität Marburg, 1527–1977* (Marburg, 1978), 43, 49; Franz Karl Theodor Piderit, *Geschichte der hessisch-schaumburgischen Universität Rinteln* (Marburg, 1842), 129–30; Wilhelm Ebert, *Die Geschichte der evangelischen Kirche in Kurhessen* (Cassel, 1860), 228–9.

at the administrative centers of Cassel, Marburg, and Rinteln retained
contact with the three cities' academic communities.[60]

The fruits of this intercourse are evident among both groups. Roughly
a fifth of the 184 civil officials in my survey continued to write and
publish after entering the government. Legal and cameral subjects preoccupied most of these men, including Kopp, Fleckenbühl, and Canngiesser,
himself a former Marburg law professor and favorite student of Christian
Wolff's. Yet social problems, such as peasant living conditions and religious toleration, also concerned several of them, most notably Adolph
Baron Knigge, who launched his career from Cassel by advocating a
universal religion in his *Allgemeines System für das Volk* (1775). The
group even included two published poets and three composers, among
them the *Kriegs- und Domänen Rat* David Philipp Apell, whose work in
ballet and comic opera was performed as far away as Paris. While many
Frederician officials indulged their scholarly and literary talents, the regime did not hesitate to utilize its professional academics for government
service. It relied heavily on its court librarians, archivists, and especially
the faculty of the *Collegium Carolinum* for research and publications on
subjects of interest to both the government and the educated public at
large. They attempted to assist government initiatives in education, poor
relief, feudal reform, agriculture, and commerce with studies designed to
enlighten the regime or the people it governed. They wrote histories,
compiled statistics, edited government directories, compendiums, hand-
books, public affairs newspapers, and journals, gave special instruction
to court residents and their children, censored private publications, and
occasionally even served on diplomatic missions. When necessary the
landgrave also consulted eminent men of letters elsewhere in the *Reich*.
Thus he retained Johann Christoph Gottsched, whose brother was a
Hessian official, for an evaluation of the country's university system.[61]
He also employed Friedrich Karl von Moser for the entire reign, both as
a special adviser on a wide range of domestic problems and as a secret
agent and envoy plenipotentiary to several central European cities, including Frankfurt, Hanau, The Hague, and Vienna.[62]

---

[60]That such interchange existed even in tiny Rinteln is borne out by an anonymous local
author's proud description of the town's "intellectual community" in "Kurze Nachricht
von den Beschäftigungen der Gelehrten in Rinteln," *HB*, 1 (1785), 641–4.
[61]Dersch, "Universität Marburg," 201.
[62]Aside from an unsuccessful mission to Hanau to effect a rapprochement with his family,
Moser's Hessian activities have heretofore totally escaped the notice of historians. The

The contact between academics and bureaucrats extended beyond government activity. In many German cities reading clubs and salons helped to forge an intellectual community from the ranks of the social elite. Hesse-Cassel's numerous Masonic lodges performed this function by bringing together not only civil officials and academics but also other components of the urban intelligentsia, including nobles, artists, and the landgrave's own princely relatives. Marburg boasted the oldest lodge, founded in 1743. Landgrave Constantin's family and top officials headed a chapter at Rotenburg, just as Frederick's sons and their ministers directed one at Hanau. Nevertheless, the greatest Masonic activity centered around the four new lodges founded in Cassel during Frederick's reign. Numbering at least 200 members, they constituted a virtual Who's Who? of Cassel's ruling elite: the landgrave, the princes of the cadet Hessian line of Hesse-Philippstal, high- and middle-ranking civil, court, and military officers, virtually the entire faculty of the *Collegium Carolinum*, and a large number of urban-dwelling nobles from Hesse-Cassel's most prominent families.[63]

Like their brethren elsewhere in Europe, the Hessian Freemasons were idealists who sincerely desired change rather than revolutionaries bent on achieving it. Indeed, in combining the espousal of abstract Enlightenment ideas like toleration, free inquiry, social justice, and equality with practical philanthropy they reflected the activities not only of Freemasonry in general but of the very Hessian regime to which many of them belonged.[64] Hence, Cassel's two largest lodges, "Zum gekrönten Löwen" and "Friedrich von der Freundschaft," built a new workhouse and donated funds to clothe its residents. In his capacity as master of "Friedrich von der Freundschaft" the landgrave even arranged for the same two lodges to underwrite a charity concert performed at Cassel's new opera house.[65] At no time, however, did this group of men who were themselves so closely tied to the government contemplate the kinds of revolutionary

narration will attempt to shed light on these activities by presenting the archival evidence that I have uncovered.
[63] Adolf Kallweit, *Die Freimaurerei in Hessen-Kassel* (Baden-Baden, 1966), 12, 63–4, 341-7; Wilhelm Kolbe, *Zur Geschichte der Freimaurerei in Kassel 1766–1824* (Berlin, 1883), 10–12, 14–15, 18, 29; Brunner, *Residenzstadt Cassel*, 294.
[64] Klaus Epstein, *The Genesis of German Conservatism* (Princeton, 1966), 84–6; Ernst Manheim, *Aufklärung und öffentliche Meinung* (Stuttgart, 1979), 89–97; Kolbe, *Freimaurerei in Kassel*, 6; Kallweit, *Freimaurerei in Hessen-Kassel*, 13; Kurt Kersten, *Der Weltumsegler Johann Georg Adam Forster 1754–1794* (Bern, 1957), 93–4.
[65] Both and Vogel, *Friedrich II.*, 86–7.

designs or activities of which Freemasonry was later accused. The same held true for those Cassel Masons who became *Illuminati*. Organized by Knigge, who was the driving force behind northern German Illuminism, the chapter drew from every professional and social group within Hessian Masonry but was dominated by such noted "free thinkers" as Georg Forster, Jakob Mauvillon, and the landgrave's son Prince Charles, who eventually succeeded Knigge as General Grand Master of the Cassel *Illuminati* and subsequently became National Superior for all Scandinavia following his appointment as Danish governor of Schleswig-Holstein. Nevertheless, although little is known of their activities, the Cassel *Illuminati* do not appear to have become engaged in anything controversial. In fact, several, including Forster, Prince Charles, and even Knigge either joined or associated with the seemingly antithetical Rosicrucians, spending much of their time dabbling in alchemy.[66]

Far from being committed to wholesale change of the established order, the Hessian Masons embodied a dualism that was typical of the entire academic and governing elite. Like Frederick himself they sincerely espoused Enlightenment ideals and utilitarian change, while simultaneously accepting most of the values and institutions of the past. In the realm of politics, they believed that government was obligated to assume an active role in providing for the popular welfare, a conviction readily borne out by the internal government correspondence of officials. They also rejected the proprietary absolutism of the past generation and were firmly convinced that, in the words of one official, "rulers are not owners, but merely administrators of state lands and income."[67] At the same time, however, they embraced the institution of monarchy without question.[68]

The same spirit of compromise was evident in their concept of religion. Whereas Hessian academics sought out the principles of natural law, their former students in the bureaucracy spent their professional lives

---

[66]Wilhelm Maurer, *Aufklärung, Idealismus und Restauration. Studien zur Kirchen- und Geistesgeschichte in besonderer Beziehung auf Kurhessen 1780–1850* (Giessen, 1930), 104–5, 108–10, 113–15; Karl, Prinz von Hessen, *Mémoires de mons temps, dictés par S. A. le Landgrave Charles, prince de Hesse* (Copenhagen, 1861), 137–8; Paul Heidelbach, *Kassel* (Cassel and Basel, 1957) 177; Kallweit, *Freimaurerei in Hessen-Kassel*, 63–4; Kolbe, *Freimaurerei in Kassel*, 5.

[67][Karl Gottfried] Fürstenau, "Zweifel gegen die Verwandlung der Domainen in Bauergüter," *HB*, 2 (1785), 507.

[68]This is not the place for a detailed profile of German political thought. For a brief but thorough analysis, see "The German Problem in the Eighteenth Century," chapter 1 of T. C. W. Blanning, *Reform and Revolution in Mainz, 1743–1803* (Cambridge, 1974).

trying to apply them to government ordinances, promoting in the process the secularization of knowledge and public welfare. Yet, with few exceptions, both groups retained their fervent faith in Christianity. Like German Protestants elsewhere they drew on the metaphysical legacy of Christian Wolff by visualizing natural law and rational thought as part of a divinely instituted cosmos. Such a feat permitted the *Wolffianer* who dominated the theology faculties at Marburg and Rinteln to reconcile federal theology with scientific method and to preach the redundancy of revealed and natural religion. It also enabled them to retain Pietist values and to employ its spirit of social activism throughout the bureaucracy and particularly those Cassel lodges that they came to dominate.[69]

Nor was Hesse's academic-bureaucratic elite inclined toward radical social change. Of late historians have tried to explain this social conservatism on a national scale. Joachim Whaley and Mary Fulbrook have suggested that the Protestant establishment's ability to coexist and ultimately integrate with the academic-bureaucratic elite not only permitted it to protect the church but encouraged it to support Germany's other entrenched institutions against rapid change.[70] Recent work by Hermann Schulz and Mack Walker has demonstrated that cameralist and juristic thought was also responsible: Although the cameralists were generally critical of serfdom and other economic anachronisms, they also valued the proven utility of existing levels of production and were reluctant to place them at risk; whereas jurists were dissatisfied with the unnatural state of human relations, they were reluctant simply to eliminate the rights and privileges of vested interests without compensation.[71] The record of the Frederician regime supports such generalizations, particu-

[69]Gerhard Müller, "Theologie in Marburg zwischen Aufklärung und Restauration," *Jahrbuch des hessischen kirchengeschichtlichen Vereins*, 28 (1977), 29–30; Heppe, *Kirchengeschichte beider Hessen*, 294–5, 335; Ebert, *Evangelischen Kirche in Hessen*, 229; Piderit, *Universität Rinteln*, 129–30; F. Ernst Stoeffler, *German Pietism during the Eighteenth Century* (Brill, 1973), 73-7, 107–8, 237–9, 246-7, 252–3, 257; Maurer, *Aufklärung*, 108.

[70]Whaley, "The Protestant Enlightenment in Germany," in Roy Porter and Mikulas Teich, *The Enlightenment in National Context* (Cambridge, 1981), 112–13, 117; Fulbrook, *Piety and Politics. Religion and the Rise of Absolutism in England, Württemberg and Prussia* (Cambridge, 1983), and "Religion, Revolution and Absolutist Rule in Germany and England," *European Studies Review*, 12 (1982), 301–21.

[71]Schulz, *Das System und die Prinzipien der Einkünfte im werdenden Staat der Neuzeit (1600–1835)* (Berlin, 1982), 207–10, 400; Walker, "Rights and Functions: The Social Categories of Eighteenth-Century German Jurists and Cameralists," *JMH*, 50 (1978), 240–5.

larly the reluctance of officials to advocate economic or social reforms that might have unfortunate short-term effects for *any* group, whether it be the guilds, the nobles, the peasants, or the government itself.

Social conservatism was, of course, hardly limited to Germany. The appeals of Locke and Montesquieu for justice and liberty were also designed to protect the vested interests of established groups. Indeed, like both Locke and Montesquieu, the bureaucracy's reluctance to overturn existing institutions extended beyond economic and social issues to the constitutional structure of the Hessian state. As in much of the *Reich*,[72] the generally stable and harmonious domestic political environment had helped promote the notion that the existence of such a *Zwischengewalt* between crown and country was a natural and beneficial part of Germany's historical tradition. The value and sanctity of corporate institutions were certainly not forgotten in Hesse-Cassel, especially among the one-third of officials who had been trained at nearby Göttingen, where the curriculum reflected strong Anglo-Hanoverian corporate traditions and the university's eagerness to attract noble enrollments.[73] Nor does it appear to have been lost on Hessian academics. In a special public "Mémoire sur la Constitution politique des Anciennes Nations," delivered at the landgrave's request, Christian Wilhelm von Dohm told his audience that a separation of power between executive and legislative institutions was indispensable to the functioning of a free society. It is highly doubtful that Frederick or Dohm's fellow professors disagreed with or were offended by his message. Within the *Collegium Carolinum* even men like Forster, Mauvillon, and Johannes von Müller extolled the virtues of traditional corporate political structures that helped preserve human liberty against despotism.[74]

---

[72]Rudolf Vierhaus, "Montesquieu in Deutschland. Zur Geschichte seiner Wirkung als politischer Schriftsteller im 18. Jahrhundert," *Collegium Philosophicum. Studien Joachim Ritter zum 60. Geburtstag* (Basel and Stuttgart, 1965), 429–32.

[73]Vierhaus, "Die Landstände in Nordwestdeutschland im späten 18. Jahrhundert," in Dietrich Gerhard, ed., *Ständische Vertretungen in Europa im 17. und 18. Jahrhundert* (Göttingen, 1974), 78–80, 92–3; Charles E. McClelland, *State, Society, and University in Germany 1700–1914* (Cambridge, 1980), 43–6; H. Christern, *Deutscher Ständestaat und englischer Parlamentarismus am Ende des 18. Jahrhunderts* (Munich, 1939), 105–207; Carol Rose Loss, "*Status in Statu*: The Concept of Estate in the Organization of German Political Life, 1750–1825," Cornell University diss. (1970), 141–3; Hanns Gross, *Empire and Sovereignty. A History of the Public Law Literature in the Holy Roman Empire, 1599–1804* (Chicago and London, 1973), 442–4.

[74]Vierhaus, "Montesquieu in Deutschland," 425, 428; Forster to Jacobi, 11 Feb. 1783, Hettner, *Briefwechsel*, 316-7; Jakob Mauvillon, *Sammlung von Aufsätzen über Gegenstände aus der Staatskunst, Staatswirthschaft und neuesten Staaten Geschichte*, 1 (Leipzig, 1776), 184, 580; Müller to Schlieffen, 30 Mar. 1782, *Sämmtliche Werke* (Tübingen,

Yet another institution that enjoyed unquestioned acceptance was the military. It is possible to find non-Hessian critics of the military establishment, among both visitors and civil officials. After his dismissal Bopp was particularly critical of the oversized Hessian military establishment. During their tenure at the *Collegium Carolinum* the Swiss Müller and Saxon Huguenot Mauvillon both lamented the excess of soldiers in Germany as a whole.[75] Yet militaristic values were more pervasive than their own critics realized. His lament notwithstanding, even Müller could not help but express his admiration for the Hessian army as it marched off to America. Nor could Mauvillon hide the evident compromise with his environment: His multiple career as a prominent Physiocrat, military scientist, and army officer represented the perfect cultural union of French lights with German arms. Moreover, the bureaucracy as a group appears to have accepted the inevitability of what one native official termed "the disposition of the Germans toward hunting and war."[76] Indeed, shortly after leaving his post at the *Collegium Carolinum*, Dohm spoke for the majority of Hessian officials in extolling the army's positive role in strengthening the economy, the treasury, and social discipline.[77] The symbiosis between cameralism and militarism was, in fact, too obvious to ignore.

The diet

What makes Hesse-Cassel so unusual among the German states is the part its *Landtag* played in the launching of domestic programs. During the nineteenth century both Heinrich von Treitschke and the Hessian historian D. B. W. Pfeiffer demonstrated some awareness of the degree to which the crown and diet worked together during the Old Regime.[78] Their observation was, however, soon forgotten. In the process of rehabilitating Frederick as an enlightened monarch, modern scholars have tended to stick to the customary practice of attributing enlightened initiatives to the landgrave and his ministers, doubtless because these have

1814), 16: 148; Karl Henking, *Johannes von Müller 1752–1809*, 2 (Stuttgart and Berlin, 1928), 10, 15, 26–7.

[75]Bopp, "Fehler," 38; Mauvillon, *Staatskunst*, 136–8; Henking, *Johannes von Müller*, 56; Henry Safford King, *Echoes of the American Revolution in German Literature* (Berkeley, 1929), 173.

[76]Ledderhose, *Kleine Schriften*, 11.

[77]Epstein, *German Conservatism*, 290–1.

[78]Pfeiffer, *Geschichte der landständischen Verfassung in Kurhessen* (Cassel, 1834), 146–67, 175–8; Treitschke, *Das neunzehnte Jahrhundert*, 519.

proven the usual sources of reform elsewhere. Although both Otto Berge's superb study of Frederick and Karl E. Demandt's groundbreaking work on the Hessian *Landtag* demonstrated a familiarity with the final protocols, or *Abschiede*, concluded between the crown and estates at the end of each diet,[79] no modern historian has ever examined either the hundreds of gravamens presented at each meeting or the extensive records of the ensuing bilateral negotiations. This is regrettable, especially since the diet usually recessed and drew up the *Abschiede* long before the crown had investigated and responded to most of its *desiderata*, electing to entrust the continuing negotiations to a smaller standing committee (*Ausschuss*) of deputies.[80] Hence, what the *Abschiede* fail to reflect is the wealth of parliamentary initiatives that the Frederician regime eventually incorporated into its extensive domestic reform program. The lists of gravamens and records of subsequent negotiations with the crown present the unmistakable profile of a parliamentary body that worked closely with the crown and virtually represented the needs of the general population, not just the enfranchised nobles and burghers who elected its deputies.

If the role of the Hessian *Landtag* was unusual, it can be attributed to the equally unique personal, fiscal, and constitutional circumstances that obtained in Hesse-Cassel. The confessional crisis certainly contributed by strengthening the landgrave's determination to get along with his subjects. Yet the collaborative relationship between crown and diet had existed for generations. Part of the reason lies in the limited power of the *Landtag*. Consisting of an upper chamber of secularized benefices and elected members of the Hessian *Ritterschaft* and a lower chamber representing the towns, it had long since lost control over the levying of taxes. Although they continued to consult the diet in all fiscal matters, the landgraves had the authority both to assess and increase all existing direct and indirect taxes.[81] The crown enjoyed such a strong constitutional position because it was already fiscally independent of the diet. Because he was *Grundherr* of two-thirds of the land and of five-sixths

---

[79]Berge, "Friedrich II."; Demandt, "Die hessischen Landstände im Zeitalter des Frühabsolutismus," *HJLG*, 15 (1965), 38–108.

[80]For example, it took the crown two years to examine and respond to the gravamens of the important diet of 1764 and three years to complete negotiations with the deputies. StAMg, 5)14726: Lennep to Riedesel, 8 Sept. 1766, 26 Feb. 1767 Actum Reg Cas.

[81]Adolf Lichtner, *Landesherr und Stände in Hessen-Cassel, 1797–1821* (Göttingen, 1913), 2; Hans Lerch, *Hessische Agrargeschichte des 17. und 18. Jahrhunderts, insbesondere des Kreises Hersfeld* (Hersfeld, 1926), 79; Both and Vogel, *Wilhelm VIII.*, 36, 38, 42.

of the population, the landgrave directly controlled substantial revenues.[82] Hesse-Cassel's century-long involvement in the mercenary trade
afforded the crown even greater fiscal leverage by giving it more revenue
than it actually needed to run the state.

Frederick's reign came at a time when the estates were particularly
vulnerable. With the destruction and exactions of the Seven Years' War
the diet was in no position to meet its customary fiscal obligations to the
crown. By contrast the landgrave had 8.5 million taler in British troop
subsidies on hand, with still more money coming in. Even without the
revenues the country normally paid into the Hessian *Kammerkasse*
(450,000 taler) and *Kriegskasse* (350,000 taler), he could expect to defray
all operating expenses for at least a decade. Later in the reign profits
turned from his involvement in the War of American Independence provided Frederick with another thirteen years' supply. His willingness to
draw on these funds to help the estates, whether by tax reductions or
moratoriums, debt assumptions, or outright grants, gave him tremendous
leverage and helped ensure the cooperation of the diet for the entire reign.
Indeed, while his generation witnessed the widespread attempts of rulers
to circumvent the fiscal privileges of corporate bodies, it was Frederick
who exercised the power of the purse in Hesse-Cassel – albeit with an
assist from Europe's greatest parliamentary institution – with his ability
to extend or deny financial aid.

The virtual absence of fiscal pressures spared the Frederician regime
from the kind of serious confrontation that characterized the relationship
between crown and country in places like Hungary, Sweden, France, England, or America and enabled it to negotiate in an atmosphere free of
conflict or mutual suspicion. Frederick's unassailable position also permitted him the luxury of showing sensitivity to the estates' remaining privileges and sensibilities. He continued his predecessors' policy of letting
them negotiate and collect taxes and made a practice of consulting with
them on most important matters. For this purpose he made – and kept –
a promise to convene diets every six years, at which time the regime gave
careful and thorough consideration to all gravamens submitted to it.[83]

The landgrave's deference extended beyond the diet to his treatment

[82]Eihachiro Sakai, *Der kurhessische Bauer im 19. Jahrhundert und die Grundlastenablösung*
(Melsungen, 1967), 7; George Thomas Fox, "Studies in the Rural History of Upper Hesse,
1650–1830," Vanderbilt University diss. (1976), 23–4.
[83]StAMg, 5)14793: 1764 Landtagsabschied, 5)14714: "Wie über die Landständischen Desideria ... zu besorgen"; Ledderhose, *Kleine Schriften*, 1: 49, 54–62.

of the *Ritterschaft* as a whole. Numbering fewer than 100 families and accounting for less than 1 percent of the population, the *Ritterschaft* consisted of those oldest Hessian noble families that enjoyed representation in the diet's upper chamber. Frederick was careful to protect its exclusivity by codifying its privileges (1763) and adding no new families to its ranks. Beginning in 1770 he extended no fewer than twenty-five personal loans totaling 331,366 taler to its members.[84] Government patronage had an even broader impact. Like other Hessian nobles, very few members of the *Ritterschaft* could live comfortably off their estates, both because of the country's poverty and because the absence of primogeniture had encouraged them to subdivide or share their inheritances. Except for the fortunate few who could find employment in the corporate hierarchy, the only remaining options were government service or employment outside the country. Fortunately, the Frederician regime provided an unusually large number of positions for a state its size, whether as civil, court, or military officers.[85] Nor was patronage limited to adults. Positions as court pages and army cadets were highly valued, since they brought in additional income together with free schooling and the likelihood of subsequent entry into government service.[86] As attractive as these opportunities were, the *Rangordnung* of 1762 also made government employment a social imperative by providing nobles residing at court with the only means of retaining equal status with bourgeois civil and military officers.[87] During the course of Frederick's reign, nearly a quarter of the *Ritterschaft* still living in Hesse-Cassel found employment abroad, repeating an odyssey that had, over time, resulted in the permanent migration of almost a third of all *Ritterschaft* families. Yet the overwhelming percentage of those who were unwilling or unable to leave the country found employment in the landgrave's service, accounting for 64 percent of all Hessian-born (224/351) and 83 percent of all Hessian-resident (224/269) members of the *Ritterschaft* (Figure 1).

The extent of government patronage was roughly the same for the thirty-four generally wealthier and more independent deputies who sat in the *Landtag*'s upper chamber (Table 5). At least twenty-two of their number held a government position before entering the diet, a group that accounts for 65 percent of all deputies and 76 percent of those with careers inside Hesse-Cassel. The percentage of deputies employed within

---

[84]Pedlow, "Nobility of Hesse-Kassel," 23, 25, 31, 122–3.
[85]Günderode, *Briefe eines Reisenden*, 228.
[86]Ruhl, *Hof Landgraf Friedrich's*, 13.
[87]Pedlow, "Nobility of Hesse-Kassel," 204–5, 209.

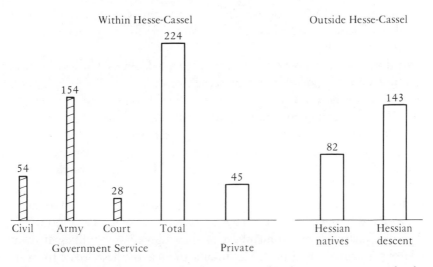

Figure 1. Ritterschaft careers, 1760–85. Eleven men combined two or more careers, thereby pushing the breakdown within the three government branches past the total of 224. Principal sources: *SAK*; Buttlar-Elberberg, *Stammbuch*; Strieder, *Gelehrten, Schriftsteller und Künstler Geschichte*.

the Hessian regime was, however, dramatically higher in Frederick's last three diets. Moreover, after 1772 the landgrave appointed six former deputies to the powerful and lucrative post of *Landrat*. Since Frederick selected all *Landräte* from a list prepared by the local *Ritterschaft*, both the landgrave and *Ritterschaft* presumably enjoyed a certain amount of leverage over these men while they were still deputies who might aspire toward future selection as *Landrat*. Including these future appointees

Table 5. *Government patronage: upper-chamber deputies, 1764–85*

	Total deputies	Officers			Total govt.	Total nongovt.	Govt. officers
		Civil	Army	Court			
1764	17	5	3	3 =	8	9	47%
1772	6	1	0	0 =	1	5	17%
1774	7	4	3	1 =	6	1	86%
1779	9	4	3	3 =	7	2	78%
1785	9	3	6	1 =	7	2	78%
Total	34	12	12	7 =	22	12	65%

Note: Individual and aggregate statistics do not correlate because several deputies either held more than one position or attended more than one diet.
Principal sources: StAMg, Landtag Abschiede; *SAK*; Buttlar-Elberberg, *Stammbuch*.

among those enjoying government employment would raise the total number of deputies in Frederick's pay to twenty-six, or 76 percent of all upper-chamber deputies.

At the same time, government patronage for deputies' family members was not only considerable but increased as the reign progressed. With 42 percent of their fathers, 63 percent of their brothers, and 74 percent of their sons securing government employment, *Ritterschaft* deputies obviously benefited from a trend toward greater patronage that reflected either Frederick's attempts to court them or simply the increased inclination of the deputies – like the rest of the nobility – to rely on the crown for their livelihood.[88] The landgrave clearly did favor *Ritterschaft* deputies with personal loans. Of the twenty-five loans he extended to members of the *Ritterschaft* after 1770, fourteen went to the relations of deputies, including ten to members of their immediate families. It is, of course, difficult to find evidence linking the use of these loans to overt government attempts to influence deputies. Nor is it plausible to assume that this was the case, given the largely consensual and advisory nature of Hessian parliamentary politics. More likely it was the deputies themselves who benefited most, using their greater proximity, intimacy, and influence with the landgrave to secure loans. Most of the twenty-five loans were, in fact, made during or immediately following meetings of the diet, suggesting that the deputies used their position and presence in Cassel to secure them, whether for themselves, their families, or their constituents within the *Ritterschaft*.[89]

The preceding evidence might explain the lack of opposition from within the Hessian nobility or the *Ritterschaft* represented in the *Landtag*. It also exposes a cozy symbiosis between the crown, bureaucracy, and privileged estates, all of whom benefited in one way or another from the *Soldatenhandel*. It does not, however, account for the initiative the diet demonstrated in urging and supporting various domestic programs. One obvious explanation is that most projects were funded with the crown's own money and, thus, posed no threat of increased taxation. Another is that, like the reforms of enlightened monarchs everywhere, they were usually aimed at bolstering the economy, hardly a controversial maneuver to the generally impoverished towns and *Ritterschaft* represented in

---

[88] These figures are based on those thirty deputies for whom genealogical information is available.

[89] I would like to thank Gregory Pedlow for providing me with much of the raw data for the loans cited here.

the diet. There is also evidence that, in their exposure to new ideas and receptiveness to change, *Landtag* deputies constituted a distinctly more progressive element not only within the Hessian nobility but within society as a whole. The presence of 65 percent of upper-chamber deputies in government service — 35 percent of them in the bureaucracy — would have predisposed them toward the regime and its policies. So might their higher degree of university training, which, at the very least, would have exposed them to the rationalist ideas that had become articles of faith within the university-trained Hessian bureaucracy. The names of 56 percent (19/34) of upper-chamber deputies appear on the published *Universitätsmatrikel*, the same percentage as for noble bureaucrats and only slightly less than the 62 percent figure for all 184 bureaucrats in my survey.[90] Though somewhat less than half of those deputies sitting in the lower chamber had received university training, they were also better educated as a group than the town constituencies they represented.

Nor is it necessarily fair to assume that the nobility in general was a hotbed of nay-saying reactionaries. They too were better educated than previous generations and thereby better exposed to the new ideas currently circulating in Germany's Protestant universities. The eighteenth century witnessed a considerable increase in the number of nobles receiving university training, drawn as they were by the social and career advantages it bestowed as well as by a genuine interest in new ideas. This was certainly the case in Hesse-Cassel, where there was a large surge in noble enrollments at both Marburg and nearby Göttingen.[91] A little more than a quarter of the Hessian *Ritterschaft* had obtained a university education level by midreign, with many others receiving instruction through private tutors or the *Collegium Carolinum*.[92] It is also worth remembering that the *Ritterschaft* as a group did elect *Landtag* deputies, including several who had already established reputations as reformers acquired from previous government service. Surely they would not have done so had they found their views objectionable.

What is perhaps most important, however, is that we appreciate the

[90]The admittedly incomplete *Matrikel* indicate the following attendance: Marburg, thirteen; Göttingen, Erlangen, and Halle, two each; Rinteln, Giessen, Leiden, and Utrecht, one each.
[91]Karl Wilhelm Justi, *Grundzüge einer Geschichte der Universität zu Marburg* (Marburg, 1827), 104; McClelland, *State, Society, and University in Germany,* 39, 52.
[92]Pedlow, "Nobility of Hesse-Kassel," 215, 222, 226.

underlying dynamic that generally governs relations between executive
and representative bodies. By their very nature as representatives of an
enfranchised group – especially one that embodies substantial vested
interests – parliamentary bodies are essentially conservative, especially
on social issues. This could certainly be said of all the eighteenth-century
congressional bodies, including those in pluralistic political systems like
Great Britain, the Netherlands, or even the fledgling United States. It was
crucial to the success of crown-diet relations that the Hessian privileged
classes as a whole – and their deputies in particular – trusted the government and were confident that it would not challenge their privileged
position. On occasions when the regime did do something aggressive,
there was sufficient residual trust and goodwill that they acquiesced,
especially since they also felt no pressure from popular unrest that might
assist or accelerate the pace of the landgrave's domestic reforms. In fact,
the experience of Hesse-Cassel suggests that, when vested interests are
not threatened, privileged corporations and individuals are capable of
embracing new ideas, acting paternalistically toward the unprivileged
classes, and virtually representing them and the general welfare.

The shape of policy

Given the breadth of the Hessian power structure and its general acceptance of existing institutions, it is not surprising that the regime was
more responsive than innovative: Far from being a broadly creative force
that applied abstract principles, it tended to govern by reacting to specific
problems as they were called to its attention. Within Hesse-Cassel the
government leaned heavily on both the reports of local bureaucrats and
the petitions of *Landtag* deputies to make it aware of existing problems.
To shorten further the already short and active lines of communication,
Frederick also traveled to outlying exclaves such as Schmalkalden and
Schaumburg to study conditions at first hand. Meanwhile, given its very
presence in Cassel the regime devoted more attention and ordinances to
correcting problems in the residence than in any other part of the country.
    It is indicative of the cautiousness – and lack of creativity – of the
Hessian regime that it often confronted local problems by first consulting
neighboring states in order to see how they had dealt with them before
actually drawing up its own solution. In fact, whenever the regime was
not reacting to specific petitions from inside the country, it was intro-

ducing ordinances modeled after the successful programs of other foreign or German states. Not surprisingly Prussia was the model most often imitated, if only because of the landgrave, who supplemented his earlier exposure to Prussia and admiration for its king with additional visits following his succession.[93] This influence was, however, also felt through the presence of so many Prussians at all levels of the Hessian administration — as well as of Hessians employed in the Prussian service, perhaps a third of all Hessian nobles living abroad.

Nor was the carryover of ideas limited to Prussia. Like most other German states, Hesse-Cassel never hesitated to model its own ordinances after those of its neighbors, even to the point of copying their laws verbatim.[94] The greatest source of such inspiration was the empire's voluminous journal literature. Public affairs journals were regularly read both by the country's academic faculties and by its bureaucrats, who were expected to search for any new developments that might be profitably applied at home.[95] In addition, the *Landtag*'s desiderata occasionally called attention to the initiatives of other states.

Foreign visitors from as far away as France, Italy, and Poland were also a source of ideas and new projects. More often, however, it was the Hessians themselves who did the traveling. The landgrave himself traveled extensively, both within the empire and to countries such as Switzerland, Italy, England, and especially France, which he visited twice before and four times after his succession. He invariably brought back new ideas that often took the form of detailed lists of proposed changes ranging from major economic initiatives to such trivial subjects as public smoking, the carriage traffic in Cassel, or the lettering on storefront signs.[96] On several occasions he dispatched fact-finding missions as far away as En-

[93]The Austrian envoy observed that Frederick was "an exaggerated admirer and imitator not only of Prussian principles but also of the king himself"; the French envoy noted that Frederick had a "mania for thinking of the king of Prussia." HHStA, RK, Berichte aus dem Reich 81: 9 Feb. 1765 Pergen report; AAE, CP, HC 13: 17 Aug. 1773 Verac report.
[94]Raeff, *Well-Ordered Police State*, 50.
[95]The failure to do so could cause quite an uproar, such as in 1774, when Frederick returned from a trip to Paris with two French pamphlets detailing a thirty-year-old Swiss technique for resuscitating drowning victims that had escaped the notice of Hessian health officials. The government immediately drafted an ordinance requiring local officials to teach the technique, though not before censuring health officials for their negligence. StAMg, 5)10551: Collegium Medicum report [Oct. 1774].
[96]StAMg, 5)1582: 27 Sept. 1775 Actum Reg Cas, 22 Oct. 1781 KDK report; "Articles pour introduire . . ." [1781].

gland to study conditions and policies in other countries. Meanwhile, Hessian agents already stationed abroad had standing orders to report new developments that might be successfully applied inside Hesse-Cassel.

The landgrave and his government genuinely thought of themselves as active participants in an age of Enlightenment. Yet in formulating policy they were influenced by no single social or economic philosophy but by a mixture of several currents of thought. Among them cameralism was clearly the dominant presence in domestic policy-making, through which all other ideas were filtered for compatibility. To be sure it shared a great deal with Enlightenment currents. Both professed the general welfare and happiness to be their primary goal and sought to achieve it by secular means, through the creation of wealth attained by greater productivity. Both were especially eager to lessen the numerous burdens on the common people, a concern expressed time and again by Hessian officials obsessed with the need "to raise the standard of living" of the peasantry.[97] Furthermore, both Enlightenment and cameralist thought believed in the ability of government to identify what Schlieffen termed the "general and immutable laws of statecraft" that, once mastered, would allow rational solutions to existing problems.[98] From time to time high government officials and even *Landtag* deputies expressed their support for such Enlightenment values as education, economic freedom, and toleration. As a rule, however, both groups tended to focus their attention on practical solutions to specific problems rather than on abstract Enlightenment principles, especially when they contradicted the tenets of cameralist science. By contrast the landgrave was prone on occasion to promote projects that were directly inspired by Enlightenment notions of freedom, equality, human dignity, and education, though they often took shape through laws that were borrowed from other states. Christian religious values also inspired all levels of the Hessian elite. Yet, having itself been integrated into the ruling elite, the Protestant hierarchy tended to reinforce rather than challenge the government's cameralist outlook. Thus,

---

[97]Ulrich Engelhardt, "Zum Begriff der Glückseligkeit in der kameralistischen Staatslehre des 18. Jahrhunderts," *Zeitschrift historischer Forschung*, 8 (1981), 42–3, 47–8, 78–9; Keith Tribe, "Cameralism and the Science of Government," *JMH*, 56 (1984), 275; Ursula A. J. Becher, *Politische Gesellschaft. Studien zur Genese bürgerlicher Öffentlichkeit in Deutschland* (Göttingen, 1978), 85; Raeff, *Well-Ordered Police State*, 40–1, 172–3; Schulz, *Prinzipien der Einkünfte*, 400.

[98]StAMg, 5)13443: 2 Jan. 1775 Schlieffen report.

the Pietist teaching that pervaded all segments of Protestant society helped legitimize government intervention by stressing the need for discipline and obedience to authority and by advocating greater social concern through utilitarian reform.[99] Not unlike our own contemporary world, the story of enlightened absolutism in Hesse-Cassel involves this interplay of statist, Enlightenment, and Christian themes.

Yet, despite their carefully molded compatibility, complete harmony was impossible. One conflict arose from the cameralist emphasis on the dynamic function performed by money, a role dramatized by J. H. G. Justi when he wrote, "Money is the blood of the state, just as government is its heart. Through taxation the blood is brought to the heart where, by wise investment, the regime recirculates it back through the arteries."[100] In practice, however, the "blood" assumed a life of its own. Although cameralism perceived the wealth of the individual and the state as common goals that together served the popular welfare, the cameralist bureaucracy's obsession with balanced budgets and the preservation of sources of revenue soon became an end in itself, occasionally superseding its empathy for popular misery. Hence it became virtually impossible to curtail proven revenue sources, whether they be the Hessian army or more traditional money-makers like tariffs, tolls, sales taxes, and monopolies, regardless of the ill effects they might have on the economy or public welfare. Despite the state's ample treasury, fiscal officials expected that public institutions such as libraries, schools, hospitals, and foundling homes would eventually be self-supporting, often by means of new taxes levied on the general public. Even the people's ability to pay taxes or avert poverty became primarily a fiscal issue as the regime's desire to meet projected revenues and curtail the expense of the welfare rolls competed with its empathy for mass suffering.[101]

Cameralism also led to conflict between government regulation and economic freedom. There is ample evidence that the Hessian regime appreciated the advantages of free trade. At the beginning of the reign

[99]Fulbrook, "Religion, Revolution and Absolutist Rule," 301–21; G. Uhlhorn, *Die christliche Liebesthätigkeit*, 3 (Stuttgart, 1890), 262; Whaley, "Protestant Enlightenment," 111–12.

[100]Quoted in Becher, *Politische Gesellschaft*, 85.

[101]For two such examples, see StAMg, 5)13446: 15 Jan. 1784 Motz report, 5)3424: 21 Feb. 1785 Comm Coll report. In the words of a 3 May 1776 ordinance, it was essential that "the people be preserved so that they may be in a position to discharge their taxes and other responsibilities." *HLO*, 864.

Frederick maintained in his *Pensées* that commerce and industry should be allowed as much autonomy as possible.[102] As early as 1766 the Saxe-Gothan minister and economist Johann Rüdiger Wegner advised the landgrave that he could best revive his country's postwar economy by restricting the monopolies and guilds, while giving local entrepreneurs a "free hand" to conduct their own affairs.[103] Frederick's ministers were, in fact, generally critical of the ill effects that monopolies and guilds had on productivity, quality, and prices and were also aware of the overall ineffectiveness of import and export barriers. Some embraced the ideal of "totally free trade" and the notion that "freedom is the soul and life of commerce."[104] Even the estates had their own practical reasons for advocating free trade, whether against monopolies or the restrictions and tariffs placed on raw wool exports, and were fully capable of arguing that they constituted a "restriction on the natural freedom of trade and movement."[105]

Yet, as in most of Germany, free trade remained principally an economic theory, while cameralism addressed itself more readily to the practical difficulties confronting government planners.[106] Above all the regime had to contend with the hostile trade environment that existed within the empire. Although it recognized that Hesse-Cassel was too small and economically underdeveloped to be self-sufficient, it could do little to eliminate the cutthroat competition among states, including the taxation, prohibition, and outright confiscation of Hessian goods by neighboring principalities. Rather, the close proximity of so many states and enclaves

---

[102]"Pensées," #30.
[103]StAMg, 5)3192: Wegner to Frederick, 26 Feb. 1766.
[104]StAMg, 5)13443: 2 Jan. 1775 GD report, 7 Jan. 1775 Bose and du Rosey votae, 5)3678: 18 Oct. 1784 KDK report. Cameralist thinkers were also critical of monopolies. See Engelhardt, "Kameralistischen Staatslehre," 79; Schulz, *Prinzipien der Einkünfte*, 316–18; Raeff, *Well-Ordered Police State*, 95.
[105]StAMg, 5)3678 "Extract Landtags Acten 1731" [1764], 5)14717: "Desideria generalia …4tes, 5tes, 7tes" [1764]; "Every monopoly, as everyone knows, is extremely harmful when it involves production and the needs of the common man, but is at its most harmful when it involves domestic output. It constitutes a genuine and widespread burden that is all the more oppressive whenever it involves life's necessities and hits hardest the poor person who is already besieged by numerous taxes and least able to pay. It benefits only the greed of those few who seek to enrich themselves at the cost of the rest of society. It corrupts the morality and character of the native, accustoms the subjects to smuggling and perjury, and injects honorable commerce with immoral implications … It is a … restriction of the natural freedom of trade and movement." 304)580: "Desiderium commune XXXIIItum" [6 Mar 1786]; Harm-Heinrich Brandt, *Von der fürstlich hessischen Commerzienkammer zur Industrie- und Handelskammer* (Cassel, 1960), 34–5.
[106]Gagliardo, *From Pariah to Patriot. The Changing Image of the German Peasant 1770–1840* (Lexington, Ky., 1969), 38.

created a siege mentality among Hessian merchants and ministers alike for which protectionism offered the only relief. Like its counterparts elsewhere in the *Reich* the regime became obsessed with the need to maintain a favorable balance of trade and stem the outflow of specie, even to the extent that Bopp criticized the retention of non-Hessian bureaucrats like himself because they exported Hessian money abroad![107]

The government was able to make limited headway against the guilds by subjecting them to closer oversight, by compelling them to admit more members, and even by occasionally authorizing cheaper outside labor in an attempt to drive down costs.[108] Yet, though their elimination might have been the best long-term solution, the government could not accept the devastating short-term effects that further reforms might have on the guilds, which were already reeling from the devastation of the Seven Years' War. Instead it continued to protect the guilds against reciprocal trade agreements and foreign imports, knowing full well that other states would retaliate against Hessian products.[109] The regime even protected the guilds against native competition from less expensive rural artisans, if only because cameralism encouraged it to compartmentalize the economy into a rural sector responsible for agriculture and an urban one devoted to commerce and industry, a rigid dualism that inclined them to protect urban guilds whenever they remonstrated against rural competition.[110]

The country's widespread poverty also mandated other forms of government intervention as well. As elsewhere in Germany the absence of private investment capital led to massive crown sponsorship of factories and other capitalist enterprises. Indeed, even as they cited the need for greater freedom against monopolies and various trade restrictions, the

---

[107]Fox, "Upper Hesse," 15, 45; Bopp, "Fehler," 181.
[108]*HLO*, 233: 15 May 1765; StAMg, 5)4009: 3 Feb. 1778 Schenck report; 5)3424: 21 Feb. 1785 Lennep and Comm Coll reports; Walter Kürschner, *Geschichte der Stadt Marburg* (Marburg, 1934), 189; C. Brauns, *Kurhessische Gewerbepolitik im 17 und 18. Jahrhundert* (Leipzig, 1911), 78–80, 83, 98.
[109]Brauns, *Kurhessische Gewerbepolitik*, 85; Ulrich Möker, *Entwicklungstheorie und geschichtliche Wirtschaft. Makroökonomische Erklärungen wirtschaftlicher Zustände und Entwicklungen der Landgrafschaft Hessen-Kassel vom 16. bis zum 19. Jahrhundert* (Marburg, 1971), 173–8, 197–8; Hans Lohse, *600 Jahre Schmalkaldener Eisengewinnung und Eisenverarbeitung* (Meiningen, 1965), 62. Thus, in 1770 it succumbed to pressure from Cassel's guilds to reject Eichsfeld's proposal for a trade agreement. StAMg, 5)6062: 1 Dec. 1769 GR protocol; 3 Jan. 1770 guild masters to Comm Coll; 15 Jan. 1770 Comm Coll report; 19 Jan. 1770 resolution.
[110]Bopp, "Fehler," 13, 180; StAMg, 5)14717: "Desideria communia der gesamten Landschaft" [1764], 5)813: 4 Aug. Eigenbrod votum, 7 Oct. 1774 rescript; *HLO*, 783–4.

estates actively sought government funds for new industry.[111] The regime also felt the need to protect the common people from the vicissitudes of free trade. Following standard cameralist practice, it closely monitored wages and prices both in Hesse-Cassel and in neighboring states, publishing exhaustive regulations that guaranteed laborers a living wage, small farmers a minimum price following good harvests, and the consumer affordable staples after crop failures.

If economic freedom was a casualty of cameralism as practiced in Hesse-Cassel, so was the freedom of the individual. In his *Pensées* Frederick stated how the "love of order" was indispensable for a ruler and, in his own notes, Bopp related how important it was that even the common people live by a systematized work schedule. Indeed, though cameralism conceded the virtues of maintaining individual freedom *when possible*, in practice the Hessian regime more readily saw enforced discipline and order as the most effective way to serve the public and individual welfare.[112] Nor did it break ranks with the body of *Aufklärer* and cameralists alike who stressed the individual's primary responsibility to society and who visualized society and the state as indistinguishable. The guidelines the regime issued to its *Landräte* made it clear, in fact, that government served the dual role of securing the happiness of the people while guaranteeing that they fulfilled their responsibility to the state.[113]

The regime's readiness to supervise so closely the lives of its subjects attests in part to cameralism's supreme confidence in the effectiveness of government as an instrument for securing the general welfare. It also reveals an unflattering view of human nature. The *Aufklärer* had been consistent with Enlightenment currents by extolling the people's intrinsic goodness as well as their natural capacities for the exercise of reason and the pursuit of pleasure.[114] Yet, like bureaucrats elsewhere, most Hessian officials saw things differently. They subscribed to an elitist view common to all educated Europeans, the philosophes included, that although all people were educable, the current ignorance of the masses rendered them

---

[111] StAMg, 5)14717: "Desideria generalia ... 4tes, 35tes."
[112] "Pensées," #3; Bopp, "Fehler," 48a; Engelhardt, "Kameralistischen Staatslehre," 52.
[113] Albion Small, *The Cameralists. The Pioneers of German Social Polity* (Chicago and London, 1909), 16, 588–9; Engelhardt, "Kameralistischen Staatslehre," 50, 70; Ulrich F. Kopp, "Von den Landräten," in [G. H.] von Berg, ed., *Hessen-Casselischen teutsches Staatsmagazin* (1796), 157.
[114] H. B. Nisbet, "'Was ist Aufklärung': The Concept of Enlightenment in Eighteenth-Century Germany," *Journal of European Studies*, 12 (1982), 81.

Sand of me

stupid, lazy, resistant to change, and excessively prone to the satisfaction of their basest instincts.[115] Harsh as it was, it conformed to the average bureaucrat's Calvinist pessimism and was readily reinforced by his daily encounters with the Hessian canaille. In the report he presented to the landgrave in 1766, Wegner recited the well-known German proverb "Wenn der Bauer nicht muss, rührt er weder Hand noch Fuss." Three decades later another official explained that the people, like children, could not be neglected without considerable risk and had to be supervised in order to save them from their natural tendencies toward lethargy and mischief:

When children are raised without close supervision they become adults who are shortsighted, less wise, and thus incapable of dealing resourcefully with adversity. The hand of authority must therefore intervene from the start and, through compulsion, require that which they refuse to do of their own volition for their own welfare, the welfare of their children and the welfare of the whole state.[116]

Such an assessment justified the regime's resolve to supervise and intervene in the lives of the landgrave's subjects, a determination that is illustrated by the single volume of the *Sammlung fürstlich hessischer Landesordnungen* that is devoted to Frederick's reign. Though it omits secret and unpublished official directives, its 1,439 public decrees and regulations alone average one new ordinance per week and dramatize the lengths to which the government was willing to go to secure the "enforced happiness" of the general population. Whatever success it attained in achieving this end must, however, be balanced against the many complaints that were leveled against the well-intentioned officials who assumed such a high profile in people's lives. One contemporary essay written near the end of the reign cited a combination of bureaucratic "despotism, slowness, and fearfulness" of bending rules as the single biggest problem confronting the Hessian peasantry. It also repeated the often-heard complaint against officials enforcing general laws that were inappropriate for local conditions.[117] Other sources decried local officials' undying passion for compiling tables and statistics. With separate cadastres and surveys for population, livestock, taxation, fire insurance, army recruiting, and feudal dues and services, Hesse-Cassel clearly was

[115]Harry C. Payne, *The Philosophes and the People* (New Haven and London, 1976), 1–41, 123, 135; Gagliardo, *From Pariah to Patriot*, 28–31, 36, 121–8; Raeff, *Well-Ordered Police State*, 78–83.
[116]StAMg, 5)3192: 25 Feb. 1766, Wegner to Frederick; Kopp, "Landräten," 134–6.
[117]"Einfälle eines Kameralisten," *HB*, 1 (1784), 200–1, 203, 207–8.

überverzeichnet. No less common was the complaint that many reforms had unintended and unforeseen side effects, many of which actually worsened the conditions they were supposed to remedy.

Finally, it is worth mentioning that Hessian officialdom exhibited a certain ideological inflexibility in its uncritical acceptance of the cameralist sciences. It adhered to all of the bromides and strategies taught in the German universities without questioning their applicability for Hesse-Cassel. Thus it proved incapable of relaxing its fiscal vigilance, even during the closing decade of the reign, when the influx of British subsidies assured a permanent reserve of funds. It was no less compulsive in its attempts to counteract what was in fact a Continentwide wood shortage by carefully rationing the country's wood supplies, even though over half of its land was covered with forests. It also failed to take the country's excess labor supply into account when it readily employed the conventional strategies for promoting population growth by seeking foreign settlers and steadfastly forbidding native emigration.

Even a casual reading of the conflicts and contradictions that troubled the Hessian regime as it drafted domestic policy suggests that its dilemma was not endemic solely to the Old Regime. While they were trying to divine the essence of natural law, Frederick and his ministers were also encountering the stress between ideology and reality that occurs naturally in all societies. Certainly the parallels with the modern world are evident enough. Armed with Justi's almost Keynesian view of monetary circulation, cameralism pitted confidence in government economic management against concurrent Physiocratic notions of economic freedom. It also placed the general interest ahead of individual freedom by taking an active role in protecting society from the imperfections of human nature. Along the way, however, it was compelled to balance competing social needs against its concern for fiscal integrity. It was also compelled to sacrifice theoretical preferences and long-term economic goals in order to spare existing constituencies such as the *Ritterschaft*, guilds, entrepreneurs, peasant farmers, and urban consumers from severe and more immediate hardships. Even public criticism of overzealous bureaucrats, their disregard for local conditions, and the limited or contrary effects of domestic programs were not without a certain timelessness.

Given such obstacles it is not difficult to understand why so much of the Frederician reform program was limited in its shape, scope, and originality – especially when we remember that the triad of crown, bureaucracy, and diet itself represented views that drew equally from the past and the future. Hence Frederick can be excused for his fatalism when, halfway through his reign, he confessed to the limited prospects for change vis-à-vis established structures, confiding in a letter to Voltaire that "in the best of all possible worlds, it is necessary to be patient and understanding of things that one does not know how to change."[118]

[118]StAMg, 4a)91,44: Frederick to Voltaire, 17 Apr. 1773.

3

The postwar recovery

The reactive nature of Hessian policymaking is illustrated by the uneven activity of government legislation over the course of Frederick's twenty-five-year reign. Domestic initiatives and reforms tended to reach peak levels of intensity during each of three crisis periods: at the conclusion of the Seven Years' War, when the regime worked to rebuild the devastated economy; at midreign, when it responded to the Continentwide crop failures of 1771–2; and during the closing years of the war in America, when it felt compelled to react to a number of recurrent problems made worse by the government's own domestic and foreign initiatives (Figure 2). Through each of these periods it is possible to trace not only the regime's reaction to existing injustices and suffering, usually after consultation with the *Landtag*, but also the evolution of new approaches to reform as it adjusted to earlier failures and mistakes with new strategies.

The common thread that ties together all three periods is the country's poverty and economic stagnation, a circumstance that both shaped and limited the success of domestic reform. At Frederick's succession Hesse-Cassel had a population of perhaps 275,000, living in roughly 2,750 square miles in central Germany.[1] It was a predominantly rural society, with three-quarters of the people living outside population centers of more than 1,000, and over 90 percent of them engaged in farming.[2] The country was not, however, well suited for agriculture. The terrain was hilly, and more than half of it was covered by forest. Arable land was in short supply, and it was also generally poor in quality. The climate

[1]There are no statistics available for the 1760s. I am repeating the estimates published for both 1740 and 1750, since wartime losses probably wiped out any demographic advances after 1750. Bruno Hildebrand, *Statistische Mitteilungen über die volkswirtschaftlichen Zustände Kurhessens* (Berlin, 1853), 40–5; Both and Vogel, *Wilhelm VIII.*, 81.
[2]Berge, "Friedrich II.," 80; Möker, *Geschichtliche Wirtschaft*, 162.

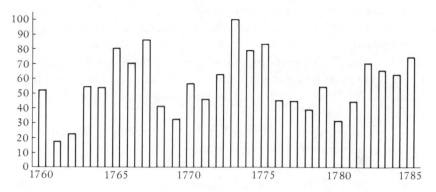

Figure 2. Frequency of publication of ordinances and regulations, per annum. Source: *HLO.*

was no more favorable, providing the country with so little sun and so much rain that Hesse-Cassel was the only state in the empire that was compelled to use covered postwagons.[3] Even the Hessian nobility lived a Spartan life, hampered as it was by relatively small and scattered plots that were difficult to cultivate and administer.[4]

If anything the country's commercial and manufacturing infrastructure was worse off. The unfavorable terrain and weather rendered the building and maintenance of roads difficult, a circumstance that explains the country's notorious reputation among travelers.[5] Though it was close to Frankfurt and Thuringia, Hesse-Cassel was bypassed by major overland and water routes that surrounded it on all sides. Its sole commercial waterway, the Weser-Fulda, was navigable only in the northernmost part of the country. Furthermore, its passage to the North Sea was hindered by two dozen tolls and the hostility of Hannoversch-Münden, whose boatmen were prone to seize Hessian goods that competed with its own industries. There was, in any event, very little of significance worth exporting. Aside from the iron production in its Thuringian exclave of Schmalkalden, Hesse-Cassel's manufacturing and export industries relied almost exclusively on textiles. Its once considerable wool and linen industries had, however, never recovered from the Thirty Years' War. Although wool manufacturing still supported the economies of Hersfeld

[3]William Mead, *The Grand Tour in the Eighteenth Century* (New York, 1914), 70.
[4]Sakai, *Kurhessische Bauer,* 6.
[5]Thielen, *Hardenberg,* 26; Both and Vogel, *Wilhelm VIII.,* 82; Apelblad, *Reise durch . . . Hessen,* 275; Adolph Freiherr Knigge, *Der Roman meines Lebens* (Liechtenstein, 1978), 66; *Briefe eines iungen Reisenden durch Liefland, Kurland, und Deutschland,* 2 (Erlangen, 1777), 81, 108.

and Eschwege, it was sufficiently moribund elsewhere that the country was very possibly a net wool importer. Meanwhile, the linen industry in both Hesse-Cassel proper and the rural northern exclave of Schaumburg was commercially insignificant. So meager was the urban economy that the Prussian Bopp was moved to observe: "There is no industry in Hesse-Cassel. . . . All Hesse is a village. The towns and cities are merely villages enclosed with walls."[6]

A look inside those walls justifies Bopp's hyperbole. The stagnant economy had devastated the guilds, whose memberships everywhere were either falling or suffering from lack of work. According to contemporary accounts, most of the country's beggars were either artisans or the unusually large number of *Betteljuden* who shared the artisans' difficulties in securing work or privileges. Even by German standards those burghers who were gainfully employed, whether guild masters or members of the tiny entrepreneurial bourgeoisie, were still generally poor, so poor in fact that one member of the General Directory claimed they were no better off as a group than common peasants.[7] With the exception of Cassel, which owed its prosperity to its court and garrison, the country's towns presented a depressing physical appearance as well. Travelers generally commented on their wretchedness. Even Hesse-Cassel's second city, the university center and one-time *Residenzstadt* of Marburg, invariably appalled its visitors. Though it had been regarded in the sixteenth century as one of the Continent's most beautiful cities, it was now routinely described by travelers as one of the ugliest.[8]

---

[6] Albrecht Eckhardt, "Die Gewerbestruktur der Landgrafschaft Hessen-Kassel um 1740," *HJLG*, 15 (1965), 175; Fox, "Upper Hesse," 28, 32; Brandt, *Commerzienkammer*, 38, and *Die Industrie- und Handelskammer Kassel und ihre Vorläufer 1763–1963* (Cassel, 1963), 19; Bopp, "Fehler," 43–4.

[7] Pedlow, "Nobility of Hesse-Kassel," 14; Lerch, *Hessische Agrargeschichte*, 32; Bopp, "Fehler," 21–2; StAMg, 5)13443: 15 Jan. 1775 Wille votum.

[8] *Beschreibung der schönsten Städte der Welt* (1572). One observer remarked that "the houses are in such wretched condition that they look like they are going to collapse at any moment . . . I believe I would become depressed if I had to stay in Marburg long." *Briefe eines iungen Reisenden*, 79; another that it was "one of the ugliest cities I saw . . . I found here not a single house in which a professor could live" (though, of course, quite a few actually did) [F. Sneedorf], *Briefe eines reisenden Dänen, geschrieben im Jahr 1791 und 1792 während seiner Reise durch einen Theil Deutschlands, der Schweiz und Frankreich* (Züllichau, 1793), 86; even the widely traveled Wilhelm von Humboldt called it "easily the ugliest and most unpleasant [city] that one can imagine [with] old and ugly houses, dirty narrow streets [and] poor lighting." Quoted in Hermelink and Kaehler, *Universität zu Marburg*, 427; *Neue Reisebemerkungen in und über Deutschland*, 3 (Halle, 1787), 60, also spoke of its ugliness. For the equally depressing portraits of other Hessian towns, see *Bemerkungen eines Reisenden durch Deutschland, Frankreich, England und Holland in Briefen an seine Freunde*, 1 (Altenburg, 1775), 6 [Hersfeld]; Heinrich König,

From this endemic poverty and economic stagnation emerged a pattern of emigration that persisted throughout the century following the Thirty Years' War. Although the inaccuracy of surviving government records does not sustain precise figures, it is clear that the combination of migration and mortality limited population growth in the countryside to modest levels, while leading to an actual decline or stagnation in most of the Hessian towns.[9]

The Seven Years' War only exacerbated the demographic and economic decline of the Hessian towns and at least temporarily set back rural areas as well. French armies invaded Hesse-Cassel three times during the conflict. Cassel itself was taken four times by each side, and Marburg changed hands on fifteen different occasions. No corner of the country escaped foreign occupation, with even the northern exclave of Schaumburg spending two years in French hands.[10] Although Empress Maria Theresa accepted Landgrave William's declaration of neutrality, assuring him that her French "auxiliaries" would spare the country and pay for supplies in exchange for free passage, the French extracted large payments wherever they went, especially in the towns.[11] In fact, though the country was treated somewhat worse than neighboring loyalist states like Waldeck, Hesse-Darmstadt, Mainz, and Fulda, its problems did not stem so much from its subsidy treaty with Great Britain as from being situated between two great armies. The Anglo-Hanoverian forces were no less brutal in ravishing livestock and crops, quartering men, and extracting money from the towns.[12]

"Althessische Silhouetten," *HJLG* (1854), 51 [Hofgeismar]; Apelblad, *Reise durch...Hessen*, 276 [Wanfried].

[9] Although modern Hessian scholarship is in agreement on this point, the Hessian cadastre and tax rolls from the sixteenth and seventeenth centuries are generally unreliable, mainly because of inconsistencies in the census tabulations and fraudulent reports of wealth provided by local communities. For what they are worth, however, they do appear to confirm these findings. A majority of the twenty-five largest towns for which data are available show declines in both hearths and taxable wealth between the end of the sixteenth and middle of the eighteenth centuries. Rural areas indicate modest increases in both categories. The most complete cadastre records can be found in the archives of the Stift Kaufungen, StAMg, 304)576 #199: "Designation der Alten Contribution der noch nicht Rectificirten Ortschaften" [1771], 304)580: "Summarischer Extract monatlichen Contributions-Betrag..." [1786]. Local population statistics are reproduced in Heinrich Reimer, ed., *Historisches Ortslexikon für Kurhessen* (Marburg, 1974).

[10] Anton Friedrich Büsching, *Neue Erdbeschreibung*, 1 (Hamburg, 1779), 1336; Atwood, *The Hessians*, 17–18; Piderit, *Schaumburg*, 159.

[11] AAE, CP, HC 12: July 1757 rescript; C. Renouard, *Geschichte des Krieges in Hannover, Hessen und Westfalen von 1757 bis 1763*, 3 vols. (Cassel, 1863–4), 1: 253–4, 311–2; Atwood, *The Hessians*, 17; Piderit, *Schaumburg*, 159; Heidelbach, *Kassel*, 160.

[12] StAMg, 4e)2665: 12 Nov. 1760 memorial; Hans-Georg Böhme, *Die Wehrverfassung in*

At the end of the war Ferdinand of Brunswick described the country as the "Hessian wasteland." Livestock had been reduced to as little as one-third its prewar level. According to official reports massive crop and livestock losses caused widespread starvation. Many peasants abandoned their farms, fleeing into the forests, begging before enemy garrisons, and even emigrating to other countries in search of food. The population loss in some areas was so great that one cavalry officer reported riding through seven consecutive villages without seeing a soul. Indeed, recent research in one village in Upper Hesse indicates that the death rate tripled in 1760, twice the rate for any other eighteenth-century catastrophe.[13]

Once again the larger towns were hit hard. In Marburg there were so many beggars that it was impossible to close the city gate without the greatest difficulty.[14] What little remained of Ziegenhain's once-thriving sixteenth-century wool industry was totally destroyed as the retreating French razed all of its remaining facilities.[15] Schmalkalden was devastated, first by 350,000 taler in payments extracted by the French, then by drastic drops in postwar iron consumption, complicated by a surfeit of weapons, debased coinage, and protectionist measures initiated by the surrounding Thuringian states.[16] Cassel shared in the falloff of commercial activity. Employment at its largest textile concern, the Landré Hat Factory, fell from 649 in 1757 to 180 by the war's end. At the same time the number of booths at its three largest commercial markets fell inexorably from 1,048 (1756) to 836 (1758) to 587 (1760) and finally to 443 (1762) at the conclusion of hostilities.[17]

Hessen-Kassel im 18. Jahrhundert bis zum siebenjährigen Kriege (Cassel, 1954), 61; L. Armbrust, *Geschichte der Stadt Melsungen* (Cassel, 1905), 65, 69–84; Wilhelm Neuhaus, *Geschichte von Hersfeld* (Hersfeld, 1927), 249–51; Piderit, *Denkwürdigkeiten von Hersfeld* (Hersfeld, 1829), 230–1; Julius L. Schmincke, *Geschichte der Stadt Eschwege* (Eschwege, 1922), 256; Jürgen Schmidt, *Melsungen. Die Geschichte einer Stadt* (Melsungen, 1978), 85-7; Lohse, *Schmalkaldener Eisengewinnung*, 60.
[13]StAMg, 4e)2665: 12 Nov. 1760 memorial, 5)7061: 31 Oct. 1763 SK report, 17II)1923: 24 Feb. 1768 report; Renouard, *Geschichte des Krieges*, 3: 869n.; Fox, "Studien zur Agrargeschichte Oberhessens 1650–1830," in A. E. Imhof, ed., *Historische Demographie als Sozialgeschichte*, 2 vols. (Darmstadt and Marburg, 1975), 2: 1030.
[14]StAMg, 5)1740: [Feb. 1764] report.
[15]Ottfried Dascher, *Das Textilgewerbe in Hessen-Kassel vom 16. bis 19. Jahrhundert* (Marburg, 1968), 50.
[16]StAMg, 5)2697: 9 June 1768, 2 June 1770 Schmalkalden Oberamt reports.
[17]Brunner, *Cassel*, 285, and *Kassel im siebenjährigen Krieg* (Cassel, 1884), 192; Dascher, *Textilgewerbe in Hessen-Kassel*, 54. Hersfeld extracted one lasting, if unintended, benefit from the war when the retreating French razed its 700-year-old Benedictine *Stiftskirche*. Used as a food magazine during the war, its burned-out frame houses Hersfeld's famous outdoor concert amphitheater, the city's number-one tourist attraction.

With the end of the war the new landgrave confronted the challenge of reconstruction. Foremost among the many problems he faced was the need to finance a recovery without placing unrealistic burdens on the taxpaying population. By the summer of 1763 both he and his revenue officials in the government Tax Office (*Steuerkolleg*) had agreed that the general population was in no condition to pay taxes and that it should be granted a tax moratorium through the following year. It was with this purpose in mind that Frederick decided to convene the estates.[18] Indeed, when the diet met, Frederick's commissioners promptly refused the customary 100,000-taler "free gift" normally granted to new landgraves and negotiated a moratorium through 1766. Although the agreement forgave only 1 million taler in taxes, it rescheduled the balance of 2.5 million over the next thirty-six years. Furthermore, the landgrave promised not to raise current levels of taxation and to convene the diet every six years.[19]

The government was able to be so generous because it anticipated the payment of 8 million taler in British subsidies, plus reparations for war damages. In fact, the landgrave promised to deduct any reparations payments from the *Landtag*'s 2.5-million-taler debt, a prospect that prompted it to dispatch a delegation to London to petition Parliament for a higher assessment of war damages.[20] Though it failed to achieve its end, the diet's London embassy constituted a quaint Hessian perversion of the customary procedures involving the power of the purse. Parliament did, however, pay the 8-million-taler minimum stipulated in the Anglo-Hessian subsidy treaty, a sum that subsequently permitted Frederick to make outright grants and some 230,000 taler in loans to individual towns that had trouble paying their taxes.[21] Little wonder that the Austrian envoy Pergen reported that in Hesse-Cassel "there is no difficulty putting the finances in good order."[22]

Although the three-year tax moratorium was the dominant issue of the 1764 diet, it was not the only matter considered. Over the next three years the regime closely considered and responded to each of the scores of desiderata presented by the deputies. One of the most important gra-

[18]StAMg, 5)7061: 31 Oct. SK report, 25 Nov. 1763 resolution, 5)14713: 7 Aug. 1763 Landtagskommission report, 5)7061: 17 Nov. 1764 SK report.
[19]StAMg, 5)14793: 1764 Landtagsabschied; Lichtner, *Landesherr und Stände*, 10.
[20]Pfeiffer, *Landständischen Verfassung in Kurhessen*, 189.
[21]StAMg, 5)13427: 30 Apr. 1768 KDK report [Rotensee], 5)14717: "Desideria Specialia ... Cassel"; Schmidt, *Melsungen*, 87; Sauer, *Finanzgeschäfte*, 28–30.
[22]HHStA, RK, Berichte aus dem Reich 81: 9 Feb. 1765 report.

vamens was another fiscal subject involving *Steuerrectification* – the revision of the country's tax cadastres. The diet had originally called for a new cadastre in 1736, both because the existing seventeenth-century registers were outdated and because some rural assessments were based on unsubstantiated (and thus understated) declarations by local landowners. In response the regime began reassessment in 1741 but had completed only about one-third of the rural cadastres when war broke out in 1756. The *Landtag* now asked the regime to eliminate the remaining tax inequities by resuming the task, stressing that only its agents were sufficiently skilled and impartial to do an accurate job. The regime agreed to resume the rectification, although it declined the *Ritterschaft*'s offer of assistance, ostensibly in order to pare administrative costs.[23]

The regime also responded positively to the deputies' call for greater efficiency and responsiveness from the bureaucracy.[24] Indeed, as it pointed out in its reply, the landgrave had already initiated several measures designed to improve administrative efficiency. Many involved the adoption of proven Prussian administrative models and practices, including the remodeling and renaming of the central treasury (*Rentkammer*) after the Prussian War and Domains Board (1760), the transferral of provincial police authority to regional *Regierungen* in Cassel, Marburg, and Rinteln (1760), and the conversion of the Privy Council into a Prussian-style cabinet (1764).[25] Others were no more than simple economies that reflected Frederick's penchant for order and attention to even the smallest detail. Thus, he attempted to reduce paperwork by ordering shorter salutations on official correspondence and worked to quicken communications between government offices by listing the names and addresses of all government officeholders in a compact *Staats- und Adresskalender* that he personally updated each year, carefully checking for errors and additions.[26]

---

[23]StAMg, 304)578 Fasc. III: "Histoire des Rectifications-Wesens", 5)14715: 4 July 1764 GR protocol, 5)14717: "Desideria communia von Prelaten und Ritterschaft, 13tes Desiderium"; *HLO*, 153–5: 19 Sept., 16 Oct. 1764.

[24]StAMg, 5)14743: "Desideria ulteriora . . . 7"; 5)14717: "Desideria Communia in Justiz Sachen."

[25]*HLO*, 9: 8 Apr. 1760; Gerald L. Soliday, "Städtische Führungsschichten in Marburg, 1560–1800," *Marburger Geschichte* (Marburg, 1980), 350. The main differences between the two War and Domains Boards were that the Hessian version was not divided into regional offices and controlled only ordinary regalian revenue but not direct tax income from the contribution.

[26]*HLO*, 34–5, 72, 107: 7 Oct. 1761, 7 Feb., 29 Nov. 1763; Vehse, *Deutschen Höfe*, 202.

Economic and social policy

In addition to fiscal and administrative matters, crown and diet shared an overriding concern for reviving the devastated economy. In its first decade the Frederician regime worked hard toward this end, placing an emphasis on commercial and industrial recovery that reflected both mid-century cameralist biases and its own sensitivity to the greater devastation suffered by the Hessian towns. Its efforts demonstrate the extent both of the regime's commitment to establishing a manufacturing economy and of the structural obstacles that stood in its way.

Many of the initiatives first employed by the regime tackled the problem of Hesse-Cassel's unfavorable economic infrastructure by attempting to create a more favorable business environment. Thus, barely one month after peace had been concluded Frederick announced his intention to establish a commerce college (*Kommerzienkolleg*) "as soon as possible." The college was, in fact, founded in the following spring partly as an immediate response to the diet's request for measures to raise the level of commerce.[27] Modeled after its Prussian namesake, the college and its branch offices in the major Hessian towns were designed to improve the coordination between the merchants and government officials who comprised its membership. Indeed, though headed by Waitz, it came to be dominated by Johann Jacob Uckermann, a flamboyant Bremen merchant who had distinguished himself as a major purveyor for the allied armies in the war and whom Frederick now appointed as a key economic adviser.[28]

Frederick also tried to stimulate the commercial environment by promoting larger and more frequent trade fairs. Acting with customary dispatch, he staged the first fair in Cassel in March 1763. To enhance its prospects of success he required the participation of all native merchants who were either receiving government privileges or intending to attend foreign fairs. Cassel's merchants were also induced to recruit their foreign counterparts, who in turn were granted subsidies and exemption from import duties. For his part the landgrave took pains to stage public

---

[27]StAMg, 5)5094: 1 Mar. 1763 resolution, 5)14717: "Desideria generalia ... 3tes"; *HLO*, 141–3: 10 Apr. 1764.
[28]Kurt Dülfer, "Fürst und Verwaltung. Grundzüge der hessischen Verwaltungsgeschichte im 16.–19. Jahrhundert," *HJLG*, 3 (1953), 197; Brandt, *Industrie- und Handelskammer*, 16, 19–22.

festivals as well as a number of operas, operettas, and plays during each fair. For added convenience he scheduled the fairs two weeks before those held in Frankfurt, hoping that foreign merchants would add Cassel to their existing itineraries.[29]

The results were, however, disappointing. The Cassel trade fairs averaged only about 250 booths, compared to the 1,000-7,000 attracted by their competitors in Frankfurt, Leipzig, and Brunswick. Participation was confined largely to Hessian merchants who had been compelled to participate and to a small number of foreign merchants from neighboring German states. Even the Hessian textile merchants from Schaumburg refused the Commerce College's request that they attend, opting instead to continue to supply their traditional market in Hanover. In 1765 the fair's sales volume of 169,000 taler was still so modest that Frederick was unable to recover his own administrative expenses. In fact, one government-owned linen factory sold only 23 taler worth of merchandise, less than its own factory outlet.[30] In desperation Uckermann approached his many contacts in Great Britain, offering to ship their goods up the Weser to the Hessian port of Carlshafen at his own expense. Nevertheless, although the British regularly sent goods up the Elbe to Leipzig and up the Rhine as far as Switzerland, they declined his offer of free transportation because they still doubted they could sell enough to make it worthwhile.[31] In relaying the British rejection to Frederick, Uckermann pointed out that, in order to make Hesse-Cassel attractive to foreign merchants, he first had to devote great effort to stimulating native industry and trade. His admonition exposed the vicious circle in which the Frederician regime was operating in its need to create both the favorable economic climate and the established commercial-industrial base that normally reinforced each other in economically developed countries. In order to overcome this handicap, much painstaking groundwork would still have to be laid.

It was toward this end that the landgrave worked, frequently in response to the gravamens of the 1764 diet. He agreed, for example, not to mint additional money and to withdraw debased coinage already in circulation, issuing in the process no fewer than fifteen coinage laws

[29]StAMg, 5)5094: 1 Mar. 1763 resolution; *HLO*, 55, 387–8: 6 Dec. 1762, 7 Nov. 1766; Piderit, *Geschichte der Haupt- und Residenz-stadt Cassel* (Cassel, 1882), 285–6; Berge, "Kassel, eine Messestadt. Ein handelspolitischer Versuch vor 2000 Jahren," *Hessische Heimat*, 13 (1963), 22–3.
[30]Berge, "Messestadt," 22–3; Brandt, *Industrie- und Handelskammer*, 19.
[31]StAMg, 5)737: Frederician [Mar. 1766] memorial, Uckermann to Frederick, 18 Mar. 1766.

between 1763 and 1768. Similarly, in removing the 2 percent tax on all exports and agreeing to maintain interest rates at 5 percent, Frederick met two additional requests of the *Landtag*.[32] In addition to these piecemeal measures the landgrave undertook to improve the country's roads, which had suffered terribly from abuse and neglect during the war. Here he made a special concession to the diet, which remonstrated for road repair on the one hand, but also complained that the customary resort to compulsory road service (*Wegebaudienst*) would place too heavy a burden on the local population. He responded by promising to excuse the local population from their service obligation, repairing the country's roads principally by wage labor paid by the state treasury.[33]

In deciding to extend the navigability of the Fulda River, Frederick went beyond the gravamens of the *Landtag*. Once again, however, the idea was not his own. During the war the French occupation forces had raised the possibility of opening the Fulda above Cassel to navigation, an idea that was immediately pressed by the neighboring bishop of Fulda. Although Frederick's ministers were initially skeptical about the project's prospects, the landgrave ordered the river dredged and two cargo ships built to ply its waters.[34] By May 1765 the work was complete. The regime began a weekly shuttle to Hersfeld, with Frederick himself sailing one of the newly built ships on its maiden voyage.[35] In the end, however, the skeptics were proved right. Hersfeld shippers who had benefited from the new link with Cassel soon opposed extending the waterway upstream to Fulda, since they would lose their new advantage as the last navigable port on the river. Protectionist sentiment also developed downstream, where Münden insisted on levying tariffs on the new shipping, despite Frederick's offer of reciprocal trade advantages. Although the regime considered constructing a canal to circumvent Münden, it was eventually discouraged by the prospect of Hanoverian retaliation – and by the twenty-three other tolls that lay further downstream. Eventually even

[32] StAMg, 5)14717: "Desideria generalia ... 7tes, 8tes", 5)14715: 18 July 1764 Actum Reg Cas. The crown had already limited interest rates to 5 percent in a 28 May 1760 edict. *HLO*, 13.

[33] StAMg, 5)14717: "Desideria generalia ... 38tes" [1764], 5)14715: 4 July 1764 GR protocol; 5)14793: 1764 Landtagsabschied.

[34] StAMg, 4f) Fulda 9: 30 June, 8 Aug. 1761 GR protocols, Fulda 36: Fulda to Frederick [1765], 5)3427: 26 June 1764 GR protocol, Feb. 1765 rescript.

[35] *HLO*, 233–4: 15 May 1765; Losch, *Zwei kasseler Chroniken des 18. Jahrhunderts* (Cassel, 1904), 141; F. Zwenger, "Hessische Städte und hessisches Land vor 100 Jahren," *Hessenland*, 8 (1894), 61.

Fulda soured on the project and discontinued its own dredging operations.[36]

The government was more likely to succeed wherever it did not have to overcome the obstacles of interstate commerce and could rely instead on its own considerable fiscal resources. Such was the case with the Fire Insurance Fund (*Brandkasse*) that it established in 1767. Although they had existed for some time in Saxony (1729), Prussia (1742), and Hanover (1750), such funds were not destined to become widespread until the 1770s. Nevertheless, the Hessian estates were impressed by what their neighbors had accomplished. During a wartime session in 1761 and again in 1764 they petitioned for a *Brandsocietät* of their own, both in order to help the landgrave's subjects obtain easier credit for investment and to preserve them from sudden loss or poverty. At the start of 1767 the diet's *Ausschuss* renewed their appeal, assuring the regime that "over half the land wants the creation of the *Brandkasse*."[37]

Frederick eventually approved the request, recognizing as he did that the local Hessian authorities did not have the financial resources to provide it by themselves. The ministry duly examined the other German insurance funds, especially the Hanoverian *Brandkasse*.[38] It was certain, however, that the estates would play a major role in running the fund. In structuring it the ministry worked closely with the diet's hereditary *Erbmarschall*, Baron Riedesel, who in turn reported back to the members of the *Ausschuss*. Once established the fund was dominated and regularly audited by the *Ausschuss* itself.[39]

As might be expected, however, the *Brandkasse* still had several obstacles to overcome. Unlike other funds, it was not compulsory. Therefore, special effort had to be made to enroll enough participants to establish the 4-million-taler equity that would make it viable. At the deputies' request Frederick got the momentum rolling by insuring progressively more crown property: first all structures that directly adjoined private dwellings, then all military facilities, finally – with a necessary

---

[36]StAMg, 5)3427: 26 Sept. 1771 Waitz, 12 June 1780 KDK reports, Brandt, *Commerzienkammer*, 31; Berge, "Der Ausbau der hessischen Handels- und Verkehrswege nach dem siebenjährigen Krieg," *Hessische Heimat*, 14 (1964), 31–2.

[37]StAMg, 5)14717: "Desideria Generalia ... 16tes" [1764], 5)10695: 15 Jan. 1767 pro memoria; Gottfried Plumpe, "Anfänge der deutschen Versicherungswirtschaft. Die hessische Brandversicherungsanstalt 1767–1885," *HJLG*, 31 (1981), 157.

[38]*HLO*, 422: 27 Apr. 1767; Kurt Günther, "Aus der Geschichte der hessischen Brandversicherungsanstalt," in *Ins Dritte Jahrhundert. 200 Jahre Hessische Brandversicherungsanstalt* (Cassel, 1967), 132.

[39]StAMg, 5)10695: Riedesel to Frederick, 24 Nov. 1766; *HLO*, 423: 27 Apr. 1767.

assist from his ministers – all church-owned buildings. Next he raised the pressure to join the fund by requiring anyone who failed to restore damaged buildings within one year of a fire to sell them. Still later he made it illegal for uninsured property owners to get a mortgage.[40] The fund's sponsors also encountered local opposition to the statewide registration of all housing that was necessitated by the insurance project. The city of Marburg protested that the *Brandkataster* violated its privileges, as did the landgrave of Hesse-Rotenburg, who enjoyed limited autonomy on his lands, known collectively as the *Quart*. The regime overcame local opposition, however, by ordering fines against anyone who resisted the registration process.[41]

By September 1768 the fund had reached 4 million taler, increasing to 17 million by the end of the reign. As early as 1771 the *Brandkasse* had insured 30,000 of the country's 57,000 structures. Given this widespread participation the insurance rate was exceptionally low, never climbing higher than 1:1,921, or .052 percent of valuation.[42] Moreover, the success of the Fire Insurance Fund ultimately inspired other government initiatives in the field of fire prevention, including the establishment of building codes, the introduction of modern fire-fighting equipment, and even the installation of Germany's first lightning rod by a University of Rinteln scientist.[43] Nor were its effects limited to Hesse-Cassel. Just as the diet had borrowed from the example of neighboring states, the *Landtag* of Hesse-Darmstadt drew from the positive experience of its sister body in beginning its own fund in 1777.[44]

---

[40]StAMg, 5)10695: 15 Jan. 1767 pro memoria, 16 Dec. 1768 rescript, 11 Apr. 1769 rescript; Staatliche Kunstsammlungen Kassel, *Aufklärung & Klassizismus*, 35; *HLO*, 544: 30 May 1769.

[41]StAMg, 5)10695: [Nov. 1767] Brandkasse-Commission report, 5)10696: 2 Oct. 1767 GR protocol; Günther, "Brandversicherungsanstalt," 140; *HLO*, 551–2: 15 Nov. 1769.

[42]Staatliche Kunstsammlungen Kassel, *Aufklärung & Klassizismus*, 35; Günther, "Brandversicherungsanstalt," 143.

[43]*HLO*, 828–35, 1139–45: June 1775, 9 Jan. 1784; StAMg, 5)1019: 16 Mar. 1781, 3 Jan. 1783, 18 Feb. 1785 resolutions, 6 Dec. 1782 GD protocol, 5)1529: 25 Apr. 1779 Münchhausen report; "Gelehrten in Rinteln," 648–9. The diet attested to the effectiveness of the new building codes by reporting at the end of the reign that straw roofs had virtually disappeared from the country. StAMg, 304)580: 8 Mar. 1786 Desiderium commune XXXV^tum.

[44]Freiherrlich Riedeselsches Archiv, Lauterbach, 64)230: 12, 23 Feb. 1778 reports. The Hessian *Landtag*'s sponsorship of a *Brandkasse* stands in vivid contrast to Johann Jakob Moser's failure to overcome opposition to a fire fund in the estates of Württemberg, whose record of intense hostility and conflict between crown and diet make it exceptional among the German states. See Mack Walker, *Johann Jakob Moser and the Holy Roman Empire of the German Nation* (Chapel Hill, N.C., 1981), 212–14.

In promoting the Commerce College, the Cassel fairs, an improved transportation network, and the insurance fund, Frederick was working to create an infrastructure that could support a better developed commercial-industrial economy. Yet, given the absence of an existing industrial base, or the private investment capital to build one, Frederick perceived the need to increase direct government sponsorship of private entrepreneurs far beyond the level of previous landgraves. His decision was not a difficult one. The *Pensées* reflect the importance he placed on industry as a dynamic force in the creation of a society's wealth. The 1764 diet was of much the same mind. Though it advocated free trade against monopolies in its gravamens, it simultaneously urged him to establish more factories, especially in the depressed textile industry, and to favor them with tax-free privileges. As early as July 1764 the Commerce College had assured the deputies that the regime had every intention of sponsoring industrial expansion.[45]

Before the month was out the regime had solicited advice from its man in Frankfurt, Friedrich Karl von Moser, who provided concrete suggestions on how to recruit qualified foreign entrepreneurs and factory workers to run new factories, especially in the well-established textile industry. By the beginning of 1765, the Commerce College was following Moser's advice, distributing advertisements throughout Germany and offering extensive privileges including twenty years' tax exemption, free land, and operating facilities.[46] Hessian officials traveling abroad, whether they were diplomats, academics, or even ailing officials taking the cure, were instructed to enlist entrepreneurs wherever they went.

The government looked for two things in its recruiting: relevant manufacturing experience among entrepreneurs and factory workers alike, and strong commercial ties with foreign markets. Among the native population Hessian Huguenots got many concessions due to their previous entrepreneurial experience and ties with France and the Huguenot diaspora.[47] It was also helpful to have connections at court. Thus concessions were granted to Landgrave Charles of Hesse-Philippstal, a finance min-

[45] "Pensées," #28; StAMg, 5)14717: "Desideria Generalia . . . 35ᵗᵉˢ" [1764], 5)14715: 4 July 1764 GR protocol.
[46] StAMg, 5)6263: 22 July 1764 Comm Coll report; *HLO*, 177–9: 1 Feb. 1765.
[47] Rudolf Schmidtmann, "Die Kolonien der Réfugiés in Hessen-Kassel und ihre wirtschaftliche Entwicklung im 17. und 18. Jahrhundert," Marburg University diss. (1928), 221–2.

ister for the landgrave of Hesse-Rotenburg, and the court posementier.
The War and Domains Board actually approved a court musician's petition for a clothing factory without even getting an opinion from the
Commerce College. There is also one instance where a Waldeck bureaucrat was awarded a textile concession in Frauensee with the understanding that he would accept a position in the local bureaucracy.[48]
Nevertheless, the regime tended to look outside the country for its entrepreneurs, feeling that natives were neither sufficiently numerous, cap-
italized, nor familiar with the latest industrial technology.[49] Once
recruited and funded by the regime, the entrepreneurs wasted little time.
By February 1765 Frederick boasted to Count Pergen that he had already
founded twelve new factories over the last year.[50]

Roughly two-thirds of all the new enterprises were set up in the Cassel
area due to the greater proximity of available labor, Huguenot and cour-
tier entrepreneurs, and markets. As Moser had suggested, the emphasis
was on textile production. The regime approved no fewer than nineteen
new petitions for textile factories in the next three years alone (1765-7),
five more than Frederick's predecessors had accepted for the entire period
of 1744–56. During the course of the reign it invested 140,000 taler into
the largely successful revival of fine linen manufacturing, nearly half of
it going into a single facility near Cassel. Yet government subsidies benefited other cities as well, including Hersfeld, which received its first wool
clothing factory ever in 1766.[51] The government also pumped money
into other popular eighteenth-century enterprises such as porcelain, plate
glass, tobacco, and tapestries. Frederick took a keen interest in a Venetian
glass factory founded by Crescentio Gallo in 1765. If he had an obsession,
however, it was to establish a silk industry in Hesse-Cassel, partly because
it required little instruction, thus enabling the weak and poor to find
gainful employment, and partly because he was convinced that there was
no scientific reason why cultivation could not take place in northern
Europe. Having already imported 700 mulberry trees and 5,400 hedglings

[48]StAMg, 5)6345: 13 Sept. 1763 privilegium, 5)3025: 17 Oct. 1765 rescript, 5)6145: 15
    Oct. 1773 rescript; Dascher, *Textilgewerbe*, 188, 218, 225.
[49]StAMg, 5)3494: 29 Nov. 1766 Comm Coll report; Brauns, *Kurhessische Gewerbepolitik*,
    100, 112.
[50]HHStA, RK, Berichte aus dem Reich 81: 9 Feb. 1765 Pergen report.
[51]Dascher, *Textilgewerbe*, 70–1, 188–231; Bernhard Heil, *Die wirtschaftliche Entwicklung
    der Stadt Hersfeld* (Hersfeld, 1924), 48.

in 1763, he readily granted a concession for silk making at Cassel four years later.[52]

The regime realized that its efforts to broaden Hesse-Cassel's industrial base would fail unless its new and existing enterprises could find markets outside the country. It was toward this end that it established a trading company at the Weser River town of Carlshafen. The Carlshafen Company was the inspiration of Uckermann, who presented the idea in 1770. Run by a mixture of government officials and private merchants, the company was funded mainly by the War and Domains Board. Nevertheless, Uckermann used his reputation to attract about thirty private investors, mostly foreign merchants as well as several government figures including Waitz and the landgrave himself.[53] One thing that attracted them was Carlshafen's advantageous location downstream from Münden, where it was free from the tariffs and disruptions of Cassel's greatest commercial adversary. To this singular natural advantage the government granted the company extensive privileges and committed itself to improve existing storage and transportation facilities, in exchange for its promise to market the products of government-subsidized enterprises and not to import any goods that might compete with native industries.

Although the Frederician regime devoted its attention and resources primarily to promoting commerce and industry, it did not totally ignore agriculture. During its first decade the regime directed schools to teach planting techniques, awarded incentives for bee and fruit-tree cultivation, and attempted to reduce crop damage caused by hunting.[54] At the diet's request the regime also acted to conserve the country's forest reserves by closing all private baking ovens in favor of communal facilities.[55] Nonetheless, this piecemeal record of agrarian ordinances doubtless made only a minimal, if positive, impression on the rural economy.

Of somewhat greater long-term significance was Frederick's establishment of an Agrarian Society (Gesellschaft des Ackerbaues) to promote

---

[52] StAMg, 5)3003: 26 July 1765 Gallo petition; "Pensées," #28; Berge, "Friedrich II.," 139.

[53] HLO, 604–5: 11 Mar. 1771 project; Dascher, "Die hessische Handlungskompagnie zu Karlshafen (1771–1789)," HJLG, 22 (1972), 234–6, 238.

[54] HLO, 88–9, 173–4, 224–6, 223–4, 379–80, 551: 28 May 1763, 22 Jan., 14, 16 Mar. 1765, 12 May 1766, 21 Nov. 1769.

[55] StAMg, 5)14717: "Desideria Generalia ... 31ᵗᵉˢ", 5)13977: Mar. 1766 KDK report; HLO, 144–5: 5 May 1764.

the development of the rural economy.[56] Historians have invariably given Frederick the credit for the *Gesellschaft*, especially since he had discussed the need for an Agrarian Society in his *Pensées*.[57] Once again, however, the immediate impetus came from within the diet, where the prominent *Ritterschaft* deputy, Adam Friedrich von Capellan, actively lobbied for it with Frederick only two months before its creation in December 1765.[58] In fact, Capellan eventually served as a director of the society, whose membership included other *Landtag* deputies, together with high government officials and faculty from the *Collegium Carolinum*.

The Agrarian Society tried to break new ground in Hessian agriculture mainly by spreading public awareness of new crops and techniques, whether through annual lectures by its members, competitions in raising crops or livestock, or prize essay contests that attracted entrants from neighboring German states and foreign countries. On occasion it also provided a forum for airing major social issues that had collateral economic significance, such as the feudal service obligation, poor relief, mass public education, taxation, and the subdivision of inheritances. The competitions themselves promoted numerous products that ranged from the exotic to the practical. Thus it awarded prizes for the production of saffron from America, tobacco from Asia, and silk from the Near East, together with prolific clovers and the common potato. Many of the contests and ideas contributed by entrants were also of uneven practicality, such as one prize-winning essay on how to make hats from goose feathers. Indeed, the society was compelled to wait eighteen years until 1803 to award the farmer who raised the most native-grown merino sheep because no one was able to acquire any in the first place.[59]

If the regime instituted anything approaching an agrarian "program" during the first decade of the reign, it was embodied in several edicts regulating and reforming the manorial dues and services discharged by the peasantry. The type and extent of these obligations varied widely within Hesse-Cassel, not just between regions but even within commu-

---

[56]*HLO*, 298–9: 17 Dec. 1765.
[57]Münscher, *Geschichte von Hessen*, 426; "Aus den Tagen der althessischen Gesellschaft des Ackerbaues," *Hessenland*, 25 (1911), 171; "Pensées," #5.
[58]StAMg, 4a)91,17: Capellan to Frederick, 5 Oct. 1765.
[59]"Nachricht von öffentlichen Gesellschaften zu Beförderung der Gelehrsamkeit und Künste in den hess. casselischen Landen," *HB*, 2 (1785), 469; W. Gerland, "Die Tätigkeit der ... Gesellschaft für Ackerbau und Kunst," *Landwirtschaftliche Jahrbücher*, 59 (1923–4), 251, 264, 270–1, 277–9; "Althessischen Gesellschaft des Ackerbaus," 171; Dascher, *Textilgewerbe*, 98.

nities. This unequal distribution caused considerable resentment among those peasants who bore the heaviest burdens. Nevertheless, the conditions of manorial servitude in Hesse-Cassel were generally mild compared to those in other parts of Germany. The Hessian peasant was not bound to the soil and was free to leave the estate on paying a small fee (*Manumissionsgeld* or *Freikaufsgeld*). He usually enjoyed de facto, hereditary ownership of the land he tilled, largely because the landgraves had historically protected him against eviction or the reversion of his own private plots to noble ownership. His obligations to his noble landlord, or *Grundherr*, essentially took the form of rent paid in dues, tithes, and labor services. Dues were numerous but small payments generally paid only in Upper Hesse and Schaumburg upon marriage, death, or departure from the land. The tithe, or *Zehnt*, was a fixed 5–10 percent (usually 10 percent) tax on peasant produce, paid in kind. Labor service, or *Frondienst*, was the most complicated, assuming a multitude of shapes (including *Jagd-, Bau-, Hand-, Spann-, Wegebau-, Fuhr-*, and *Walddienst*) that fit into two general classifications: limited (*gemessen*) and unlimited (*ungemessen*) labor service. Both forms were significant, but unlimited service was dreaded the most since it frequently consisted of time-consuming tasks such as construction work that could be levied at irregular intervals without notice and, perhaps even more irksome, unequally distributed within a community. When levied, both forms of labor service could compel peasants to spend three to four hours a day in transit between the *Grundherr*'s scattered plots (*Vorstreckdienst*). Yet, because it did not permit the peasant to plan ahead, unlimited labor service was far more likely to oblige him to neglect necessary work on his own plot of land. When all labor service for the landlord was added to parallel obligations to the community (usually construction) or state (construction or hauling for the military), the total burden could, in some instances, consume up to half of a peasant's available time.[60]

Since the landgrave was *Grundherr* of about two-thirds of all Hessian farmland and a proportionate percentage of the peasantry, the regime

[60]Cf. Hugo Brunner, "Rittergüter und Gutsbezirke im ehemaligen Kurhessen," *Jahrbücher für Nationalökonomie und Statistik*, 115 (1920), 52, 57–62; Gerland, "Gesellschaft für Ackerbau," 255-7; Lerch, *Hessische Agrargeschichte*, 38-72; Pedlow, "Nobility of Hesse-Kassel," 166-7, 170–1; Hans L. Rudloff, "Beiträge zur Geschichte der Bauernbefreiung und bäuerlichen Grundentlastung in Kurhessen," *Jahrbücher für Nationalökonomie und Statistik*, 105 (1915), 802–3, and "Die gutsherrlich-bäuerlich Verhältnisse in Kurhessen," *Schmollers Jahrbuch*, 41 (1917), 120–32; Sakai, *Kurhessische Bauer*, 6, 9–10.

could have a big impact on peasant living conditions. It was obliged, however, to weigh its own genuine concern for peasant hardship against at least three other competing considerations. The regime was constrained to balance the prospects of reform against its own fiscal and labor needs. It was also sensitive to the rights of noble landlords, whose manorial privileges it respected as property that could not simply be forfeited without compensation, especially since they accounted for between one-third and half of all noble landed income.[61] Finally, there was the pervasive sense within the administration that it would be unwise to change too much too fast, lest "the whole constitution in Hesse be overturned."[62] The value the regime placed on fiscal integrity, property rights, and stability guaranteed that the reform of service obligation would be piecemeal and ultimately incomplete.

Nonetheless, progress was made. As early as 1763, Frederick moved against hunting and forest labor service (*Jagd- und Walddienst*), informing the ministry in his own hand that it was exercised too arbitrarily, with local officials often conscripting more peasants than necessary, and that "it is my sincere desire that, hereafter, my subjects no longer be burdened with it and consequently have their all-important work disrupted by it." He did not, however, entirely eliminate either service. In order to combat the purported wood shortage, peasants could still be recruited for tree planting. Indeed, an ordinance published three months later merely limited service to the absolute minimum numbers of peasants needed and available for work, although they now had to be paid wages. Moreover, Frederick limited his decrees to those lands for which he was *Grundherr* by exempting the estates of the nobility and the cadet line of Hesse-Rotenburg.[63] This pattern repeated itself two years later, when Frederick became aware of peasant dissatisfaction with hauling service (*Fuhrdienst*) in the district of Bauna, where the construction of Weissenstein palace had led to a great deal of unlimited service.[64] Once again he stopped short of abolishing the *Fuhrdienst* obligation itself, because he needed peasant labor to complete the construction. Instead, he moved

---

[61] As estimated by Pedlow, "Nobility of Hesse-Kassel," 184.
[62] StAMg, 5)3064: 1 July 1767 Grimmel report.
[63] StAMg, 5)18798: 11 Mar. 1763 pro memoria, 11 Mar. 1763 GR protocol; *HLO*, 90–1, 158: 10 June 1763, 10 Oct. 1764.
[64] Paul Heidelbach, *Kassel*, 46, and *Die Geschichte der Wilhelmshöhe* (Leipzig, 1909), 184–8.

to ease the burden by commuting *Fuhrdienst* and some other obligations into a cash payment, and then personally set a favorable wage rate for all hauling activity.[65]

At the very least the Bauna affair helped focus Frederick's attention on the problems posed by unlimited labor service. In fact, in 1766 he instructed the *Kammerrat* Johann Grimmel to draw up plans for commuting all unlimited labor service performed for the crown and local communities into a cash payment, intending thereby to end "not only all inequity and oppression, but also the entire underlying problem, so that each subject who must perform labor service ... gets enough time off for his own work." With this purpose in mind he had the War and Domains Board undertake a detailed, district-by-district survey of all labor service in Hesse-Cassel, assessing in the process the effect that conversion would have on government revenue.[66] The study was ready by 1767, at which time Frederick accepted Grimmel's upbeat prediction that cash commutation of unlimited labor services not only would free the peasant to work his own land more productively but would thereby benefit the treasury both by yielding higher taxes and by enabling him to feed his livestock from his own, more plentiful crops rather than from the crown's meadow and forest land. By the end of the year the regime had issued a *Punctatio* establishing reasonable conversion payments for previously unlimited labor services involving construction work performed for the crown, the military, and local communities.[67]

Over the next few years Frederick issued additional regulations restricting limited labor service performed on domain lands according to each peasant's wealth and, thus, his ability to perform it.[68] Meanwhile, in the exclave of Schaumburg he facilitated the peasants' ability to buy their freedom by lowering the cost of *Freikaufsgeld*, often to less than a single taler, despite government records indicating that most of the 1,000 peasants who left his domain lands by the end of the reign resettled outside Hessian territory.[69] At no point, however, did the landgrave's reforms actually eradicate unlimited labor service performed on the pri-

[65]StAMg, 40)7 Amt Bauna 14: Waitz to Frederick, Waitz report, 11 Apr. 1765, 4 June 1765 rescript.
[66]StAMg, 5)3064: 7 Oct. Grimmel petition, 17 Oct. Vorstellung, 19 Oct. [misdated Aug.] 1766 rescript.
[67]StAMg, 5)3064: Punctatio, Grimmel report, 1767.
[68]*HLO*, 509–12: 31 Aug. 1768.
[69]StAMg, 5)3907: KDK reports 1760–86.

vate estates of the local *Grundherr*, whether he was a nobleman or the landgrave himself. In addition, Frederick also passed over Grimmel's suggestion that he consider a broader agrarian program that would end limited labor service and address other causes of peasant suffering such as depressed grain prices and crop failures. Admittedly he did intervene from time to time to reduce labor services wherever local officials reported them to be too much of a burden.[70] Nevertheless, in its first decade the Frederician regime stopped short of adopting a more comprehensive, coordinated program to change the face of Hessian agriculture.

As the only concrete agrarian program of the 1760s the reform of labor service illustrates the Hessian government's greater sensitivity to those specific problems that had been called to its attention, whether by the estates or local officials, than to general abstract principles. Internal memoranda dealing with labor service also suggest that the regime was at least initially more concerned with preserving the peasantry's living standards than with boosting agricultural productivity. In this sense these initiatives comprise part of a fairly extensive series of postwar poor relief measures that complemented the regime's efforts to revive the economy. Like the reform of labor service, many of Frederick's early initiatives, such as the tax moratorium and reductions negotiated with the estates, the Fire Insurance Fund, and even the expansion of the bureaucracy's widows' and orphans' fund were valuable in either reducing or preventing the spread of poverty. From his *Pensées* it is quite clear that Frederick even valued the salutary effect that new factories and public works projects would have in employing the poor and the weak.[71]

To these measures can be added a number of other individual steps the regime took to afford immediate relief to the poor, such as distributing free bread, livestock, and seed grain, or in closely monitoring food prices by requiring police officials to fill out and return preprinted price charts every two weeks.[72] To a great extent it attempted to revive the spirit of public charity on which previous regimes had relied. No fewer than three ordinances directed against the country's surfeit of beggars and vagabonds admonished the public to give more generously. The regime also

[70]Lerch, *Hessische Agrargeschichte*, 56.
[71]"Pensées," #26, 48.
[72]StAMg, 5)7061: 31 Oct. 1763 SK report; Fox, "Upper Hesse," 135, 137.

instructed local officials to use all available means to pressure creditors into stretching out debt collection from those impoverished by the war. To set a good example Frederick listed the names of almsgivers prominently in the local gazette and let it be known that he was passing the poor box at his own table twice each week.[73]

Yet the most celebrated public-welfare measure was Frederick's establishment of Germany's first comprehensive center for expectant mothers and foundlings, the *Accouchir- und Findelhaus*. Frederick had already discussed the need in his *Pensées*, moved as he was by a wartime epidemic of illegitimate births and infanticide.[74] By 1763 he had established the twin facility in adjoining buildings directly across from the Cassel orphanage. Modeled after Berlin's home for unwed mothers, the *Accouchirhaus* accepted poor married women as well as the unwed once they were in their last trimester of pregnancy. To encourage them to come unwed mothers were promised complete anonymity, including exemption from fines, public penance, and health care costs. As the first such establishment in Germany the *Findelhaus* borrowed from its counterpart in Paris. In order to guarantee their anonymity parents could place their child in a turnstile that had been built into a windowless outer wall of the foundling home. When turned, the device delivered the foundling to the director's heated office, sounding a bell to alert the staff. Although the government endeavored to entrust its foundlings to paid foster parents, many lived at the foundling home until age nine, at which point they graduated to the orphanage, where they were taught a trade.[75]

From the start Frederick took a great personal interest in the facility, receiving monthly reports from the director, visiting it regularly, and even stipulating the children's clothing, diet, and hygiene.[76] He soon enlisted the scrutiny of local officials as well. After one incident in which local officials suspected an unwed girl was pregnant but failed to prevent her from killing her baby, he ordered fines for neighbors or employers who failed to report any suspicions of an unwed pregnancy to the *Accouchirhaus*.[77] The government's difficulty in attracting foster parents led to

[73] *HLO*, 72–6, 227, 242, 382: 13 Feb. 1763, 28 Mar., 21, 28 June 1765, 15 Aug. 1766.
[74] "Pensées," #5.
[75] *HLO*, 20–3: 3 Mar. 1761; Karl Stein, "Das Waisenhaus in Kassel von seiner Entstehung bis zum Ende der kurhessischen Herrschaft 1690–1866," University Frankfurt diss. (1923), 97, 113; Günderode, *Briefe eines Reisenden*, 130, 133.
[76] StAMg, 5)16523: Frederick's notes [n.d.]; Frederick to Wittorf, 21 Sept. 1775.
[77] StAMg, 5)1559: 31 Aug. 1765 Actum, *HLO*, 281–2, 445: 10 Sept. 1765, 25 Aug. 1767.

a second edict requiring not only relatives but even neighbors to assume responsibility for orphans, albeit in exchange for a government pension.[78]

Enlightenment constructs: education, justice, and religion

Although hardly inconsistent with contemporary philosophical currents, the regime's record of administrative, economic, and public-welfare initiatives was largely reactive in its ad hoc response to pressing problems raised by the Seven Years' War. By contrast, its activities in the fields of education and justice demonstrate that the landgrave occasionally attempted to superimpose Enlightenment ideas on existing institutions, both out of conviction and out of a desire to be known as an enlightened ruler.

No idea was more central to the *Aufklärung* than education, whether as a weapon against prejudice and superstition or as a vehicle for creating a more virtuous and ultimately happier world.[79] Frederick himself strongly believed in it. In his correspondence with Crousaz and Burlamaqui, he expressed the conviction that education was vital to nurture goodness and overcome human flaws. Later in the *Pensées* he exclaimed that "everything depends on education" and emphasized the need for advanced secondary and university-level instruction. Shortly after his succession, he even issued a public declaration in which he proclaimed the importance of education for everyone, including the common people, stating that it was central to the development of individual character and therefore of general utility to society.[80] As happened with much else in his reign, Frederick's achievements in the field of education fell short of the goals he set. Nevertheless, more than any previous landgrave, he actively championed education at all levels, as well as in all major disciplines, and was especially helpful in emphasizing the central role of the humanities.

Frederick spent his first decade as landgrave focusing on the educational needs of the country's ruling elite. This was partly because the *Assekurationsakte* had removed him from management of the Hessian school system, which was run by the country's Calvinist-dominated Consistory.

---

[78]*HLO*, 439–42: 24 July 1767; Berge, "Friedrich II.," 45.
[79]Nisbet, "'Was ist Aufklärung'," 80–4.
[80]StAMg, 4a)90,13; "Pensées," #2, 5; W. J. C. G. Casparson, *Aeltern und Vormündern eine Anstalt bekannt, in welcher Junge Manns-Personen von Stand und Range sollen erzogen werden* (Cassel, 1764), 4–8.

In addition, Frederick's concentration on higher education also reflected the pedagogical elitism prevalent among Enlightenment thinkers and educators during the 1760s. One major concern was the sad state of the Hessian university system. Whereas Rinteln had always been a university of modest pretensions, its sister institution at Marburg had clearly fallen on hard times. Like Marburg itself, Germany's first Protestant university had begun to decline in the seventeenth century, following the court's transfer to Cassel, the establishment of a rival Hessian university at Giessen, and the Thirty Years' War. Though it had revived briefly with the arrival of Christian Wolff, its troubles resumed with his return to Halle, the growing popularity of the new university at Göttingen, and the destruction of the Seven Years' War. Although most German universities suffered from small enrollment, hard times had reduced Marburg to one of the empire's smaller institutions, and Rinteln to little more than a seminary school. Funds were in such short supply that Marburg could afford neither to pay its shrunken seventeen-man faculty (compared to Göttingen's sixty) nor to spend more than 100 taler annually on its tiny 5,000-book library.[81]

Already in the first year of his reign Frederick had sought Gottsched's advice on how to revive Marburg. Once the war had ended he put the matter before the diet, which assured him that the university would collapse without considerable outside support.[82] While they agreed to raise funds for its postwar rehabilitation, Frederick himself issued six decrees over the next seven years that closely followed the recommendations of Gottsched and the Hessian diet. The remedies they prescribed dealt with the threat posed by rival universities like Göttingen in much the same fashion that the regime dealt with all foreign competition: with a combination of protective legislation, increased government investment, and regulation. To promote attendance at native institutions the landgrave forbade Hessian university students from studying abroad without prior permission and raised the number of semesters they needed to spend at a Hessian university from one to four.[83] To attract new students and

---

[81]McClelland, *State, Society, and University*, 28, 63–8; Hermelink and Kaehler, *Philipps-Universität*, 388–97, 408, 412–13, 415; Dersch, "Universität Marburg," 168. Nicolai would remark in 1761 that there were never any books for him to review from Rinteln except Bibles and catechisms. Gerhard Schormann, *Academia Ernestina. Die schaumburgische Universität zu Rinteln and der Weser (1610/21–1810* (Marburg, 1982), 251.

[82]Dersch, "Universität Marburg," 165-7, 198–203; StAMg, 304)573: 8 May 1764 petition, 5)14793: 1764 Landtagsabschied.

[83]*HLO*, 517, 605–6: 8 Dec. 1768, 12 Mar. 1771.

faculty he increased the number of government fellowships, funded new laboratory equipment, and attempted to lure several Leipzig and Halle professors with the promise of high salaries. Unfortunately, the landgrave was turned down by all of the faculty he approached, including Gottsched himself.[84] Moreover, like the governments of other German states, Frederick took advantage of his universities' financial dependence to oversee their operations more closely. Within a very short time he was prescribing everything from the curriculum, academic schedule, and teaching loads to the treatment of student misbehavior and indebtedness.[85]

Notwithstanding his aid to Marburg and Rinteln, Frederick lent far more assistance to the country's other institution of higher learning, Cassel's *Collegium Carolinum*. Founded as a two-year preparatory school for the children of Cassel's social elite, the college had also fallen upon hard times.[86] Yet the preferential treatment it received mirrored not only Frederick's greater sensitivity to problems in Cassel but also the association he made between the intellectual life of his residence and his own image as an enlightened ruler. The college's rehabilitation certainly gave him another opportunity to express his faith in education and the pursuit of knowledge. The published revisions of the curriculum extolled the landgrave's faith in "sound reason, which is the basis and fulcrum of all other knowledge, art and science." He also put this faith into practice. Drawing from the curricula of the Berlin *Realschule* and Brunswick's own *Collegium Carolinum*, the landgrave mandated a broad knowledge of both German and French literature, history, and culture, and placed particular stress on the mastery of philosophy, science, and additional foreign languages.[87]

The landgrave's attempts to revive the college's sagging enrollments were no less dramatic. Once again he expanded the number of fellowships, personally scrutinizing each application for the dozen awards that he now made available for non-Hessian students.[88] He was, however,

[84]*HLO*, 256-7: 20 Aug. 1765; StAMg, 40)Kammer 24 Rinteln: KDK to Wittich, 14 June 1765; Schmitz, *Naturwissenschaften an der Philipps-Universität*, 49–50.

[85]StAMg, 5)16142: 12 Mar. 1765, 5)8079: 14 Nov. 1766 rescripts; *HLO*, 256-77, 306–11, 550, 572: 20 Aug. 1765, 17 Jan. 1766, 8 June, 20 Oct. 1769; McClelland, *State, Society, and University*, 69-70, 91.

[86]Hermann Schelenz, "Über das kasseler Collegium Carolinum," *Hessenland*, 18 (1904), 78.

[87]*HLO*, 374–9, 714–26, 740–8: 9 May 1766, 17 Sept., 23 Nov. 1773; Casparson, *Eine Anstalt bekannt*, 14; Heidelbach, *Kassel* 172.

[88]StAMg, 40)24 Cassel 38: 16 Jan. 1767 rescript, 5)2910: "Nachfolgende am Carolino studierende . . ."

especially eager to enrich the education of young Hessian nobles and army officers, particularly those destined for careers at court. By 1770 college faculty had begun giving special instruction to young army officers and cadets since they, unlike most court and civil officers, rarely had an advanced education. Within a year their numbers had swollen to sixty-one students, more than the college's entire civilian enrollment.[89] By then Frederick had also managed to increase the college's faculty from seven to nineteen. Though he was turned down by some of Germany's brightest luminaries, including Winckelmann and Lessing, he was able to attract several important figures including the portrait painter Tischbein (1762), a pioneer in obstetric medicine, Georg Wilhelm Stein (1763), the writer and antiquity scholar Rudolf Erich Raspe (1767), the widely published Hungarian mathematician Johann Matthias Matsko, and one of Germany's most prominent Physiocrats, Jakob Mauvillon (1771).

The landgrave was so successful in recruiting new faculty for the college because Cassel, unlike Marburg, was a thriving and beautiful city with an attractive court. Yet he also enhanced its popularity by funding several adjunct institutes. Matsko's decision to join the college was influenced in part by the establishment of a mathematical-mechanical institute (1762) that survives today. Similarly, Frederick assisted Stein's work by appointing him director of the *Accouchir- und Findelhaus*, which now became a training facility where midwives could receive free instruction for practice throughout the country.[90] Though he had ignored similar requests from the Marburg faculty, the landgrave founded a botanical garden in 1765 for the research and extraction of pharmaceutical products. Within two years it housed 600 plants, far more than the 359 originally requested by the college pharmacologist.[91] Similarly, by 1771 purchasing for the college's anatomical theater earned it the reputation of having the most extensive stock of medical instruments in Germany.[92] Cassel's most exotic scientific collection was, however, the menagerie that Frederick founded at the end of the decade. The landgrave personally

[89]W. Grotefend, "Die Ergänzung des hessischen Offizierkorps zur Zeit Landgraf Friedrich's II.," *Hessenland*, 14 (1900), 2–3; Atwood, *The Hessians*, 47.
[90]*HLO*, 481–3, 486–93: 21 Dec. 1767.
[91]StAMg, 5)12624: Boettger [Aug. 1765] petition, "Specification der sämtlichen Pflanzen . . ." [1767]; Dersch, "Universität Marburg," 167–8.
[92]*Briefe eines iungen reisenden*, 100; [Johann Heinrich Merck], "Über einige Merwürdig-keiten von Cassel," *Der teutsche Merkur* (1780), 217–18.

directed acquisitions through his foreign envoys and even handled some of the feeding arrangements for its worldwide muster of 400 animals.[93]

Nor did the landgrave's patronage stop here. Beginning in 1771 he made available funds to enable college faculty to publish their research, albeit in German in order to maximize their local exposure and impact. It was with these same goals in mind that he soon issued and personally enforced a directive requiring the faculty to deliver regular public lectures.[94] No less important was his decision to support several new journals. Throughout Germany periodical literature provided a necessary medium for spreading useful public information regarding government ordinances and commercial transactions, as well as a welcome platform for giving academic and literary work greater exposure. At the same time, however, it is quite likely that Frederick's enthusiasm was further whetted by reminders from people like Raspe that such journals "befördert die Glorie der Landherrschaft" by increasing both his and his country's exposure abroad.[95] Thus journalism provided yet another avenue that served his twin goals of educating the Hessian elite and promoting his own enlightened image abroad. Once again it was Cassel that provided the focus for activity. Although the city was already well-served by one public affairs magazine, the *Casseler Commercien- und Polizeizeitung*, the college's faculty began no fewer than three new journals dedicated to a medley of political, commercial, and literary interests. In the end, however, none of the new journals survived more than a few issues, each having failed to establish a sufficient readership from within the limited base of bureaucrats, merchants, and academics.[96]

Given the record of his private utterances and public actions, it is difficult to deny Frederick's commitment to Enlightenment notions of education and learning. The same can be said for his stance toward the country's justice system. Here too the landgrave not only addressed existing prob-

[93]StAMg, 5)12730: 17 Oct. 1773 Frederician memorandum, "Nahmen der Thiere."
[94]StAMg, 5)2918: 21 Jan., 31 Dec. 1771 rescripts.
[95]StAMg, 5)2634: Raspe to Frederick [Feb. 1768].
[96]For more about each journal, see StAMg, 5)2634: 29 Aug. 1769 GR protocol, 1 Sept. 1769 Lennep votum (*Hessen-Casselischen Zeitung*), 5)2633: 24 Aug. 1779 resolution (*Politische Zeitung*); John Carswell, *The Prospector. Being the Life and Times of Rudolf Erich Raspe*, (London, 1950), 71–2 (*Casseler Zuschauer*). A similar fate befell the *Intelligenz-Blätter* founded by Rinteln faculty in 1762. See StAMg, 5)16362: [Nov. 1762] rescript, 13 June 1769 GR protocol, 25 Jan. 1771 report.

lems that had been aggravated by the war but also demonstrated his readiness to superimpose Enlightenment constructs on established institutions.

Even before the restoration of peace the landgrave was compelled to deal with a countrywide crime epidemic that had been fueled by the widespread poverty and chaos generated by the war. From the very beginning he involved himself in efforts to deal with the crisis to the point of sitting in on minor criminal cases.[97] By 1763 the regime had resorted to a number of strategies that included the deployment of military forces and even a mandatory night watch in every Hessian town.[98] When Frederick convened the estates the following year, the focus shifted from the problems of crime prevention and law enforcement to the failings of the Hessian judiciary itself. For three years the diet and its deputized *Ausschuss* discussed its shortcomings, finally presenting a comprehensive twenty-two-point proposal that served as the blueprint for Frederick's efforts to improve the quality, equity, and efficiency of the Hessian legal system.

The diet's principal complaint was that the length of judicial proceedings and the proliferation of appeals involving minor civil awards had slowed the courts to a virtual halt, causing delays of up to five years.[99] In response the regime issued a series of decrees designed to streamline the judicial process. At Frederick's behest it reduced the number of steps involved in most trials and actively encouraged judges to budget their time and set deadlines for certain cases.[100] Lawyers became subject to fines for dragging out litigation but were otherwise encouraged to ferret out hopeless cases and appeals by properly advising clients whenever their prospects were poor. Toward this end Canngiesser published a compendium of legal precedents in order to assist litigants in judging the viability of their suits and appeals beforehand. In any event the regime restricted the number of times an appeal could be heard and adopted the

---

[97]Such as one trial involving the theft of some bees by four teenage boys that resulted in a two-week jail term. StAMg, 5)11188: 7 Feb. 1761 resolution.
[98]StAMg, 17II)1923: 27 Dec. 1762 Actum Reg Cas, 18 Jan. 1763 GR protocol; *HLO*, 72–6, 88–9: 13 Feb., 28 May 1763.
[99]StAMg, 5)14722: "Protocol von Land-Tags Sachen, 19," 5)14717: "Desideria Communia in Justiz Sachen, 19ᵗᵉˢ."
[100]StAMg, 5)11116: 9 June 1767 GR protocol, 6 July 1770 Ordnung, 5)11968: 23 Dec. 1774 GD protocol, 17 Jan., 4 Feb. 1775 Actum; *HLO*, 406–8, 582–5, 814–15: 17 Mar. 1767, 6 July 1770, 28 Feb. 1775.

diet's request that all appeals for damages under fifty taler be disallowed.[101]

The regime also reacted positively to the estates' criticism of the men who practiced law in Hesse-Cassel. It responded to their complaints about high legal fees, first by limiting the fees that lawyers could charge, then by retaining peasant advocates at its own expense.[102] To improve their professional competence lawyers were soon made subject to proficiency examinations. The regime also ratified the diet's request that judges' salaries be raised in order to improve their quality after a comparison with neighboring states had disclosed that "no salary schedule is so wholly inadequate as the one here." It also promised to relieve local bureaucrats of their judicial powers on the grounds that they had little professional competence.[103] Finally, when the estates repeated a forty-year-old complaint that the seigneurial courts never received copies of new ordinances that were routinely disseminated among crown officials, Frederick approved their request that future laws be published for general use. Within a year the first volume of the monumental *Sammlung fürstlich hessischer Landesordnungen* appeared, its foreword clearly acknowledging the inspiration of the 1764 *Landtag*.[104]

In remonstrating with the crown, the estates raised issues based on practical, everyday problems faced by the general population. Moreover, in carrying out these reforms Frederick was largely reacting to practical societal needs as presented to him by the estates, something he did throughout the reign. The extensiveness of the landgrave's reforms suggests, however, that he was acting as much from conviction as in compliance with the *Landtag's* wishes. Indeed, like his administrative, economic, and educational initiatives, Frederick's legal reforms went beyond the original desiderata of the estates by instituting solutions that he himself had either devised or borrowed from neighboring states. His Prussian namesake had, for example, already streamlined judicial procedures, raised professional standards, and stripped local bureaucrats of

---

[101]StAMg, 5)17726: 26 Feb. 1767 Actum; *HLO*, 406, 409–10, 578–9, 586: 17 Mar. 1767, 6 July 1770; Leonhard H. L. G. von Canngiesser, *Collectionis notabiliorum Decisionum supremi tribunalis appellationum Hasso-Cassellani*, 1 (Cassel, 1768).

[102]StAMg, 5)14717: "Desideria Communia in Justiz-Sachen", 5)14726: 26 Feb. 1767 Actum, 5)11116: 9 June 1767 GR protocol; *HLO*, 409–10: 17 Mar. 1767.

[103]StAMg, 5)14717: "Desiderium Communia in Justiz-Sachen, 4tes, 6tes", 5)14715: 18 July 1764 Actum; *HLO*, 409: 17 Mar. 1767; Berge, "Friedrich II.," 192.

[104]StAMg, 4h)3503: 6 Dec. 1764 Kriegskolleg report, 4h)3503: 14 Dec. 1764 resolution.

their judicial prerogatives. Similarly, although Frederick may have been the first ruler to provide free legal representation for peasants, other German states had already limited lawyers' fees and given general legal advice.[105]

Frederick's attempts at law enforcement and judicial reform did, in fact, encounter some opposition both within the *Landtag* and his own ministry. Throughout the reign many smaller Hessian towns protested the mandatory night watch as a drain on human resources that reduced productivity and increased costs beyond actual losses suffered from banditry. Even larger towns such as Hersfeld complained about the overzealousness of officials who locked the town gates so early that farmers could not return to their homes and doctors could not reach patients living in the countryside.[106] Several ministers also fought in vain against fining tenacious lawyers who attempted to draw out trials, as well as against the establishment of trial deadlines, arguing with likely justification that trial length was impossible to predict. The Supreme Court also questioned whether the Prussian models the landgrave embraced were "either practical or beneficial to the general welfare."[107]

Both the ministry and *Landtag* also opposed certain aspects of Frederick's decision to adopt the modern form of criminal punishment eventually popularized by Cesare Beccaria. Once again the landgrave had drawn his inspiration from Prussia, where Frederick the Great had implemented the ideas of Christian Wolff by restricting the use of torture, gradually replacing corporal punishment with milder and more proportional penalties, and stressing the advantages of prevention over correction.[108] The ministry generally concurred with Frederick's faith in the effectiveness of preventive measures. The notion of *Präventationsrecht* was, in fact, already broadly accepted by German jurisprudence.[109] Within Hesse-Cassel the decision to establish the *Accouchir- und Fin-*

---

[105]Hubert Johnson, *Frederick the Great and His Officials* (New Haven, 1975), 66; Berge, "Friedrich II.," 196; Gagliardo, *From Pariah to Patriot,* 44–6.

[106]StAMg, 5)14717: "Special Desideria der Stadt Zierenberg" [1764], 5)14721: "Desideria der Stadt Hof-Geismar" [1772], 5)40: 11 Oct., 13 Dec. 1784 petitions, 5)5746: 14 Mar. 1785 Actum, 17e) Bad Hersfeld 150: 15 Oct. 1782 petition.

[107]StAMg, 5)11116: 27 June 1767 Regierung report, 16 July 1767 Ober App Ger report.

[108]O. Fischl, *Der Einfluss der Aufklärungsphilosophie auf die Entwicklung des Strafrechts in Doktrin, Politik und Gesetzgebung* (Darmstadt, 1973), 85–6; Walther Hubatsch, *Frederick the Great of Prussia. Absolutism and Administration* (London, 1973), 41; Reinhold Koser, "Die Abschaffung der Tortur durch Friedrich den Grossen," *Forschungen zur brandenburgischen und preussischen Geschichte,* 6 (1893), 236.

[109]Eberhard Schmidt, *Einführung in die Geschichte der deutschen Strafrechts-Pflege,* 3d ed. (Göttingen, 1965), 225.

delhaus stemmed partly from the desire to prevent serious crimes such as infanticide, as did Frederick's insistence on publicizing all punishments, whether by posting bulletins in the *Polizei- und Commerzienzeitung* or by requiring convicts to perform public-service work such as street sweeping or road construction.[110] Moreover, certain strategies in crime prevention were closely allied to cameralist teaching since both identified the elimination of poverty as a major goal, either in reducing criminal behavior or the fiscal burden posed by poor relief. It is in this light that we can appreciate the symbiotic nature of one Frederician decree that not only reduced fines but canceled them totally whenever they could only be raised by compelling the defendant to surrender his livestock or other means of livelihood. Indeed, the landgrave advocated quicker trials partly because they saved the defendant (or litigant) money, minimized lost worktime, and reduced government detention costs.[111] Nevertheless, Frederick's insistence that fines be reasonable and adjusted according to the defendant's own resources was ultimately opposed by the *Landtag*, which protested his elimination of heavy fines and long jail sentences.[112]

The landgrave encountered considerably more difficulty in reducing the incidence of pretrial torture and corporal punishment. He had advocated eliminating the "absurdity" of torture as well as long imprisonment and capital punishment in the *Pensées*, repeating the stock criticism that it not only was inhumane but did not prevent or reduce crime. With the conclusion of peace he informed his ministers that physical punishment had already been eliminated in several states and directed them to lay the necessary groundwork for abolition within Hesse-Cassel.[113] They immediately expressed their opposition. Though conceding that torture "is a dangerous, unsure and fraudulent method" of investigation, they argued that it was often necessary to keep criminals off the streets and that corporal punishment was more humane than long prison terms. A few weeks later the Supreme Court joined the fight with its own list of objections, predicting that the abolition of torture and corporal punishment would make it almost impossible to identify accomplices, while serving as an *invitatio ad delinquendum* that would "multiply the number of robbers and thieves." Within the ministry only

---

[110]StAMg, 5)11998: 19 Feb. 1765 Actum; Joachim H. Balde and Leopold Biermer, *Medizin in Kassel* (Cassel, 1973), 50; Both and Vogel, *Friedrich II.*, 40.
[111]*HLO*, 412–13, 814: 17 Mar. 1767, 28 Feb. 1775.
[112]StAMg, 5)14722: "Protocol von Land-Tags Sachen, 16" [1772].
[113]"Pensées," #4, 12; StAMg, 5)2299: 14 Feb. GR protocol, 10 Apr. 1764 Actum.

Kopp supported the landgrave in calling for the abolition of pretrial torture and corporal punishment, arguing that both practices were incompatible with natural law. Yet even he joined the Supreme Court in supporting corporal punishment for criminals already convicted of major crimes as well as torture if it was needed to effect restitution of stolen property or locate accomplices.[114]

Faced with this opposition, the landgrave opted to accept a compromise proposed by the Supreme Court that was already in practice in Prussia. Instead of outright abolition, he merely directed judges to issue more fines and prison sentences, meanwhile requiring that they secure his prior approval before ordering torture or corporal or capital punishment.[115] Even this half step was too much for the estates, which protested the restraint on corporal punishment when they met again in 1772.[116] Frederick was not finished, however. Three years later he applied the same restraints to the seigneurial courts, which had been exempted from the original decree. The final blow came in May 1776. Pointing to the example of other states and reiterating his earlier arguments that torture only distinguished between the obdurate and the timid, Frederick directed Kopp to issue an edict banning torture and restricting corporal punishment to the flogging of hardened and convicted criminals. Lest there be any truth to previous arguments that corporal punishment was a deterrent against the commission of crimes, he ordered that the rescript be kept secret from the public and "locked up in the archives."[117]

Frederick's limited retention of flogging paralleled similar qualifications within Wolffian jurisprudence and the Prussian legal code. He was, in fact, determined to eliminate all other instances of corporal punishment, however minor they might be. This becomes evident from studying the landgrave's deliberations over the retention of *Drehhäuschen*. These were small, enclosed cubicles situated on a turntable into which an individual was placed and given a whirl after being convicted of a misdemeanor. In August 1776 the *Commissarius Loci* for Eschwege, Theopholis Christian Becker, dutifully reported the existence of *Drehhäuser* to Frederick because they tended to make their victims motion sick. Becker's report is noteworthy, if only because he was a former proponent of corporal

[114]StAMg, 5)2299: 10 Apr. 1764 Actum, 26 May 1764 Ober App Ger report, Kopp Votum [1764].
[115]*HLO*, 412: 17 Mar. 1767.
[116]StAMg, 5)14722: "Protocol von Land-Tags Sachen, 16" [1772].
[117]StAMg, 5)2299: Frederician memorials [n.d.], 10 May 1776 rescript.

punishment who had utilized Christian teaching to advocate the death penalty, but who now felt constrained to report even a trivial violation of the ban on corporal punishment. Although the Cassel *Regierung* recommended keeping the *Drehhäuschen* since the resulting "sea sickness" was only minor and temporary, Frederick ordered them closed down.[118]

His efforts notwithstanding, the landgrave did not totally eliminate all incidences of torture or corporal and capital punishment. He did manage to persuade Landgrave Constantin to eliminate them in the *Quart*, disarming his cousin's only reservation – the lack of alternative jail space – by offering to provide the facilities and pay for the costs of incarceration. Yet he was unable to get the landgrave of Hesse-Philippstal to comply until October 1785, just a few days before his own death.[119] On occasion some seigneurial courts appear to have ignored the ban.[120] Frederick himself retained corporal punishment for army deserters, though this represented an improvement over the previous penalty of death and was the only military offense not punished with imprisonment.[121] Moreover, contemporary observers reported that Frederick, like his Prussian namesake, did permit the execution of criminals in exceptional cases such as those involving the murder of children or entire families.[122] Nevertheless, by the end of the reign more humane forms of punishment had clearly triumphed in Hesse-Cassel. As the *Justizrat* Hans Adolph Friedrich von Eschstruth remarked in one ministerial meeting in 1784, the horrible injustices committed against people like the Family Calas were a thing of the past: "The voice of the people and our enlightened writers are no longer divided, [having at last put an end to] the inhuman barbarism and ignorance of our forefathers, at least in our enlightened fatherland."[123]

Though Frederick attempted to superimpose current Enlightenment notions of education and jurisprudence on Hessian society, he had no such delusions about the prospects of achieving greater religious toleration. The *Assekurationsakte* had taken care of that. He did, however, appre-

---

[118]StAMg, 5)11138: 16 Aug. 1776, GD protocol, 10 Sept. 1776 Actum; Becker's book was entitled *Commentum Theologorum evangelicorum haud esse doctrinam de poena capitali homicidis doloris necessario infligenda* (Marburg, 1747).
[119]StAMg, 5)2299: Kopp to Constantin, 2 Aug. 1776; Berge, "Friedrich II.," 176.
[120]StAMg, 5)2299: 5 Oct. 1785 report; Berge, "Friedrich II.," 172, 176.
[121]AAE, CP, HC 13: "Observations" 1 June 1773 Verac report.
[122]Knigge, *Roman meines Lebens*, 54; Losch, *Kasseler Chroniken*, 51–2, 136–372; Dietrich Tiedemann, "Etwas zur Schande der Menschheit," *HB*, 2 (1785), 351–4.
[123]StAMg, 5)2299: Eschstruth Votum [Nov. 1784].

ciate and address the need to <u>disarm the fears of his Protestant subjects.</u> Upon his succession he promptly reaffirmed the *Assekurationsakte* at the estates' request and made no effort to intervene on behalf of the country's one thousand Catholics. When he published his *Pensées* in 1776 he even went out of his way to extol the advantages of religious uniformity.[124] Meanwhile, any major initiatives on behalf of greater religious toleration, including any innovation in the complicated and tense confessional division between the country's dominant Calvinists and the Lutheran minority, would have to come from Cassel's Calvinist Consistory. In reality the Consistory was more tolerant than the Hessian church or its people and tended to reflect the more enlightened and secular notions of the government ministers who dominated its membership. Thus there was some movement toward greater religious toleration during the opening decade of Frederick's reign, though it was essentially accomplished without the landgrave's participation.[125] The primary beneficiaries were the country's Lutherans, who benefited from a limited expansion in their religious, social, and economic privileges. In addition, the Consistory did introduce *Aufklärungstheologie* into the churches by forcing both Protestant communities to accept a common hymn book that replaced divine with natural revelation.[126]

Frederick's abstention from confessional matters had the desired effect. His subjects soon realized that their fears of Catholic tyranny had been unjustified and that they could trust his commitment to the confessional status quo. Meanwhile, his efforts and accomplishments in assisting the country's postwar recovery had totally rehabilitated him in their eyes. As early as 1764 the Calvinist preacher de la Porte was assuring Boswell that he was "a good prince [who] needs only sensible and clever people to guide him."[127] Within a couple of years it was impossible to find a foreign observer who had anything but praise for the new landgrave. In

---

[124]StAMg, 5)14793: 1764 Landtagsabschied; "Pensées," #29.
[125]The only exception appears to have been Frederick's appointment of Lutherans to the Calvinist-dominated Rinteln *Regierung* in 1760. When the Schaumburg estates protested that the number of Lutheran appointees exceeded the quota established by William VIII, Frederick replied that appointments were decided only by ability, not confession. It is difficult, however, to imagine that the new landgrave could have stood firm against the Schaumburg estates without the complete support of his ministers and the Cassel Consistory. StAMg, 5)5173: 24 Oct. 1760 resolution.
[126]Heppe, *Kirchengeschichte beider Hessen*, 340; Vehse, *Deutschen Höfe*, 181; Maurer, *Aufklärung*, 76–81, 90; Wilfried Reininghaus, "Vereinigung der Handwerksgesellen in Hessen-Kassel vom 16. bis zum frühen 19. Jahrhundert," *HJLG*, 31 (1981), 124–8.
[127]Pottle, *Boswell on the Grand Tour*, 154; Münscher, *Geschichte von Hessen*, 425.

his reports to Versailles the French envoy Hennenberg wrote that "the landgrave's conduct with his estates and subjects is so noble and beneficial to the interests of his country that they are reduced to remonstrating over matters of little importance." Six months later Moser informed Maria Theresa that "the landgrave of Hesse-Cassel rules his land rather well, loves his subjects, and is loved by them," an assessment that was echoed by other foreign observers, such as the young Hanoverian Knigge, the future Prussian minister Hardenberg, and the Genevan state councillor DuPan, who assured Frederick's confidante Madame Gallatin that he was "loved in this country." Yet another traveler went so far as to classify him as one of the "most excellent" princes in the empire.[128]

Nor was Frederick's performance lost on the leaders of the Hessian diet, who resolved as early as 1771 to construct a memorial in his honor. As it had in the past the *Kriegskasse* eased the estates' financial embarrassment, on this occasion by lending them 20,000 taler for the purpose. The project was, in fact, duly ratified at the next meeting of the Hessian *Landtag*, which made a point of thanking the landgrave for "having brought prosperity to the entire country."[129]

Admittedly neither Frederick's foreign admirers nor his *Landtag* deputies came from the masses of rural poor who composed the greatest number of his subjects. Still, in the absence of any evidence to the contrary, it is hard to imagine the people's being disappointed with a monarch who had reduced the dual burdens of taxation and labor service while increasing government spending on numerous commercial and humanitarian projects. Rather the available evidence suggests that the postwar crisis was now over. After a decade of feverish activity Frederick had not only helped the country to recover from the war, he had helped himself to recover from his past.

---

[128]AAE, CP, HC 12: 18 Mar. 1766 Hennenberg report; HHStA, RK, Kleinere Reichsstände 163: 30 Sept. 1766 report; Knigge, *Roman meines Lebens*, 53; Peter, *Madame Gallatin*, 35; *Briefe eines iungen Reisenden*, 82; Thielen, *Hardenberg*, 26.

[129]StAMg, 5)5528: 11 Dec. 1773 Pro Memoria. Hessian scholars have always claimed that the memorial project was conceived by the diet in 1774, doubtless because it was authorized in the *Abschied* that was drawn up in that year. Yet the *Ausschuss* had already secured the loan from the *Kriegskasse* in 1771. StAMg, 12) Kriegszahlamtsrechnungen, 1771.

4

The famine years

Notwithstanding Frederick's attempts to impose Enlightenment ideas on education and justice, the Hessian government had devoted its first decade primarily to rebuilding the economy and living standards after the cataclysm of the Seven Years' War. By 1770 it stood on the threshold of two new challenges: an anticipated exhaustion of cash reserves following the end of British subsidy payments, and a very real shortage of food caused by the crop failures of 1770–1. Whereas the fiscal crisis could be resolved by administrative belt-tightening and ultimately by Hessian involvement in the American Revolution, the agrarian crisis elicited new strategies in addressing the country's economic and social problems. During the previous decade the regime had stressed helping the masses of poor people, mainly by remedial relief, and building industry and commerce. At midreign the regime shifted its approach to the problem of poverty from remedial relief to prevention, primarily by boosting peasant productivity. It also gradually began to identify and correct some of the flaws in its mercantile policy, adopting a more balanced approach that placed greater emphasis on agricultural development.

Once again, however, a subsistence crisis coincided with concern over money, with the shortcomings of the fiscal and administrative system inspiring the government's immediate attention and ultimately coloring its approach to economic and social reform. Frederick had been eager to set up a more efficient *Staatssystem* since the mid–1760s. This concern continued to grow, especially after Great Britain had completed its subsidy payments in 1770. With the *Kriegskasse*'s reserves sinking to less than a million taler there arose, in the words of the French envoy Verac, a "spirit of economy that appears to dominate all of the landgrave's financial operations."[1] As he had in the past Frederick drew much of his inspiration from neighboring states, and especially from Prussia, which had already undertaken major fiscal reform during the immediate postwar period (1763–72). After asking Berlin about its system of tax collection, he sent a circular letter to all of his envoys and agents abroad, instructing them to report quarterly about any new developments in the field of state finance.[2] In 1773 Frederick finally hired Bopp away from the Prussian government and began to work closely with him in introducing many of the fiscal strategies and offices already in place there.[3]

Major changes were immediately forthcoming. In May Frederick appointed Bopp to head a new General Directory that, like its Prussian counterpart, directed the major fiscal offices such as the War and Domains Board.[4] By autumn he had instituted a number of cost-cutting strategies, including closer bookkeeping standards and sharp cuts in the number of court and administrative personnel. Indeed, according to Verac Frederick even reclassified one cavalry regiment as dragoons because the latter received fewer incidental payments and then committed the ultimate sin of delaying the "indispensable" appointment of a new envoy to Versailles in order to save the 40,000 florins in start-up costs.[5] No less innovative was the landgrave's reaction when the Rinteln *Regierung* replied to a directive requiring greater efficiency by complaining that its staff was too old and ill to work faster. He immediately awarded them early retirement, replacing them with younger family members who received the same salaries – minus the sum of their elders' pensions.[6] In addition to slashing expenses, Frederick and Bopp also attempted to generate increased revenue through the more efficient collection of taxes. Following Prussian models they gave the *Steuerkolleg* much greater control over tax collection in the towns and introduced tax farming to the royal domains, closely

[1]HHStA, RK, Berichte aus dem Reich 81: 9 Feb. 1765 Pergen report; AAE, CP, HC 13: 15 Oct. 1773 Verac report.
[2]StAMg, 5)2709: 10 Sept. 1773; Berge, "Friedrich II.," 80.
[3]StAMg, 4a)92,15: Frederick to Philippine Amalia, 14 Aug. 1773.
[4]Several central offices were restructured and renamed to correspond with their Prussian equivalents. For more on the administrative reforms see Friedrich Israel, "Die Kriegs- und Domänenkammer Landgraf Friedrichs II. und ihre Wurzeln," *Mitt* (1925–6), 90; Felix Rosenfeld, "Geheime Kanzleien und Kabinett in Hessen-Kassel," *ZHG*, 51, N. F. 41 (1917), 117–48; Dülfer, "Fürst und Verwaltung," 205, 212.
[5]StAMg, 5)15886: 15 Oct. 1773 GD protocol; AAE, CP, HC 13: 25 Sept. 1773, 15 Oct. 1773 Verac reports.
[6]StAMg, 5)5160: Rinteln Regierung to Frederick, 9 Nov., 16 Nov. 1772 resolution.

imitating the *Régie* system that had been established by Frederick the Great in 1772.[7]

Finally, Frederick's administrative reforms also led to the most dramatic personnel change of the reign, the fall of Jakob Sigmund Waitz. Waitz's resignation has customarily been attributed to his opposition to the administrative reorganization and to the reduction in his influence at the hands of Bopp. Yet, if we are to believe Verac, Waitz was actually forced to resign, having brought on his fall by enriching himself in his office, an indiscretion most unfortunate in the climate prevailing at court in 1773.[8] Whatever its causes Waitz's fall benefited a number of individuals. Though Bopp assumed command of economic policy, some of Waitz's former posts were also entrusted to Kopp and to Wackenitz, another veteran of Prussian service, who now became finance minister.

What is perhaps most striking about Frederick's shake-up of the government's existing administrative offices, practices, and personnel is that it was not needed to avert fiscal catastrophe. As Verac pointed out in his reports to Versailles (which was quite experienced in these matters), the Hessian fiscal crisis was not that severe, the state's finances were sound, and they would be responsibly administered so long as Frederick himself was landgrave.[9] Rather, the landgrave was concerned about the long-term prospects of running into debt, a specter that had been raised by the state's steadily diminishing surplus. Perhaps he was merely exercising more foresight than most rulers, a cautiousness that was partly justified by the erratic, boom-to-bust pattern of the *Soldatenhandel*. Nevertheless, the intensity of his concern and the measures he introduced exemplify the high priority that the entire Frederician regime placed on fiscal integrity.

Nor are the fiscal reforms without a certain touch of irony. Although the numerous austerity measures appear to have stemmed the flow of red ink,[10] the administrative changes may have cost the treasury more money than they saved. The central Prussian administrative system that

---

[7] StAMg, 5)2295: "Extract ... 8 Oct. 1773," 20 Oct. 1775 report, 3 May 1776 rescript.
[8] "Others compare the fortune that he enjoyed at the start of his ministry with that which he has amassed and with the present financial state of the prince, and it is felt with justification that he has not been very discreet in the means by which he enriched himself." AAE, CP, HC 13: 4 June, 13, 25 Sept. 1774 Verac reports.
[9] AAE, CP, HC 13: D'Aiguillon to Verac, 3 Oct. 1773.
[10] The *Kriegskasse* actually added 350,000 taler to its surplus between 1771 and 1775. StAMg, 13) Kriegszahlamtsrechnungen, 1771–5.

the landgrave sought to introduce best conformed to Frederick the Great's own requirements, including the need to detach as many offices as possible from his "insubordinate" core bureaucracy, something that was not a problem in Hesse-Cassel. It was needlessly complicated for a small state like Hesse-Cassel and probably resulted in decreased efficiency and increased operating costs. Locally there were problems too. Like the Prussian *Régie*, the Hessian tax farmers ended up alienating the peasantry with their ruthlessness, as well as those local bureaucrats who resented their interloping. Unlike their Prussian counterparts, however, the Hessian tax farmers actually succeeded in collecting less revenue than before.[11] Yet, if Prussianization was a failure at least it outlasted Bopp, who was demoted at the end of 1776, his Hessian career cut short by his inability to increase receipts and by the discovery of a diary filled with condescending comments about the country and its people.

The agrarian challenge and reform

The government's interest in increasing revenue persuaded it to examine the productive potential of Hessian agriculture. By then, however, the regime had found a more compelling reason to undertake a thorough reform of the country's agrarian economy. The crop failures in 1770 and 1771 had created a second subsistence crisis on a scale comparable to the effects of the Seven Years' War. The price stability in staples that the government had achieved by 1765 was shattered. In Cassel grain prices doubled in 1770, tripled again in 1771, and then sextupled in 1772. Long lines of burghers besieged the town's bakeries, often going two or three days without eating. By 1772 the mortality rate had risen by 70 percent and did not return to normal levels until 1775.[12] Conditions were little better outside the residence. From the Diemel Valley in the north to Schmalkalden in the east local officials reported numerous cases of death by starvation and large-scale emigration abroad.[13] The government immediately initiated several stopgap measures to stave off widespread starvation by freezing staple prices, canceling tax collections, and forbidding

[11]Berge, "Friedrich II.," 70–4.
[12]Möker, *Geschichtliche Wirtschaft*, 251; Losch, *Kasseler Chronik*, 135–8; "Tabelle von den Getauften, Begrabenen und Geehlichten in der Stadt Cassel, von den Jahren 1765 bis 85," *HB*, 2 (1785), 679.
[13]StAMg, 5)13446: 15 Jan. 1784 Motz report; Lohse, *Schmalkaldener Eisengewinnung*, 62.

all exports of grain.[14] By a stroke of luck Frederick had just begun building
a countrywide system of granaries modeled after Prussia's. Although the
granaries themselves were not yet fully stocked, their existing stores
helped minimize the extent of starvation.[15] The country was also well
served by the newly established Carlshafen Company, which, on Uckermann's own initiative, secretly purchased 230,000 taler's worth of foreign
grain for shipment back to Hesse-Cassel.[16] Meanwhile, to boost productivity the government provided peasants with free seed grain, released
them from labor service during the harvest, and permitted Sunday
farming.[17]

As was his custom the landgrave also turned to the estates. When it
convened in November 1771, the *Landtag* vented its wrath on the two
most hated groups in the Hessian countryside: lawyers and Jews. The
lawyer problem stemmed directly from Frederick's decision to afford the
peasants free legal aid. At the time he believed that legal aid would give
them access to the judicial system that they could not otherwise afford
due to the cost of fees, travel, and lost income by letting a lawyer act as
their surrogate in court. But the diet now pointed out that, in practice,
lawyers had flooded the countryside and induced peasants to initiate
trivial litigation since it was all at the government's expense. Not only
had the surfeit of court cases defeated the landgrave's hope of expediting
justice, it had also so attracted the peasants' interest that they were now
devoting less time to their work than before. Worst of all, lawyers were
still saddling them with debts by charging unreasonable travel costs from
Cassel, which were not covered by the government. Over the next three
years the regime labored to eliminate these unexpected consequences of
the legal aid program, first by punishing lawyers who promoted trivial
litigation, then by withdrawing the entire program (as the estates had
requested), and finally by reinstituting it along with restrictions against
frivolous suits and the levying of travel costs by lawyers.[18]

---

[14]StAMg, 5)799: 30 Apr. 1771 rescript; 5)13163: 4 June 1771 Actum; 5)2697: 20 Sept.
1772 KDK report, 18 Feb. 1772 resolution; *HLO*, 623–5: 5 Oct. 1771.
[15]StAMg, 5)13193: 22, 23 Nov. 1769 KDK reports; Fox, "Upper Hesse," 239, 246–50.
[16]StAMg, 5)10600: 5 Dec. 1771 KDK report. Although much of the grain came from
outside Germany, Uckermann's success in purloining the harvests of neighboring states
resulted in considerable resentment among the population of Paderborn. Dascher,
"Karlshafen," 239–40.
[17]StAMg, 5)8746: 22 Aug. 1771 GR protocol; 40b) Generalia 37: Verzeichnis; *HLO*, 616:
22 Aug. 1771.
[18]*HLO*, 661, 685, 785–6: 22 Aug. 1772, 13 Apr. 1773, 25 Oct. 1774; StAMg, 5)11109:
Kopp votum [n.d.]; Berge, "Friedrich II.," 187.

Like its remonstrances against country lawyers, the diet's complaints about the Jews were directed against the impact of previous government decrees. This is not the proper place for a detailed profile of eighteenth-century attitudes toward the Jews. Suffice it to say that Christian hostility was general within every country and segment of European society. Though they opposed religious persecution, most philosophes such as Voltaire, Diderot, and Holbach were disdainful of what they saw as the Jews' religious barbarism, together with their unprincipled and mercenary nature.[19] This was also the case among Germans, and certainly Hessian academics, including the future *Collegium Carolinum* professors Christian Wilhelm von Dohm and Georg Forster.[20] All levels of Hessian officialdom, like the Hessian people themselves, sincerely believed that the Jews competed unfairly with Christian merchants and unscrupulously exploited the ignorant and hard-pressed peasantry. Bopp was convinced that they were the principal cause of poverty in Hesse-Cassel.[21] Indeed, the country's economic malaise may have exacerbated anti-Semitic feeling by intensifying the competition for survival. Given its greater concern for the Christian community's economic well-being, the Frederician regime had heretofore limited itself to a few ordinances easing the numerous restrictions on the country's 7,500 Jews.[22] It was, however, a 1730 decree permitting them to settle in the countryside that the diet now sought to repeal. The *Landtag* had made the same request in 1764, at which time it had decried the business practices of rural-dwelling Jewish settlers.[23] Although it now repeated these arguments, it was also able to point to the example of Frederick the Great, who had recently decided to expel all propertyless Jews from the Prussian countryside.[24]

In August 1773, Frederick and his ministers concluded a nine-month-

---

[19]Arthur Hertzberg, *The French Enlightenment and the Jews* (New York, 1968), 282–6, 292, 309–12.
[20]Justus Friedrich Runde, "Über die bürgerliche Verbesserung der Juden," *HB*, 1 (1784), 63; Joseph S. Gordon, "Georg Forster und die Juden," *Jahrbuch des Instituts für deutsche Geschichte*, 7 (1978), 218, 221, 226; Epstein, *German Conservatism*, 221–2.
[21]Bopp, "Fehler," 179.
[22]Abraham Cohn, *Beiträge zur Geschichte der Juden in Hessen-Kassel im 17. und 18. Jahrhundert* (Marburg, 1933), 31, 35–40, 61–3, 69; H. Metz, "Die Juden in Hessen," *Hessenland*, 10 (1896), 74.
[23]StAMg, 5)14715: 4 July 1764 GR protocol; 5)14717: "Desideria der Stadt Hofgeismar, 4." [1764]; 5)13427: 30 Apr. 1768 Actum.
[24]StAMg, 5)14722: "Protocol von Landtags Sachen, 20." [1772]; 17II)1153: 21 Feb., 27 Nov. 1772 GR protocols; Selma Stern, *Der preussische Staat und die Juden*, 1 (Tübingen, 1971), 95.

long investigation by approving the diet's request.[25] Important as the decree was for the hundreds of Jewish families living in the countryside, the decision itself rested on certain calculations and priorities that exposed the underlying mind-set of the Frederician regime. As the *Regierungsrat* Ludwig August von Berner had made clear back in November, one indispensable consideration was that expulsion not affect tax receipts. In addition was the regime's sensitivity to the implacable hostility of the Christian peasantry and to the lack of sufficient arable land to support the growing number of Jewish settlers. What seems to have been most decisive, however, was the Jewish settlers' apparent reluctance to become farmers and forsake those commercial activities through which they might exploit the peasantry's ignorance and financial difficulties. Under such circumstances the government concluded that their presence in the countryside represented an "extremely dangerous situation and a major reason for the deteriorating living conditions in the countryside."[26] Quite apart from their reputed unscrupulousness, the Jews' engagement in commerce corrupted the customary distinction that needed to be made between the separate economic roles of town and country. Such was the message that Frederick conveyed to Landgrave Constantin when he informed him that "like all merchants, which the Jews are after all, they belong in the cities, not in the villages."[27] Indeed, although the expulsion edict forbade further Jewish migration to the countryside and required younger children to return to the towns, it did permit firstborn sons to remain there so long as they forsook all commercial activities and learned a truly "rural" profession such as farming. The government reiterated this commitment to a vocational distinction between town and country when it issued a second edict one year later that forbade even Christian artisans, entrepreneurs, and merchants to settle in the countryside unless they somehow served the agrarian economy, and placed immediate restrictions on those artisans already located there.[28]

Whether it was justified or not the action taken against country lawyers and Jews was the panacea that the estates sought for the current agrarian crisis. In addition, however, they planted the idea for another major

---

[25]StAMg, 5)5528: 11 Aug. 1773 protocol.
[26]StAMg, 5)5528: 10 Dec. 1772 Actum, Kopp to Riedesel, 11 Aug. 1773; 17II)1153: 27 Nov. 1772 GR protocol.
[27]StAMg, 5)5528: Frederick to Constantin, 17 Aug. 1773.
[28]StAMg, 5)5528: 10 Dec. 1772 Actum; 5)813 and *HLO*, 783–4: 7 Oct. 1774 rescript.

initiative by seeking the appointment of provincial commissioners to assist in the equitable collection of taxes. When Frederick approved this request in September 1772 he already had much more in mind than tax administration.[29] In convening a new session of the diet in the fall of 1773, he announced his intention to create ten *Landräte*, two for each of the country's five river valleys. Although they would lend assistance in the administration of taxes and in the forthcoming expulsion of the Jews, he stressed that their primary goal would be to help the peasantry.[30]

The estates were already familiar with the *Landrat* concept, since the landgrave and Bopp had borrowed it from Frederick the Great. Indeed, as in Prussia each *Landrat* was to be a local noble chosen from a list of two nominated by the *Ritterschaft* and was to perform many of the same functions as his Prussian counterpart. There were, however, significant differences. Given his overriding concern with economic development Frederick chose to apportion the *Landräte* along geographic rather than historical and political lines. Moreover, unlike in Prussia where he was paid by the crown but represented the nobility, the Hessian *Landrat* was to receive his 1,000-taler salary from the *Ritterschaft*, even though he was responsible to the crown.[31] Although it grumbled that the special 10,000-taler levy needed to pay for the *Landräte* violated Frederick's earlier pledge not to raise additional taxes, the diet did not oppose the new positions and even managed to express its satisfaction over his plan to utilize them to assist the peasantry.

The diet's limp response to the creation of the *Landräte* (and of a parallel group of *Commissarius Loci* in the towns) attests in part to its impotence as a legislative institution. Yet, when viewed in conjunction with the crown's own willingness to rely on the *Ritterschaft* to provide direct assistance to the peasantry, it dramatizes once again the existence of a long-standing reciprocal relationship based on trust and cooperation. Indeed, in seeking resident, landholding nobles who were familiar with local problems, Frederick perceived a common interest with the *Ritterschaft* in serving the welfare of the Hessian peasantry. The contrast could not have been greater with Prussia, where the *Landräte* identified and

---

[29]StAMg, 5)14794: 22 Aug. pro memoria, 22 Sept. 1772 concordat.
[30]StAMg, 5)14795: "Landtags Abschied de 10 Feb. 1774."
[31]StAMg, 5)5528: 20 Dec. 1773 report, 5)14795: "Landtags Abschied de 10 Feb. 1774"; Dülfer, *Die Regierung in Kassel, vornehmlich im 19. und 20. Jahrhundert* (Cassel, 1960), 169.

sided with their fellow nobles against the interests of both the king and the peasantry.[32] A look at the *Landräte* nominated by the diet and appointed by the landgrave suggests that Frederick's trust was well placed. Although nearly half of them were former *Landtag* deputies, more than a third were also former or current crown officials, and more than half were university educated. Moreover, their official correspondence with the regime furnishes ample evidence of their support for the landgrave's reforms and the peasantry's needs. Whenever problems did arise with the *Landräte*, they usually concerned their overzealousness in executing government policy and involved complaints from local sources, rather than from Cassel.

It was not long before the *Landräte* emerged as Frederick's principal representatives at the local level and the key instruments in the implementation of agrarian reform. From the very start he had envisioned them as the primary vehicle for improving rural productivity and living standards by protecting the peasantry from various forms of exploitation, ensuring proper cultivation, and keeping him informed about conditions in the countryside.[33] Within time the regime came to regard them as surrogates who could advocate the peasantry's interests in Cassel despite its lack of representation in the *Landtag*.[34] Once established their functions steadily mushroomed until they covered the entire domain of government responsibilities and public welfare. In one way or another they were involved in tax collection, military recruiting, the dissemination of new ordinances, crime prevention, education, the Agrarian Society and Commerce College, even in the promotion of subscriptions to the Insurance Fund. They became the regime's eyes and ears in each of the country's five river valleys, visiting each town and village at least once a year, from where they were expected to file semiweekly reports and tabulate statistics on every economically significant subject such as crops, soil fertility, livestock, population, income, taxes and tax arrears, labor obligations, and other dues.[35]

As he had done following his first diet in 1764, Frederick not only strove to satisfy the deputies' requests but initiated programs and strat-

---

[32]Kopp, "Landräten," 115–16; Dülfer, "Fürst und Verwaltung," 219; Johnson, *Frederick the Great and His Officials*, 12, 59–62; Robert M. Berdahl, "The *Stände* and the Origins of Conservatism in Prussia," *Eighteenth Century Studies*, 6 (1973), 305–6.

[33]StAMg, 73)266: 24 Sept. 1773 rescript.

[34]"Einfälle eines Kameralisten," 200–1; Kopp, "Landräten," 113–14.

[35]StAMg, 5)4293–4: "Landraths Instructiones," 5 May 1780; Kopp, "Landräten," 130–72; Gerland, *Gesellschaft für Ackerbau*, 249.

egies of his own devising. Thus, in addition to moving against country lawyers and Jewish settlers, he launched his own agrarian program, beginning with the establishment of the *Landräte*. The forces at work in Cassel were many – so numerous in fact that it is difficult to determine which were the most influential. Since midcentury cameralist theorists had increased their emphasis on the role of agriculture. By 1770 Physiocratic ideas from France had already found their way into their writing as well as into the domestic policies of states like Baden-Durlach.[36] Yet, tempting as it might be to attribute the growing emphasis on agrarian issues to these ideas, considerable circumstantial evidence indicates that practical needs played a decisive role. The government remained determined to avert a future fiscal crisis by preventing the erosion of its agrarian tax base and minimizing the fiscal burden of poor relief. At the same time the widespread crop failures of 1770–1 compelled the regime to readjust the priority it had formerly given to the promotion of commerce and industry, and to give greater attention to current notions of agrarian development.[37]

Despite these trends Frederick still retained his faith in the country's industrial potential. The welcome combination of peace and government aid had helped to revive production in several areas, such as steel, plate glass, and especially textiles. By 1774 the attractive quality and prices of Hessian linen had netted 700,000–800,000 taler in sales through the Carlshafen Company alone, roughly triple the annual prewar figure for all linen exports.[38] Although it was still dwarfed by its major competitors, the Cassel Fair had nearly doubled in size to include 400 participating merchants.[39] It was in the face of such growth that the 1773 diet could thank Frederick for bringing prosperity to the country even while it was bemoaning the effects of the recent crop failures.

Yet the landgrave's mercantile policies had hardly been an unqualified

[36]Gagliardo, *From Pariah to Patriot*, 34–40; Schulz, *Prinzipien der Einkünfte*, 402; Ulrich Muhlack, "Physiokratie und Absolutismus in Frankreich und Deutschland," *Zeitschrift historischer Forschung*, 9 (1982), 40; Wilhelm Bleek, *Von der Kameralausbildung zum Juristenprivileg. Studium, Prüfung und Ausbildung der höheren Beamten des allgemeinen Verwaltungsdienstes in Deutschland im 18. und 19. Jahrhundert* (Berlin, 1972), 288.

[37]Jakob Mauvillon, *Physiokratische Briefe an den Herrn Professor Dohm* (Brunswick, 1780), 2.

[38]P. Cauer, "Zwei heimatliche Glashütten des 18. Jahrhunderts," *Unsere Heimat*, 21 (1929), 5; *Briefe eines iungen Reisenden*, 100; *HB*, 1 (1784), 658; Dascher, *Textilgewerbe*, 167, and "Karlshafen," 151.

[39]StAMg, 5)10674: "Designation Kaufleute..."

success. By midreign it had become clear that even many "successful" enterprises would survive only if government aid were continued far longer than originally anticipated. It was equally evident that the practice of granting privileges to new or struggling concerns had a ripple effect throughout the whole industry as established businesses demanded matching concessions in order to remain competitive. When faced with the prospect of a business failure that would reduce production and employment, the regime almost invariably elected to continue its support. As a result, concessions originally granted to specific enterprises for a limited period of time usually became automatically renewable, industrywide privileges.[40] In addition, the abundance of money that the landgrave had made available for entrepreneurs had led to several instances of mismanagement, graft, and fraud. Notwithstanding Uckermann's considerable ability as a purveyor of foreign grain and Hessian textiles, even the Carlshafen Company was plagued by sloppy planning and money management.[41] Meanwhile, many new enterprises had failed altogether, despite government privileges and direct financial aid. Frederick's venture into silkworm breeding had died within two years, thereby defying his earlier intuition and subsequent attempts to keep it alive.[42] The new porcelain factory proved wholly unable to compete abroad with better-quality products, or even to find a sufficiently large captive domestic market. By 1770 it was forced to liquidate its unsold inventory through porcelain lotteries and auctions, where it could be purchased for as low as one-seventh of actual cost.[43]

Frederick reacted to the mixed results of his mercantile policies with renewed enthusiasm. He expanded the existing list of native products protected by import tariffs and prohibitions with a dozen new edicts between 1771 and 1775. He also redoubled his efforts to attract foreign craftsmen and entrepreneurs by promising tax freedom and dropping the minimum wealth requirement for admission into the Hessian towns.[44] He continued to use his foreign contacts and Hessian officials traveling abroad to recruit entrepreneurs and prospect for new industrial techniques.[45] In 1773 he even expanded the scope of the Agrarian Society

[40]For a profile of these problems see StAMg, 5)3918, 5)3632, 5)3652, 5)6019–21.
[41]StAMg, 5)3495: 22 May 1769 rescript; 5)6347: 2 May 1793 Oberrentkammer report; Dascher, "Karlshafen," 242, 251.
[42]HLO, 564–5: 16 Feb. 1770.
[43]StAMg, 5)1490: 5 Apr. 1770 report; 5)10485: 13 Sept. 1773 GD report; Siegfried Ducret, *Die landgräfliche Porzellanmanufaktur Kassel 1766–1788* (Brunswick, 1960), 183–5.
[44]HLO, 629, 734–5: 26 Nov. 1771, 1 Nov. 1773.
[45]Thus Frederick employed Raspe and Dohm during research trips to Hanover and the

to include commerce and industry, renaming it the *Gesellschaft des Ackerbaues und der Künste* "because trade and traffic are the source of wealth."[46]

At the same time, however, he did become more cautious in founding new industries. During 1773 he drastically reduced the size and competence of the Commerce College, turning over the supervision of all government-owned and -subsidized factories to the War and Domains Board. The move reflected not only Frederick's shaken confidence in the merchants who had dominated the college but also the victory of the fiscally conscious board, which had clashed with the college over the latter's generosity in approving subsidies and its own reluctance to forgo revenue-bearing trade imposts such as tolls and tariffs in the interests of increased trade.[47] It now became important for entrepreneurs to demonstrate the existence of an established local consumer market and to present a proven record, as did Crescentio Gallo, whose successful Venetian glassware factory earned him privileges for two new factories for making hats (1773) and perfume (1778).[48] Otherwise the board limited itself more than ever to such safe industries as textiles. After having granted only two new requests since 1767, the government now approved nineteen new textile privileges over the next two years and a total of thirty-six by 1777, including the country's first cotton factory founded in 1774. By 1775 it was even instructing the *Landräte* to foster textile production by encouraging more flax cultivation and by setting up spinning classes in the villages.[49]

Moreover the Frederician regime now began to draft a comprehensive agrarian program that assumed an importance equal to the promotion of industry. As had its efforts at industrialization, the government's in-

Palatinate, as well as the *Steuerrat* Johann Georg Lorentz when he went on a tour of Rhenish health spas. He also utilized his agent in Geneva to recruit emigrants following the city's latest outbreak of civil unrest. These efforts notwithstanding, Frederick's recruiters appear to have had no more success than Lorentz, who reported that, despite his glowing description of the country's industrial climate and privileges, his pitch "very rarely made a deep impression." StAMg, 5)6522: Frederick to KDK [Oct. 1773]; 5)4015: 26 Aug. 1774 rescript; 5)13467: Lorentz to Kopp, 29 Aug. [1775]; 5)13302: 20 Feb. 1778 KDK report; Albert Duncker, "Drei Briefe Rudolf Erich Raspe's and den Landgrafen Friedrich II. von Hessen," *ZHG*, 20, N.F. 10 (1882), 139; Dascher, *Textilgewerbe*, 33.

[46]*HLO*, 736-7: 16 Nov. 1773.
[47]*HLO*, 713: 9 Sept. 1773; Brandt, *Commerzienkammer*, 36-7, 39; Dascher, "Karlshafen," 232, 240.
[48]StAMg, 5)3003: 22 June 1773 GR protocol, 27 Mar. 1778 resolution.
[49]Dascher, *Textilgewerbe*, 222-7; Kopp, "Landräten," 153; StAMg, 5)6167, 5)6292, 5)3194: 31 Mar. 1775 resolution.

itiatives embraced all of the standard eighteenth-century strategies of boosting production by increasing investment, maximizing use of available resources, labor, and technology, and developing new products and markets. Once again it derived most of its inspiration from abroad by reading about or dispatching observers to other states, especially Prussia.[50] If it distinguished itself in any way from the other German regimes, it did so by the sheer volume and extensiveness of its initiatives, the degree to which it elicited the cooperation of the estates, and the closer oversight and intervention it enjoyed at the local level through the presence of the *Landräte*.

One broad approach to boosting production was to increase the amount of land under cultivation, a strategy that corresponded to the general view among cameralist thinkers that Germany's arable land was undercultivated, but was also a source of particular concern in Hesse-Cassel, where farmland had actually been lost to forestation in the first half of the century.[51] Beginning in 1774 crown officials such as the *Landräte* and cadastre surveyors had standing orders to report any uncultivated plots of arable land. When discovered, their peasant owners were generally given the choice of putting them under the plow, renting them out to someone else, or losing possession. The requirement was even extended to clergymen whose pastoral duties prevented them from tending to their own or church-owned plots.[52] It was characteristic of Frederick's thoroughness and obsession with detail that no one was spared the responsibility for cultivating fallow land. At one point in 1781 he directed his subordinates' attention to a particular church plot across the Fulda from Cassel that he felt should be planted with legumes. He even issued a decree requiring all newlyweds to plant four fruit trees on fallow land or along roadsides following their nuptials.[53] Yet the government's effort to enlarge the amount of land under cultivation found its greatest expression in the sponsorship of crop rotation and colonization.

Converting the country from the three-field system to crop rotation was not an easy task. To begin with, the government had to overcome the lack of fertilizer that was necessary to convert to continuous culti-

---

[50]For the multiplicity of reforms already in place elsewhere see Gagliardo, *From Pariah to Patriot*, 41–50, 55–6; Hubatsch, *Frederick the Great*, 101–11, 81–2, 170, 172, 175.
[51]Small, *The Cameralists*, 594; Möker, *Geschichtliche Wirtschaft*, 123.
[52]HLO, 770: 8 July 1774; StAMg, 5)3243: 2 Jan. 1777 Actum Cassel Consistory, 11 Feb. 1777 resolution.
[53]StAMg, 4a)90,12: "Articles pour introduire..."[1781]; Berge, "Friedrich II.," 117.

vation. In response it encouraged the stockpiling of dung through stall feeding, while also seeking to increase the number of livestock by promoting stud farms, better disease control, and the widespread planting of clover for use as fodder. Nor was it easily discouraged when a second obstacle emerged in the form of popular resistance to these initiatives. Town residents who owned livestock but no grazing land protested in vain that they now had to purchase fodder for stall feeding instead of being able to bring their animals to the town common.[54] Moreover, when the peasantry refused to plant two superior imported varieties of clover, Esparcette and St. Foin, the government immediately resorted to a combination of incentives and compulsion, offering free seed, exemptions from taxes and tithe, and even a subsidy to those peasants who introduced the new clover – while demanding that they do so.[55] In the end the government appears to have made some progress. Although the imported clovers were generally ignored and the three-field system endured in some areas until the next century, its persistence did lead to greater soil cultivation. In addition, livestock surveys initiated in 1773 to gauge the success of government programs recorded a dramatic increase from 525,352 to 810,265 by 1781.[56]

If anything Frederick's attempt to increase cultivation through the establishment of immigrant colonies proved more difficult than his efforts on behalf of crop rotation. Hesse-Cassel had already successfully settled foreign colonists when Landgrave Charles welcomed several thousand Huguenot refugees at the turn of the century. In addition, large European states such as Prussia, Austria, and Russia had long sustained major colonization programs of their own. Yet, the Frederician regime does not appear to have considered following suit until the possibility was called to its attention by a chance encounter in the autumn of 1775. At that time Hessian officials intercepted forty-one people from Trier who were on their way to new settlements in Prussia and offered them identical concessions if they agreed to settle in Hesse-Cassel. After they had been

[54]StAMg, 17e) Kassel 608: [21–2 Oct. 1776] Lennep votum.
[55]StAMg, 5)13250: 25 Feb. 1773 SK report, 26 Nov. 1782 KDK report, 17 June 1783 petition; 5)3194: 9 Feb. 1775 rescript; *HLO*, 692–4: 4 June 1773. Thus one *Landrat* gave a community eight days to explain why it had not planted Esparcette on its fallow land, and a 1783 ordinance required peasants who did not plant sufficient fodder to feed their animals to liquidate their excess livestock. StAMg, 17e) Leidenhofen 13: 1 Feb. 1777 report, 10 Feb. 1777 Schenk notes, Kleinschmidt to Schenck 15 May 1777; *HLO*, 1133: 24 Oct. 1783.
[56]Dascher, *Textilgewerbe*, 163; StAMg, 5)10597, "Land- und Viehverzeichnis ... 1781"; *HLO*, 1097: 17 Dec. 1782.

established in their new settlement at "Friedrichsfeld," the landgrave decided to launch a concerted effort to attract and settle other foreign colonists on Hessian soil. Not surprisingly, operating procedures were modeled after the Friedrichsfeld experiment, which had itself been copied from the Prussians. Prospective colonists were offered free building material, firewood, seed grain, 100 taler for livestock, thirty *Acker* of land (eighteen acres), and exemption from taxes and military service.[57]

By any standards, the results were modest. The government was able to recruit fewer than a thousand settlers for sixteen *Friedrichsdörfer*, a far cry from the 250,000 that populated Prussia's 1,500 village colonies. Yet the worst problem concerned those who did come. Government officials soon discovered that most of the settlers were destitute, unskilled, or lazy (and often all three) and could make little headway on the inferior land that was still available for cultivation. To make matters worse, many tended to misspend their cash advances so that they had to be given additional funds to afford them adequate food and shelter when winter arrived.[58] At the same time nearby towns protested that the unrestricted admission of foreign settlers had attracted a large number of petty criminals and freeloaders who used community mills, schools, and other services without having to contribute taxes for their upkeep.[59] Given its own priorities the government generally agreed that "the state is not served by the reception of destitute and beggar-poor foreigners." By 1779 it was expelling deadbeats from the colonies and requiring that future settlers have useful skills. To weed out the destitute it later introduced a Saxon ordinance that levied a ten-taler fee on all prospective settlers.[60] Nevertheless, despite these efforts the regime was unable to achieve its goal of making the colonies self-sufficient. Like so many of the entrepreneurs it had recruited from abroad, the colonists were able to retain their annual subsidies and renew their tax and other privileges at regular intervals well into the next century.[61]

[57] StAMg, 5)2641: 28 Sept. 1775 KDK report, 21 Feb. 1776 punctation; 5)2637: 4 Nov. 1777 SK report.
[58] StAMg, 5)2637: 4 Nov. 1777 SK report; 5)2639: 17 Mar. 1780 rescript, 23 Nov. 1782 SK report.
[59] StAMg, 5)2964: 4 Feb. 1779 desiderium, 5)14739: 23 Mar. 1779 desiderium; 17II)2055: [Feb. 1778] petition.
[60] StAMg, 5)2643: 10 Dec. 1779 resolution, 17II)2055: 8 Apr. 1785 Baumbach report, 17 June 1785 GD protocol.
[61] StAMg, 5)2641: 26 Oct. 1785 report, 19 Apr. 1805 GD protocol, 5)2638: 4 June 1804 rescript; 5)2637: 19 June 1805 rescript; Gottfried Ganssauge, "Bauernsiedlungen des Landgrafen Friedrich II.," *Hessische Heimat*, 5 (1939), 19. Berge estimates that the col-

In addition to increasing the amount of land under cultivation, the government employed other widely used strategies in its attempt to boost agricultural production, often with the same mixed results. To expand the number of workdays Frederick approved a petition from the estates of Schaumburg that called for a reduction in the number of religious holidays. He then applied the reduction to the entire country with a series of decrees closely patterned after similar laws in Hesse-Darmstadt and Brunswick, thereby eliminating at least two dozen non-Sabbath church observances and holidays, some of which had customarily lasted up to a week. Later the War and Domains Board attempted to schedule all of the country's church fairs for the same three-day period in late October to prevent peasants from wasting worktime by leaving their villages to attend fairs in neighboring towns. Fragmentary evidence suggests, however, that the peasantry resisted each of these initiatives.[62]

The government also encouraged the introduction of new crops and farming techniques. The recent famine favorably disposed many peasants to its efforts on behalf of potato cultivation. By the end of the reign it had become a staple in at least some areas.[63] In 1775 the landgrave also imported 10,000 grapevines from Switzerland at his own expense in an attempt to establish a wine-producing industry. Three years later he also introduced madder after Dohm had returned from a fact-finding trip to Swabia with glowing reports about its success in the German southwest. Nevertheless, both of these projects foundered miserably in the country's raw climate.[64]

As had been the case with its mercantile program, the regime's agrarian policies were most likely to succeed whenever it needed only to rely on its own considerable resources and could ignore such unfavorable independent factors as market conditions, climate, and popular resistance to change. For this reason it was able to employ successfully two common tactics for boosting agricultural investment. In 1774 it established the General Deposit and Assistance Fund (*General-Depositen- und Assistenzkasse*). Though initially intended for livestock purchases, the fund

onies cost Frederick 108,000 taler. Berge, "Aus der Entstehungsgeschichte der hessischen Friedrichsdörfer," *Hessische Heimat*, 5 N.F. (1955–6), 9.
[62]Heppe, *Kirchengeschichte beider Hessen*, 315; HLO, 663, 669-70, 687: 29 Sept. 1772, 15 Jan., 13 May 1773; StAMg, 5)3194: 7 Mar. 1775 KDK report; Maurer, *Aufklärung*, 95.
[63]HLO, 586: 12 July 1770; StAMg, 5)13446: 15 Jan. 1784 Motz report.
[64]Ilsegret Dambacher, *Christian Wilhelm von Dohm* (Frankfurt, 1974), 102; Berge, "Friedrich II.," 116.

assisted farmers who wished to improve their plots by advancing loans at rates of 1–2 percent. Moreover, unlike the Prussian Credit Institutes after which it was modeled, it did not concentrate its loans among noble landowners but spread them evenly throughout the general farming population.[65] One year later the government awarded lifelong, hereditary leases to all crown tenants. The move contradicted a Europe-wide trend toward short-term leases that had become popular among landlords because they could take advantage of their tenants' financial problems through periodic negotiations. The awarding of *Erbleihe* was, however, already the rule in neighboring Saxony, Prussia, and Hanover, because the German cameralists realized that they boosted productivity by giving peasants greater incentive to improve their plots. Such was the effect of the decree on noble landlords that virtually all peasant leases in Hesse-Cassel guaranteed lifelong possession by the end of the century.[66]

By instituting hereditary leases the government aimed to boost productivity by increasing the peasantry's incentive to work harder. It was this same strategy that inspired it to take a second look at feudal dues and services. Back in 1767 Grimmel had urged Frederick to follow Denmark's example in parceling up the demesne land on which limited labor service was performed into *Erbleihe*, predicting that free wage labor would be so much more productive that it would simultaneously benefit both the peasantry and the crown's domain revenues.[67] Although nobody was ready for such a bold move at that time, the agrarian crisis inclined the regime to act. In January 1773 it finally executed Grimmel's recommendation by establishing hereditary plots in exchange for a small annual payment in cash or *natura*. As usual the decree applied only to crown domains. Nevertheless, in one fell swoop labor service had been sharply reduced on two-thirds of the country's arable land and had set an example that many nobles emulated over the next few years.[68] Other actions followed. In February the government commissioned its second detailed survey of labor service in less than a decade, directing officials

---

[65]HLO, 781–3: 7 Oct. 1774; Staatliche Kunstsammlungen Kassel, *Klassizismus & Aufklärung*, 35.

[66]StAMg, 5)15487: 16 June 1775 resolution; Brauns, "Agrarpolitik," 83; Lerch, *Hessische Agrargeschichte*, 13, 17, 23; Olwen Hufton, *Europe: Privilege and Protest, 1730–1789* (Ithaca, N.Y., 1980), 27; Schulz, *Prinzipien der Einkünfte*, 402; Gagliardo, *From Pariah to Patriot*, 53–7.

[67]StAMg, 5)3064: 1 July 1767 Grimmel report.

[68]StAMg, 5)3064: 29 Jan. 1773 GR protocol; Ulrich Friedrich Kopp and Carl Friedrich Wittich, *Handbuch zur Kenntnis der hessen-casselischen Landes-Verfassung und Rechte*, 7 vols. (Cassel, 1796–1808), 4: 188.

to answer twenty-one specific questions about its nature and fairness in every community. One month after that it decreed that remaining labor services could not be required whenever the peasant needed the time to perform work essential for his livelihood such as sowing, reaping, or even other labor services for which he was being paid. Before the year was out Frederick abolished altogether the exaction of *Handdienst* (sowing, fertilizing, reaping) on crown lands. Later on he directed the *Landräte* and other officials to monitor closely the local allocation of labor service in order to eliminate existing abuses.[69]

The government's decision to move against labor service inspired new interest in the problems posed by feudal dues and services. As late as 1772 the Agrarian Society had sponsored a prize essay competition on labor service reform only to receive no contributions. In 1774 the reorganized society took up the question again and this time received seven submissions in response to its question asking how labor service could be converted into cash or natura payment "so that the landlord loses nothing and the peasant profits."[70] Indeed, the government was willing to reform labor service in the first place because it was convinced that the enhanced productivity of free labor would benefit both the peasant and the state without harming the interests of the *Grundherr*.

It was with this same notion in mind that it also began to contemplate the conversion of the tithe into a fixed payment. Like labor service, the tithe clearly limited productivity by encouraging peasants to leave their less fertile land fallow.[71] The government theorized that conversion would benefit everyone by providing the landlord with a steady income, by eliminating the expense of negotiating, collecting, and shipping the tithe payment, and by encouraging the peasant to place more land in production. By the summer of 1774 the Tax Office officials entrusted with the project were already predicting that "a solution can be achieved whereby the *Zehndt-Herr* loses nothing and the *Zehndtpflichtige* can only gain." After spending six months testing their ideas in the Diemel River district of Trendelburg, they submitted a plan calling for the replacement of the tithe with a fixed payment based on soil quality.[72]

---

[69]StAMg, 40)7 Generalia 42: 4 Feb. 1773 rescript; 5)8723: 15 Oct. 1773 GD protocol; HLO, 679–80, 794, 810–11: 19 Mar. 1773, 23 Jan., 10 Feb. 1775.
[70]Gerland, *Gesellschaft für Ackerbau*, 260–1.
[71]StAMg, 40)19 Generalia 33: 26 Jan. 1777 Wakenitz votum; Sakai, *Kurhessische Bauer*, 23.
[72]StAMg, 40)19 Generalia 33: 20 May 1774 GD protocol, 5)8831: 1 Aug. 1774, 21 Jan. 1775 SK reports.

After studying the plan, however, the War and Domains Board was far less sanguine. Though it favored conversion in principle, agreed that it would lead to greater productivity, and freely confessed to an overriding desire to help the peasants, it foresaw numerous drawbacks that threatened to backfire on all the parties involved. Its pessimism stemmed in large part from an unflattering view of the Hessian peasantry. The board feared, for example, that the peasants' spendthrift nature would incline them to loaf and consume the money they had saved after a bumper crop, thereby depriving them of a cushion to fall back on after a poor harvest. The *Kammerrat* August Ludemann even suggested that some peasants would spend the proceeds of a good harvest so quickly that they would not even be able to pay the tithe conversion payment that came due a few weeks later, thus immediately falling into debt to the landlord. Quite aside from the problems such indebtedness posed for both peasant and landlord, the board was also concerned that tithe conversion would deprive landlords of higher future payments in the likely event that crop yields increased over time. Finally, the government's ongoing difficulties with the new cadastre helped raise the specter that the new registers and procedures necessitated by conversion would lead to burdensome administrative difficulties and costs. Ludemann addressed this fear in comparing the conversion plan to Vauban's *Dîme Royale*; while conceding that "this work has earned widespread popularity with most administrative and fiscal experts" and would theoretically benefit the peasants, landlords, and government by replacing complex dues with a single, simple payment, he pointed out that it "has never been put into practice, perhaps because legions of tax and fiscal officials great and small have never been able to figure out how to make it work."[73]

The War and Domains Board's negative judgment did not end the matter. When it submitted its final report to the General Directory in February 1777, the landgrave and his ministers simply told it to come up with a better conversion plan. Shortly afterward, however, the General Directory received an equally pessimistic report from the Diemel *Landrat* Stockhausen, whose inquiries with Trendelburg's magistrate and peasants confirmed the board's suspicions about the impracticality of any conversion project.[74] Any hope of converting the tithe was now dead, so dead in fact that, when one landlord subsequently sought the govern-

[73]StAMg, 40)19 Generalia 33: ministerial votae, 26 Feb. 1777 KDK report.
[74]StAMg, 5)8831: 26 Feb. 1777 KDK report, 40)19 Generalia 33: 14 Mar. GD protocol, 21 July 1777 resolution.

ment's advice about a fair rate for converting the tithe into a cash payment on his estates, it advised him that he would be better off keeping the existing system in place.[75]

With the stillborn tithe-conversion project the government reached the limits of agrarian reform. Although it launched numerous and sometimes expensive programs designed to boost the productivity of Hessian agriculture, it was reluctant to risk any venture that threatened to open a Pandora's box of unforeseen and unwelcome consequences. One reason for its caution was that the many initiatives it was willing to undertake worked reasonably well without sacrificing stability. The remedial measures that began in 1773 successfully addressed the country's fiscal and agrarian problems, just as the reforms of the past decade had helped revive the commercial economy after the Seven Years' War. As early as 1777, the War and Domains Board was, in fact, speaking of steady, if unspecified, increases in crop yields throughout the country.[76] The fact remains, however, that the government was committed to working within the established system. Nowhere did it challenge the socioeconomic structures of Hessian society. Nor did its actions hurt any group or vested interest, except the Jews, the one group the government felt no need to represent. Indeed, it was unwilling to impose any reform that threatened undesirable side effects for any of those groups whose welfare it was trying to serve, whether it be the peasants, their noble landlords, or the state itself. Such were the dynamics – and the limitations – of governmental policy.

The assault on poverty

Frederick's new agrarian program, like the commercial-industrial projects that had preceded it, reflected the government's desire to create wealth both in order to enhance individual welfare and to reinforce the state's own fiscal strength. This same dualism of humanitarian and fiscal objectives emerges from the government's efforts to stem the growing numbers of poor and needy. The Hessian regime realized that poverty not only increased human suffering but also consumed public funds. In confronting this problem it was really fighting on both fronts. An examination of the numerous programs that it devised reveals three basic

[75]StAMg, 40)19 Rauschenberg 10: 5 Jan. 1782 KDK report.
[76]StAMg, 5)8831: 26 Feb. 1777 KDK report.

Table 6. *Poverty statistics for Cassel, 1765–76*

Itinerant beggars			Poor rolls		
1765	810		1765	518	
1766	1015	+25%	1766	464	−10%
1767	1553	+53%	1767	511	+10%
1768	2152	+39%	1768	531	+ 4%
1769	2959	+38%	1769	537	+ 1%
1770	3289	+11%	1770	644	+20%
1771	4631	+41%	1771	659	+ 2%
1772	3980	−14%	1772	725	+10%
			1773	740	+ 2%
			1774	753	+ 2%
			1775	794	+ 5%
			1776	828	+ 4%

Sources: Stein, "Das Waisenhaus in Kassel," 121; W.J.C.G.C [asparson], "Ueber das schäd-liche Betteln der sogennanten Passanten oder Vagabunden," *HB* 1 (1784), 603.

strategies: remedial public assistance, sumptuary laws, and income preservation.

In its first decade the Frederician regime attempted to sustain the country's voluntary system of public charity by encouraging greater support from private sources. When it did intervene it tended to take a Band-Aid approach that concentrated more on remedial aid than on prevention. As was the case elsewhere in Germany, the recent famine raised the government's awareness and determination to do more on behalf of the poor. Yet even before then the existing instruments of public charity were clearly straining under increasing burdens. In Cassel the number of itinerant beggars and native residents on the poor rolls grew steadily during the country's postwar recovery (Table 6). The prodigious increases in the number of itinerant beggars do not necessarily reflect increasing poverty, but rather the residence's emergence as a magnet for poor people fleeing the Hessian hinterland and neighboring states right up until the famine years. The poor roll records do, however, indicate that things were not uniformly good among Cassel's indigenous population. With annual increases averaging 7.7 percent and a rise of 56 percent between 1767 and 1772, poverty had resumed its wartime march, gaining even greater momentum with the crop failures. By then government studies had revealed that voluntary contributions to the *Armenkasse* would not solve the problem by themselves. Not only were Cassel's wealthier families shirking their share of almsgiving but the burghers as a group were actually donating less than they had prior to the war, providing less than a third of the funds needed to support the city's poor. So great was the shortfall that the government feared that private foundations, which "can serve the state as useful citizens," would have to close.[77]

The situation was also desperate at the state-run *Accouchir- und Findelhaus*. Frederick had originally intended its operations to be supported roughly equally by private charity and government subsidies. For this purpose, he had committed funds generated by excise tax fines, a state-run lottery, and a printing press located in the orphanage basement. To his dismay, however, Cassel's burghers contributed less than 1 percent to the facility's operating costs, thereby compelling him to make special annual gifts to sustain operations.[78] The deficit was exacerbated by the very success of the *Accouchirhaus*, which was regularly delivering eighty to a hundred babies each year. Despite extreme overcrowding it had maintained an excellent survival record for both newborns and their mothers. Yet the *Findelhaus*, which was already having difficulty handling the large number of foundlings it received through its turnstile, was unable to absorb the additional transfers from the *Accouchirhaus*. The situation worsened dramatically after the crop failures, when it took in a total of 100 children in a single year, roughly three times its capacity. Although half of all foundlings usually died within a year and some babies were entrusted to foster families, the remainder were compelled to live in unhealthy conditions until they could be sent across the street to the equally overcrowded orphanage. Most never survived long enough to graduate. By 1773 Stein reported that overcrowding was so bad at the *Accouchir- und Findelhaus* that it might have to close.[79]

The widening gap between the numbers of poor and the funds available to support them presented the government with a dilemma between the needs of public welfare and its own concern for fiscal integrity. It was determined to assist the growing legions of the poor and helpless, both

[77]StAMg, 5)10852: 29 July 1773 AW report, 5)10853: 10 Nov. 1775 AW report.
[78]StAMg, 5)10852: 29 July 1773 AW report, "Überschlag von Einnahme ..." [1773].
[79]StAMg, 5)10852: 20 Dec. 1773 AW report, 27 Apr. 1774 pro memoria; Käthe Heinemann, "Aus der Blütezeit der Medizin am Collegium illustre Carolinum zu Kassel," *ZHG*, 71 (1960), 94; Stein, "Waisenhaus in Kassel," 96, 98, 106-7, 111. The problems of overcrowding and high mortality experienced by the Cassel *Findelhaus* closely parallel those of its counterparts in London and Paris, especially during the famine. Claude Delasselle, "Abandoned Children in Eighteenth-Century Paris," in Robert Forster and Orest Ranum, eds., *Deviants and the Abandoned in French Society* (Baltimore, 1978), 48-9, 54, 73; Peter C. Hoffer and N. E. H. Hull, *Murdering Mothers: Infanticide in England and New England 1558–1803* (New York and London, 1981), 140.

in order to control crime and to reintegrate them into the productive part of society. It was, however, unwilling to do so by constantly borrowing from existing cash reserves. Yet the alternative was to levy new taxes that would provide public-welfare operations with a reliable source of revenue, but at the expense of placing additional burdens on the already hard-pressed population, driving still more people onto the poor rolls.

In their reluctance to introduce a compulsory poor tax, government officials searched for ways to cushion the blow. Frederick himself admonished his ministers that his poorer subjects not be forced to raise money to the point that they would have to pawn their own means of income. In response one proposal suggested allowing people to postpone their payments, or finding them additional work and income sources with which to defray the cost. Another advocated adopting Hesse-Darmstadt's levy on inheritances over 200 taler as a painless way of shifting the burden to those who could afford to pay.[80] In the end, however, the regime decided on a compulsory tax that would nonetheless be individually negotiated with each burgher according to his ability to pay. Decreed in August 1773, the mandatory *Wochensteuer* applied to all major towns and was designed to enable each local *Armenkasse* to support the poor, while also rescuing institutions such as the *Accouchir- und Findelhaus* from collapse. Enforcing it was a system of ward commissars (*Quartierkommissare*) copied from existing Prussian and Parisian models who were responsible for negotiating and collecting the tax from the burghers, while closely supervising and making payments to the towns' indigent population.[81]

The poor-relief system ushered in by the *Wochensteuer* represented the centerpiece of the government's new program of public assistance. Yet, for much the same reason the government also lent considerable remedial aid to those in need of health care. Like poor relief, the government had afforded health care minimal attention during its first decade but was now intervening forcefully because of the imminent collapse of private or church-run institutions. The government also perceived a causal relationship between poor health, poor productivity, and poor subjects. Hence, by the end of 1772 it had begun to construct a *Charité* hospital for the indigent that mimicked its namesakes in Paris and Berlin. Once

---

[80] StAMg, 5)3542: 20 Mar. 1772 SK report; 5)10852: 2, 10, 20 Mar. 1772 SK report, 29 July 1773 AW report; 5)10853: 10 Nov. 1775.
[81] *HLO*, 707–10: 6 Aug. 1773; StAMg, 5)10726: 12 Nov. 1773 GD protocol.

again the government established a permanent revenue base for its creation with a presumably incongruous trio of new taxes on dogs, butchered meat, and marriages.[82] It also addressed the need for more and better-trained midwives in rural areas, first by raising their salaries, then by transferring several private and military surgeons to teaching duties in the countryside.[83] Following the outbreak of a number of epidemics at the beginning of the decade the government also made free medical care available for their victims.[84]

In its most ambitious undertaking, the government soon established substantially greater supervision and control over health conditions and medical care throughout the country. By 1770 it had already more closely centralized its scrutiny over health conditions in various parts of the country by subordinating all medical professionals to Cassel's *Collegium Medicum*, a government authority dominated by the medical faculty of the *Collegium Carolinum*.[85] The most important step came, however, in 1778 when Frederick invited Christoph Ludwig Hoffmann, personal physician to the bishop of Münster, to his summer residence at Hofgeismar to tell him about Münster's new health code. After comparing it with the older ordinances in force elsewhere in Germany, he adopted it for Hesse-Cassel. The new thirty-five-page health code moved to eliminate the practice of medicine by so-called *Empiraker*, barbers, and other laymen who learned their trade solely by trial and error to supplement their principal source of income. Henceforth all medical personnel, including surgeons, doctors, pharmacists, and midwives, were classified according to their level of competence, as defined by regular examination and enforced by visitation and the public display of diplomas. Meanwhile, they were limited to prescribing drugs that had been tested, approved, and priced by the *Collegium Medicum*.[86]

While the government was affording remedial assistance to the poor and the sick, its assault on poverty assumed a second dimension that delved

---

[82]*HLO*, 662–3: 4 Sept. 1772; N. Neuber, "Über das Landkrankenhaus zu Bettenhausen," *Mitt* (1898), 45.
[83]StAMg, 5)1228: 15 Mar. 1770 Actum; 5)7732: 20 Dec. 1771 GR protocol; 5)1214: 13 May 1774, 27 Jan. 1775 GD protocols.
[84]StAMg, 5)1206: 28 Oct., 18 Nov., 9 Dec. 1774 GD protocols.
[85]StAMg, 5)1450: 1 Oct. 1770 resolution.
[86]*HLO*, 919–54: 31 July 1778; Balde and Biermer, *Medizin in Kassel*, 54–5; Hans Braun, "Hessische Medizinalverhältnisse im 18. Jahrhundert," *Hessenland*, 17 (1903), 102–4, 126–8, 144–5; Berge, "Friedrich II.," 228.

even more deeply into the lives of the landgrave's subjects: prevention by manipulating the people's environment and regulating their life-style. Such an attempt at "social engineering" derived its sustenance from the government's perception of the causes of poverty, an insight that reflected a distillation of Calvinist pessimism, cameralist teaching, and the bureaucracy's long experience in dealing with the common people. It was an article of faith at every level of the Hessian government from the landgrave down to the local *Beamte* that poverty stemmed from a natural inclination toward hedonism and lethargy and that individuals succumbed most fully to these instincts once caught in a chain of events that led from hardship, to indebtedness, despair, lost incentive, and ultimately to complete surrender.[87]

The government understood, however, that well-executed *Polizei* could preserve the people from their vices by diverting them from ruinous complacency and consumption when times were good, and preserving them from debt when they turned bad. Hence it instructed the *Landräte* to supervise closely the activities of both agricultural and industrial workers, pressing them to apply themselves and looking for evidence of lack of application. In their vigilance they were told to pay particular attention to poor building maintenance "because a poor worker reveals his true character no more openly than through the improper upkeep of his possessions." They were also given full authority to approve all church festivities and to forbid music and other forms of entertainment that threatened to undermine worker productivity.[88]

A major thrust of government intervention found expression through the intensification of existing sumptuary laws. The government strengthened its prohibitions on expensive clothing to the point of mounting house-to-house inspections. It also tightened its ban on the purchase of both chocolate and coffee on the grounds that the social ambience surrounding their consumption undermined public morality, while promoting idleness and lethargy. The government justified a particularly intensive campaign against coffee because it was also associated with numerous health hazards ranging from insomnia and jitters to sterility

[87]StAMg, 5)813: 4 Sept. 1774 Münchhausen report and votum, 5)13443: 17 Jan. 1775 Wille votum; 5)3542: 26 Jan. 1778 SK report; 5)3542: [Aug. 1778] Frederician rescript; 5)2755: 16 May 1783 Pappenheim report; 5)13446: 15 Jan. 1784 Motz report; Bopp "Fehler."
[88]StAMg, 5)4294: "LandRaths Instruction"; *HLO*, 845: 21 Oct. 1775 rescript; Kopp, "Landräten," 137–8.

in men and both menstrual hemorrhaging and miscarriages in women.[89] In 1774 it even took the unpopular step of forbidding the children of both peasants and burghers from enrolling at a university unless they could prove that their parents could afford the expense and loss of their labor, and that they had sufficient academic potential. Although such prohibitions existed in other German states, the decision was a difficult one for the regime, which feared it "could cause a sensation abroad" that would damage the landgrave's reputation as a patron of education.[90] In fact, the law is remarkable because it also compelled the government to confront conflicting priorities between its attempts to promote education and university enrollments and its efforts to forestall poverty through inessential consumption and the diversion of teenage labor.

Nor was it the only instance where the government was obliged to weigh conflicting priorities. Sumptuary laws like those issued against finer clothing, coffee, and chocolate were not only aimed at safeguarding personal wealth and character but also directed at discouraging the purchase of imported goods. Thus *Kleiderpracht* ordinances compelled people to wear Hessian-made clothing and the coffee ban promoted the drinking of Hessian-brewed beer, claiming that it was "without a doubt the healthiest" beverage available, ideally suited toward maintaining "the robust constitution of the common man."[91] By limiting wasteful consumption and the export of specie, these prohibitions benefited the Hessian economy in two separate ways. Yet, whenever such goods and services were produced inside the country or otherwise generated income for the state, the government was obliged to choose between sustaining worker productivity and some other facet of its revenue base. In such instances, the all-pervasive desire to preserve existing sources of state income usually took precedence over poverty prevention. For a brief two-year period beginning in 1771 the government actually halved its prohibitive duties on imported coffee in order to boost foreign participation and trade volume with both the Cassel fairs and the Carlshafen Company. Ten months later it also reversed its opposition to tobacco consumption following the establishment of a state-owned factory. The War and Domains

[89]Brunner, *Kassel*, 300; August Woringer, "Zoll und Schmuggel in Hessen im 18. und 19. Jahrhundert," *Hessenland*, 20 (1906), 62; StAMg, 5)1598: 4 May 1775 Coll Med report, 5)4039: 30 Dec. 1785 KDK report; D. Busch, "Ueber den Kaffee," *HB* 1 (1784), 607, 610–11.
[90]StAMg, 5)7750: 7 May 1774 Kopp votum; *HLO*, 769-70: 2 July 1774.
[91]StAMg, 17II)1335: 21 Dec. 1765 protocol.

Board did subsequently levy a 50 percent tariff on imported tobacco, but only to protect the new enterprise and generate outside revenue.[92]

Perhaps the most obvious conflict between the attempts to reduce wasteful consumption and the search for revenue is provided by the government's position toward gambling. During its midreign crisis the regime sharpened the existing ban on all games of chance. Except for the small *Klassenlotterie* operated by the *Accouchir- Findel- und Waisenhaus* authority, it outlawed all cash lotteries and also prohibited participation in foreign lotteries because, like purchases of imported luxury products, they helped to impoverish both the country's people and the economy by exporting money.[93] Yet the government routinely granted retroactive exemptions to any native Hessian who actually won a foreign lottery in order to enable him to import his winnings and spend them inside the country.[94] Furthermore, at the suggestion of a visiting Polish diplomat Frederick even committed himself to the establishment of a state lottery at the height of the famine in the summer of 1771.

At the time he justified his decision by pointing out that the threat it posed to the financial integrity of poor people was counterbalanced by the hope and fantasies it would inspire among a great number of people, the fortunes it would afford to a lucky few – and the additional income it would bring the state. The entire operation was designed to be especially attractive. Unlike a *Klassenlotterie* the new *Zahlenlotto* permitted each participant to bet as much as he wished, paying up to 60,000 times his investment. Moreover, no fewer than five winners were announced twice each month to the accompaniment of trumpet fanfare. To no one's surprise the lottery was an instant success, attracting enormous crowds of people from throughout the Cassel area for each of its biweekly drawings. That was the problem. Local officials complained that working people all over northern Hesse were taking the day off to attend the drawings, one of them estimating that they cost the peasantry more in lost productivity than hail, forestation, or crop failure. It also became evident that all too many poor people were investing everything they had in the lottery, thereby victimizing the people it was designed to benefit. Nevertheless, its tremendous popularity and the 12 percent net profit it afforded

---

[92]*HLO*, 596, 635, 689: 31 Dec. 1770, 3 Mar. 1772, 14 May 1773; StAMg, 5)3757: 26 Oct. 1771 KDK report.
[93]*HLO*, 764–5: 28 Apr. 1774.
[94]StAMg, 5)1792: 22 Apr. 1768 report, 26 Apr. 1768 rescript, 5)1782: 25 Apr. 1770 report.

the treasury inclined Frederick not only to retain the *Zahlenlotto* but to establish a second operation in Marburg in 1779.[95]

Indeed the lottery was not the only instance where the government confronted the choice between a popular and profitable venture that hurt the poor and an unpopular and unprofitable sumptuary ordinance that benefited them. The reestablishment of a coffee ban in 1773 brought widespread smuggling, hundreds of private petitions, and sharp protests from merchants who claimed that it was crippling the Hessian porcelain industry and the Cassel fairs by eliminating the sale of popular coffee services.[96] When the government responded with higher penalties and stricter enforcement, large numbers of people simply began frequenting cafés in the many Hanoverian and Mainz enclaves in Hessian territory, prompting shopkeepers and excise officials in border areas to complain about sharp drops in sales on the Hessian side of the frontier. Although it soon reduced the prohibitions for burghers "in the interests of commerce," official reports of lost sales and tax revenues, smuggling, and popular defiance continued to the end of the reign.[97]

Other sumptuary ordinances were no less unpopular. One law prohibiting peasants from wearing cotton and calico created burdensome inventories for the country's textile merchants and brought retaliation from neighboring states against Hessian-made products.[98] Meanwhile, the new restrictions on entering university students so devastated peasant enrollments at Marburg that university officials were not even able to give out the increased number of fellowships recently allotted by the government for the indigent. It was in vain that they pointed out the impossibility of assessing accurately the potential of students, whether "late bloomers" or "overachievers," before they had matriculated.[99]

Just as the government tried to mold the common people's cultural and material environment, it also attempted to reduce the risk of poverty by

[95]August Woringer, "Das kasseler Lotto 1771–1785," *ZHG*, 47 (1914), 20–1, 31, 34–9, 46-7; Friedrich Dott, "Ein Zahlenlotto in Kassel, 1771–1785," *Hessische Heimat*, 14 (1964), 24.

[96]StAMg, 5)832; 5)10485: 13 Sept. 1773 GD report; 5)10484: 13 Sept. 1773 Waitz report, 17 Sept. 1773 GD protocol.

[97]*HLO*, 756, 761–2, 827, 851, 997: 11 Feb., 5 Apr. 1774, 6 June, 21 Dec. 1775, 21 Feb. 1780; StAMg, 5)831: 18 Mar. 1774 GD protocol; 5)3427: 11 Oct. 1774 KDK report, 5 June 1775 pro memoria; 5)3217: 10 Jan. 1780 petition; 5)2699: 18 Aug. 1783 KDK report.

[98]StAMg, 5)7423: 28 July Comm Coll report, 13 Aug. 1773 resolution.

[99]StAMg, 5)7750: 10 Nov. 1776 Univ. Mg. petition.

trying to expand or preserve existing sources of income. This assumed many forms, ranging from the creation of jobs for the needy to reducing, delaying, or even forgiving the discharge of tax and debt obligations when they threatened to destroy the livelihood of those already gainfully employed.

The government's efforts applied to both the urban-commercial and rural-agricultural sectors, as befitted the new balance in Hessian economic policy. In the towns Frederick and his ministers continued to look on industrial labor as an ideal income source for the weak and the poor, especially if it involved textile work. For several years the inmates at the state orphanage had worked textiles and had even engaged in silk weaving following the planting of several mulberry trees outside the building. The government also employed from 15 to 20 percent of Cassel's growing itinerant community in various textile enterprises.[100]

It also closely monitored the living and working conditions of workers who were already employed. Hence, at one point the War and Domains Board warned that flax workers performing piecework were so underpaid that they were "being reduced to beggary," despite their labor. To prevent this it threatened the entrepreneurs who exploited them with stiff fines and jail terms unless they paid a living wage. On the other hand the board felt that it was the flax workers' responsibility to seize every opportunity to save themselves by enlisting the assistance of their families. The husbands of female flax workers were advised of the folly of spending "long winter nights in idleness" and admonished to join their wives in spinning. The message was even less ambiguous for their sons, who were subjected to fines for refusing to assist their mothers.[101]

Since 90 percent of the population was engaged in agriculture, most of the government's efforts focused on preserving existing peasant income levels by protecting farmers from losing the land, livestock, and implements they needed to survive. It would be a mistake to assume that this represented a new approach that stemmed from Enlightenment or Physiocratic thought. Like many of its German counterparts, the government had been trying to preserve the integrity of peasant-operated farmland since the sixteenth century in a strategy that mixed

---

[100]Martin Eckel, "Das kasseler Werkhaus 1782–1823," *ZHG*, 75–6 (1964–5), 433; Stein, "Waisenhaus in Kassel," 124–5; Dascher, *Textilgewerbe*, 90.
[101]StAMg, 5)3194: 9 Feb., 1, 7 Mar. 1775 KDK report.

humanitarian motives with its determination to maintain an adequate income for the nobles, food supply for the towns, and tax base for the state.[102]

A case in point is the inheritance regulation that outlawed the Hessian practice of subdividing farmland equally among all surviving children whenever it led to the creation of unprofitably small plots. Like some of its neighbors Hesse-Cassel had passed its first such *Hufen-Edikt* in the sixteenth century, only to see it totally ignored. By the eighteenth century as much as a third of all peasants were cultivating plots of less than five *Acker* (about three acres). In their defiance of government attempts to institute primogeniture, many farmers had subdivided their land into parcels as small as one-eighth and even one-sixteenth of an *Acker*, despite government studies indicating that the average family needed at least twenty to thirty *Acker* (twelve to eighteen acres) in order to eke out a subsistence living.[103]

In an attempt to compel greater compliance with the existing laws, the 1764 diet had appealed for stronger penalties. Yet, although it directed local officials to enforce the law, the government feared the effect that fines would have against the already hard-pressed peasant population.[104] The agrarian crisis finally prompted it to take action, both to save peasants from further hardship and indebtedness that might cost them their property and to sustain their ability to discharge existing tax and manorial obligations.[105] In fact the new *Hufen-Edikt* of November 1773 avoided the threat of fines or other penalties and merely reiterated existing ordinances by prohibiting the subdivision of farmland into parcels under one *Hufe* (thirty *Acker*, or eighteen acres). What made it different from past measures was effective enforcement through a combination of greater government determination and the close oversight of the newly installed *Landräte*.

---

[102]Möker, *Geschichtliche Wirtschaft*, 108; Brunner, "Rittergüter und Gutsbezirke," 57; Raeff, *Well-Ordered Police State*, 112–13.
[103]StAMg, 17II) 1434: 20 Apr. 1765 report; "In wie weit ist es rathsam, durch die Landpolizei der Veräuserung und Vertheilung der Bauergüter Schranken zu setzen?" *HB*, 2 (1785), 434; Möker, *Geschichtliche Wirtschaft*, 113–14, 146; Brunner, "Rittergüter und Gutsbezirke," 57; Sakai, *Kurhessische Bauer*, 13.
[104]StAMG, 5)14717: "Desideria communia ... 9tes," "Desideria generalia ... 19tes"; 17II)1402: 19 July 1764 Actum Reg Cas, 17II)2404: 12 Apr. 1766 rescript; *HLO*, 411: 17 Mar. 1767.
[105]StAMg, 304)578: 23 Mar. 1779 petition, 5)13446: 19 Mar. 1779 GR protocol; 5)13287: [n.d.] report, "Project einer Resolution..."; *HLO*, 737–40: 10 Nov. 1773.

The government also worked to insulate peasants against the consequences of their unpaid debts. Seven days after issuing the *Hufen-Edikt* it decreed an ordinance at the urging of the Tax Office, awarding peasants a four-year moratorium on all farm debts. Over the next few months this was supplemented by two additional decrees that forbade the pawning of livestock and enjoined tax collectors from seizing farm animals or other productive capital such as land, buildings, or implements for a period of four years for nonpayment of taxes.[106] In the following October peasants received additional insurance against foreclosure from an ordinance obliging creditors to pay for most of the court costs involved in debt litigation. Even in those instances where liquidation did take place the government began employing tactics designed to keep the land in the hands of peasant smallholders, such as by reselling foreclosed land cheaply at public auctions and by requiring noble landlords to get its permission before buying out their peasants.[107]

In addition to protecting peasant smallholders against divided inheritances and debt foreclosure, the government moved to protect their capital against catastrophic loss with a series of edicts issued in the mid–1770s. Beginning in 1774 it passed out seed grain to peasants whose previous harvest had been too meager to enable them to save for the next planting. One year later it gave them detailed instructions on how to protect their livestock against disease. By 1776 it actually began reimbursing them for one-third of all livestock deaths and for crop failures inflicted by natural causes such as hail, fire, floods, rodents, or blight, while simultaneously reducing all financial obligations to both the crown and private landlords in proportion to their losses.[108]

The government had clearly demonstrated a certain amount of courage and determination in its ambitious attempts to strengthen the security of peasant farmers and resolve the problems of individual poverty. Thanks largely to the greater loyalty and closer oversight afforded by the *Landräte*, its efforts to protect the country's smallholders against their creditors and noble landlords compare favorably to Frederick the Great's failure to overcome the opposition of the Prussian nobility to his vain attempts

[106]HLO, 749–55: 26 Nov. 1773, 11 Feb. 1774; StAMg, 5)13169: 21 Jan. 1774 GD protocol.
[107]HLO, 785–6: 25 Oct. 1774; StAMg, 5)4294: "LandRaths Instruction"; Möker, *Geschichtliche Wirtschaft*, 108.
[108]HLO, 760, 825–6, 851–6, 863–6, 915–17: 26 Mar. 1774, 18 May, 28 Dec. 1775, 3 May 1776, 14 Apr. 1778.

to forestall their amalgamation of peasant lands.[109] Yet the absence of a powerful and conservative opposition in Hesse-Cassel did not by itself guarantee the successful outcome of reform. Before long some of these initiatives had given rise to unexpected and unwelcome consequences that actually worsened some of the problems the government was trying to correct.

Problems immediately surfaced with those tactics designed to discourage foreclosure. In their eagerness to find peasant buyers government auctioneers often resold foreclosed land so cheaply that creditors were unable to recoup their original investment. As a result investors simply stopped extending farm loans, thereby making it difficult for peasants to obtain credit for purchasing or improving land. Although the regime corrected the situation by fixing a minimum auction price, it was still unable to soothe investors who were also being harassed by delinquent peasants who openly dared them to sue, knowing that creditors now had to pick up the tab for all the legal costs.[110] Peasants were equally brazen in dealing with government tax collectors. In the past many would claim to be too poor to pay their taxes but then would pay once threatened with the seizure of their livestock. Now they merely hid their harvested crops in the field while claiming poverty, knowing full well that the tax collectors could not seize their capital.[111]

Worse yet were the effects of the new *Hufen-Edikt*. With strict enforcement came hundreds of protests and petitions for exemption from families that were unwilling to disinherit their daughters and younger male children. The problem was exacerbated by confusion among officials and families alike, many of whom assumed that the new edict forbade subdivision or female inheritance in all cases, instead of just those involving plots under one *Hufe*.[112] Over the next few years local crown officials and the representatives of the estates began to report many unfortunate consequences that aggravated some of the agrarian problems that the government had hoped to correct. Begging and vagabondage increased as the number of disinherited youths gradually grew. The number of marriages dropped sharply, because younger male offspring could not support a family and prospective brides had no dowry to offer. Rather

---

[109]Berdahl, "The *Stände*," 304–5.
[110]StAMg, 5)3542: 17 Aug. 1778 Actum.
[111]StAMg, 5)3542: 26 Jan. 1778 SK report, 21 May 1778 report.
[112]StAMg, 17II)2404: 28 Oct. 1777 rescript. Surviving petitions fill five thick fascicles at the StAMg, 17II)2405–8, 5)13283.

than improve the farmland that would go to their eldest son, peasants started saving what money they could in order to have something to pass on to their disinherited children. Meanwhile, potential investors were now even less interested in advancing credit because the inheritance restrictions had collapsed the value of land that could no longer be freely disposed of.[113]

By 1776 the new agrarian crisis created by the *Hufen-Edikt* had become the subject of widespread discussion. The Agrarian Society sponsored a prize essay competition on how to reverse the 50 percent fall in land values caused by the edict, followed by a later competition that questioned whether the subdivision of farmland should be governed by *Polizei*.[114] The *Landräte* were suggesting that the edict be repealed – and were soon to be joined by the very estates that had inspired it in the first place.[115]

Yet for the moment Frederick and his ministers stood firm. Through the *Hufen-Edikt* they were boldly attempting to effect a massive shakeout that would save the poorest peasant farm families from steadily deepening poverty by forcing younger children into more promising careers, while enabling elder offspring to salvage a subsistence living from agriculture. Notwithstanding all the undesirable and largely unexpected side effects, the edict also seemed to be doing what it was intended to do. Significant numbers of disinherited peasant youths of both sexes had already left the countryside "because they expect little or nothing from their parents." Although his estimate was likely exaggerated, the new French envoy Grais even reported that the *Hufen-Edikt* "has caused a considerable emigration to the extent that the population is not half what it should be."[116] If there was anxiety within the government, it concerned where the country's youths were going. Few appear to have drifted to the towns, which were in no position to provide them with alternative employment. Rather, they were heading in two directions. Many peasant youths of both sexes simply left the country for other German states, a population shift that made the cameralist purists in Cassel wince. Nevertheless, most young men reacted to the *Hufen-Edikt* as they were expected to by enlisting in

[113]StAMg, 5)14743: "Desideria ulteriora ... 5"; 5)13446: 15 Jan. 1784 Motz report; 5)3242: Dec. 1784 Lennep/Meyer report.
[114]Strieder et al., *Gelehrten, Schriftsteller, und Künstler Geschichte*, 4: 234; Gerland, *Gesellschaft für Ackerbau*, 286.
[115]Brauns, "Agrarpolitik," 85; StAMg, 5)14743: "Desideria ulteriora ... 5" [1778].
[116]AAE, CP, HC 14: 14 Mar. 1776 Grais report.

the Hessian army. Even here, however, the government was not spared yet another unpleasant surprise. What no one could have foreseen in 1773 was the promise of a new life that the army would soon offer the Hessian poor, thereby involving the country in a demographic crisis far greater than the government ever could have anticipated.

5

Foreign and military policy

Nowhere was the continuity with the past and acceptance of existing attitudes and institutions more evident than in Hessian foreign and military policy. Although Frederick brought new ideas and inclinations to the throne, he did very little to change the direction of foreign policy or the role of the army in society. He also discovered once again that, as in his domestic policy, even the most carefully considered initiatives could lead to the most unexpected and unwelcome repercussions.

The Hessian diplomatic and military system

Like most other small states Hesse-Cassel was very much subject to the limitations posed by its small size. Despite its 12,000-man standing army, it enjoyed little diplomatic leverage. Instead, it generally blended in with the bulk of smaller states that abided by the *Reichsfriede*, valued the stability afforded by the status quo, and helped make imperial institutions work, especially at the regional, *Kreis*, level. Like other small states it also had an established relationship with certain other states that largely predetermined its policies within the empire. Two centuries of defending German Protestantism against the Counter-Reformation and then Germany itself against French aggression had cemented Hesse-Cassel's membership in a "Protestant System" that embraced not only the northern German states but also Great Britain, the Netherlands, Sweden, and Denmark. By midcentury it was a relationship with which the dynasty, ministry, and people felt comfortable. It had also given rise to a tradition of keeping a strong military in order to maintain the country's security against foreign threats.

The Seven Years' War and Frederick's succession had undermined the commitment to the Protestant System. In 1757 William VIII had briefly considered remaining neutral or even enlisting his army in the imperial service in order to save the country from the ravages of both sides, but had finally dropped the idea because he feared that the French might seek repeal of the *Assekurationsakte*.[1] Obviously Frederick had no such fears or inhibitions against working with Catholic Austria and France if it would prevent further destruction. He was, moreover, also moved by what can only be described as a love-hate relationship with Hesse-Cassel's traditional allies. Despite what the French envoy accurately termed a "zealous admiration of everything that is Prussian," the new landgrave deeply resented his great namesake, who had humiliated him during the conversion crisis and had never hesitated thereafter to ridicule him and his eccentricities. At the same time he still felt alienated from Great Britain owing to the British government's residual ill feeling over his failed marriage with Princess Mary. To his credit Frederick also recognized that Prussia's strength and proximity compromised Hesse-Cassel's freedom of movement and ultimately threatened its existence. For these reasons, he sought to gain independence from the Prussian alliance and actually opened wartime negotiations with the French in order to secure Hessian neutrality and a French subsidy.[2]

Yet the obstacles to such a diplomatic *volte face* proved overwhelming. As his father's ministers explained in a memorial presented shortly after his succession, deserting the Protestant alliance would cost the government extensive British subsidies that were needed both to pay its troops and to finance the country's eventual economic recovery. They also pointed to the "undying hatred" the Hessian people felt toward their French and Austrian occupiers, and the likely revenge that its current allies would wreak on those parts of the country they continued to hold. Indeed, it is altogether probable that Frederick feared the violent reaction of Prussia and of his own subjects, who probably would have interpreted a French subsidy treaty as a precursor to Catholicization, especially since it would have violated the *Assekurationsakte*'s ban against allying with a Catholic state against a Protestant one.[3] Notwithstanding his bold designs, the new landgrave remained a spectator in a war fought largely in his country. With peace imminent, he pleaded with his allies not to

[1]Renouard, *Geschichte des Krieges*, 1: 294; Demandt, *Geschichte*, 278.
[2]HHStA, RK, Kleinere Reichsstände 163: 23 Sept. 1766 Moser report, Berichte aus dem Reich 81: 9 Feb. 1765 Pergen report, 106: 1 Nov. 1771 Neipperg report, 134: 7 Oct. 1784 Trauttmansdorff report; AAE, CP, HC 12: 10 May, 3 June 1766 Hennenberg reports.
[3]StAMg, 4e)2665: 12 Nov. 1760 memorial; HHStA, RK, Kleinere Reichsstände 163: [1766] Moser report, RK, Berichte aus dem Reich 81: 9 Feb. 1765 Pergen report, 106: 1 Nov. 1771 Neipperg report.

besiege Cassel, only to watch them deliver "the last fatal blow" to the city in the closing days of the war's final campaign.[4] Though he eventually declared Hessian neutrality at the start of 1763, he did so only at the suggestion of the Hanoverian ministry, after Britain and France had suspended hostilities.[5]

Following the conclusion of peace Frederick continued to work for Hessian neutrality because he was convinced that war would break out again and wanted to save the country from further destruction.[6] Curiously enough the new Prussian junta shared his premonition of war and preference for neutrality. Yet their efforts to gain Hesse-Cassel a measure of independence were equally unsuccessful. Despite the landgrave's enthusiastic support, Schlieffen's plan to create a nonaligned bloc of German states foundered because no other states had the financial resources to furnish troops.[7]

Concurrent attempts to effect an alliance with France and Austria proved equally unrealistic. From his listening post in Frankfurt Moser warned Frederick that French policy was currently in such confusion that even the French envoy there felt Great Britain would make a more reliable ally![8] Meanwhile both the landgrave and his ministers were so apprehensive Hesse-Cassel might suffer the fate of Saxony should it make any attempt to cut its ties with Prussia that they refused to take any risks whatsoever.[9] Thus, when the French asked the landgrave to dispatch the Francophile Wittorf to Paris to negotiate the alliance, he balked out of fear that the appointment of such a high-ranking minister would immediately alienate and alert Berlin to his intentions.[10] At the same time the French also held back, alternately suspecting that he could not withstand the opposition of his father's ministers and that his Francophilia was inspired only by a desire "to seek a prompt and pecuniary advantage in all his dealings." In the end it was the French who rejected the Hessian proposal for a subsidy treaty.[11]

[4]PRO, SP 87/45: 14 Sept., 26 Oct. 1762 Clavering report.
[5]StAMg, 4e)2522: Frederick to Brunswick, 11 Jan. 1763.
[6]HHStA, RK, Kleinere Reichsstände 163: [1766] Moser report, "Extract Schreibens ... 18 October 1766."
[7]Christian von Dohm, *Denkwürdigkeiten meiner Zeit*, 3 (Hanover, 1817), 94.
[8]StAMg, 4f) Frankreich 1680: 17 Dec. 1765 Moser report.
[9]StAMg, 4h)3020: 6-7 Oct. 1766 Althaus, Canngiesser, and Waitz votae, Frederick to Althaus, 22 June 1767; AAE, CP, HC 12: 30 Apr. 1763 Contades report, HC 14: 10 May 1776 Grais report; HHStA, RK, Kleinere Reichsstände 163: 23, 30 Sept. 1766 Moser reports.
[10]AAE, CP, HC 13: 15 Oct. 1773 Verac report, D'Aiguillon to Verac, 18 Nov. 1773.
[11]AAE, CP, HC 12: 22 Sept. 1766 Aigremont instructions, HC 13: Aigremont to Verac, 20 May 1772, 15 May 1773 Verac report, D'Auguillon to Verac, 18 Nov. 1773.

The same combination of ministerial opposition and fear of Prussian reprisals also destroyed what chance there was of an Austrian alliance. In fact, when Moser arrived in Vienna in 1766 to tender the landgrave's offer of an alliance before Prussia could find out, he warned his hosts that "because the landgrave is surrounded by Prussophiles and fears this king more than anything else in the world, I can only conclude that, even if I remain quiet from this day onward, Berlin will not forget or rest until I have been driven from [Hessian] service."[12] Though they never doubted the sincerity of Frederick's hopes for a Hessian-style diplomatic revolution, the Austrians understood until the end of the reign that he would never take such a risk and that, should Frederick the Great "beckon him to camp, he would show up immediately."[13]

Frederick's failure to attain some measure of independence from Prussia became even more evident at the beginning of 1772 following the death of his estranged wife Mary. Since he was now free to remarry, the landgrave immediately let it be known that he hoped to wed a Catholic princess, preferably an Austrian archduchess.[14] Instead, widespread public sentiment and pressure from Berlin compelled him to choose a Calvinist cousin of Frederick the Great, Princess Philippine of Brandenburg-Schwedt, and to submit to a marriage contract that committed him to raise all of their children Protestant. The Schwedt marriage proved to be a fiasco for the luckless landgrave as his new bride made little attempt to win his affections, neglected court functions, and spent most of her time with other members of Cassel's considerable Prussian contingent drawing unflattering comparisons with Berlin. The couple remained childless and soon began living apart, a fate that symbolized the sterility of Frederick's Prussian misalliance.[15]

Indeed Frederick's sacrifices won him little leverage within the Protestant alliance in securing his main dynastic goals, if only because its members were currently at peace and not in need of immediate military assistance. It continued to frustrate his attempts to secure the reversion of Hanau, which now passed on to his eldest son, William.[16] It also failed

[12]HHStA, RK, Kleinere Reichsstände 163: 23 Sept. 1766 Moser report.
[13]HHStA, RK, Berichte aus dem Reich 81: 9 Feb. 1765 Pergen report, 106: 1 Nov. 1771 Neipperg report, 134: 7 Nov. 1785 Trauttmansdorff report; AAE, CP, HC 12: 3 June 1766 Hennenberg mémoire.
[14]AAE, CP, HC 13: 20 May 1772 Aigremont report, "Mémoires et observations ... " [Jan. 1773]; HHStA, RK, Kleinere Reichsstände 163: Emmerich Joseph to Colloredo, 12 July 1772.
[15]AAE, CP, HC 13: 9 Mar. 1772 Aigremont, 30 July, 7 Aug. 1773 Verac, 14: 10 Aug. 1776 Grais reports; Vehse, *Deutschen Höfe*, 185–6.
[16]For much of the past decade Frederick had tried to regain Hanau by promising his

to support Frederick's efforts to obtain the electoral dignity, a traditional Hessian goal that had been reawakened by the imminent extinction of the Bavarian Wittelsbachs.[17]

Frederick's impotence surfaced most dramatically following his attempt to succeed to the Polish throne. The British and Prussians had ridiculed his hopes of someday being elected its king during the opening years of his reign.[18] Yet a Polish confederation actually offered him the crown in 1770, telling him that his well-trained army, full treasury, and enlightened reputation made him ideally suited for the throne.[19] This flattery notwithstanding, Frederick was realistic enough to hinge his acceptance on the support of the great powers. When this support failed to materialize, Schlieffen and the other ministers had no difficulty dissuading him from a foreign venture that at best would have resulted in his permanent absence from the country.[20] When the first Polish partition was consummated a few months later, Frederick gave up all hope of election, commenting prophetically to the French envoy that there was "no guarantee that the king of Prussia would not do the same thing to Hesse someday, and that this example should make all of the princes of the empire tremble."[21]

Frederick's quest for the Polish throne reminds us that the smaller lay princes were no different from their more powerful relations, except in their inability to realize their dynastic objectives independently. It also demonstrates that the country's precocious financial and military strength was still insufficient to make it a significant force within the empire. If

estranged family the continued use of the county's income and residence. The support of the emperor and Louis XV was, however, insufficient to convince the Protestant powers to acquiesce. For the reactions of the great powers, see HHStA, RK, Berichte aus dem Reich 81, 84, 106, Kleinere Reichsstände 162–3; AAE, CP, HC 12: Louis XV to Frederick, 24 Apr. 1762, 19 Apr. 1766 Hennenberg report; PRO, SP 81/165: Butte to Clavering, 7 Aug. 1761.
[17]Hans Philippi, "Zur diplomatischen Vorgeschichte der Erhebung des Landgrafen von Hessen-Kassel zum Kurfürsten," *ZHG*, 84 (1974), 11–13.
[18]PRO, SP 87/45: 30 May 1763 Clavering report; HHStA, Berichte aus dem Reich 81: 9 Feb. 1765 Pergen report.
[19]Otto Forst-Battaglia, *Eine unbekannte Kandidatur auf dem polnischen Thron. Landgraf Friedrich II. von Hessen-Kassel und die Konföderation von Bar* (Bonn, 1922), 33.
[20]Asseburg, *Denkwürdigkeiten*, 382; Forst-Battaglia, *Polnischen Thron*, 35, 43; Walter Wagner, *Hessen-Kassel und der Fürstenbund vom Jahr 1785* (Darmstadt, 1932), 27. In the end only Louis XV lent his support, whereas Catherine II delivered a stern warning against Hessian intervention. AAE, CP, HC 13: 20 May 1772 Aigremont, 3 July 1773 Verac reports., Verac Instructions, 13 July 1773.
[21]AAE, CP, HC 13: 30 July 1773 Verac report.

the large Hessian military was of tangible value to the landgrave, it was as an instrument not of diplomacy but of economic and fiscal policy.

The army had, in fact, demonstrated its utility long before Frederick's succession. Although Landgrave Charles had originally maintained sizable forces solely for security, his decision to lend troops to such traditional allies as Great Britain, the Netherlands, and Sweden brought immediate and largely unexpected benefits. The eighteen subsidy treaties he concluded provided alternative employment for younger sons, thereby easing the burden of poverty in the countryside and putting an end to the constant exodus of young people to other parts of Germany while also attracting foreign exchange that could be used for industrial investment.[22] As we have already seen they also became a primary source of state revenue that could be generated and deployed without the need to consult the estates. Although exact figures are unavailable, the thirty conventions concluded between 1702 and 1763 may have earned over 25 million taler, enough to meet half of the government's needs over that period. No wonder that William VIII, who concluded eleven treaties of his own, exclaimed in 1745 that "these troops are our Peru. In losing them we would forfeit all our resources."[23]

The flow of foreign subsidies not only relieved the landgrave of the need to pressure the estates, it also helped reduce the burden of taxes for his subjects. A combination of increasing population and foreign subsidies actually reduced financial obligations payable to the state from about 3 taler per capita early in Frederick's reign to a low of 2.2 taler in 1784. These figures compare favorably with the level of taxation in other German states, such as Prussia (4.1), Bavaria (3.8), Baden (4.2), Cologne (5.3), and Zweibrücken (6.2). The income from subsidies also permitted the government to limit military spending to about 60 percent of its budget, roughly the same as in Prussia, even though its army was proportionally larger.[24] Although the generally poorer Hessian taxpayer

[22]Both and Vogel, *Wilhelm VIII.*, 65, Möker, *Geschichtliche Wirtschaft*, 222; Hans Philippi, *Landgraf Karl von Hessen-Kassel 1654–1730* (Marburg, 1980), 6, 8, 11–12.

[23]Philippi, *Landgraf Karl von Hessen-Kassel. Ein deutscher Fürst der Barockzeit.* (Marburg, 1976), 484, 536, 660–4; Both and Vogel, *Wilhelm VIII.*, 11, 108, 215; Möker, *Geschichtliche Wirtschaft*, 217.

[24]Population and taxation statistics taken from W. O. Henderson, *Studies in the Economic Policy of Frederick the Great* (London, 1963), 66–8; Eberhard Weis, *Montgelas 1759–1799. Zwischen Reform und Revolution* (Munich, 1971), 164-7; Hans Speier, "Militarism in the Eighteenth Century," *Social Research*, 3 (1936), 320; D. Stutzer, "Das preussische Heer und seine Finanzierung in zeitgenössischer Darstellung 1740–1790," *Militärgeschichtliche Mitteilungen*, 24 (1978), 39.

needed this advantage and doubtless felt he was already being taxed to the limit, it is not difficult to envision how the lower rates helped preserve his tenuous position on the land and thereby ensure domestic tranquillity.

Of course Hesse-Cassel had to pay a price for these benefits. Above all there was the human cost in lives lost campaigning abroad in nearly half of the years between 1702 and 1763. It is also worth noting that much of the money never materialized. Sweden co-opted nearly 5 million taler during Landgrave Frederick I's reign as king. In addition, most of Hesse-Cassel's clients failed to pay all of their obligations until their need for Hessian troops to fight in a subsequent war forced them to do so. Thus, as late as 1764 Moser was in The Hague trying to get the Dutch to repay part of 325,000 taler owed from the War of the Spanish Succession.[25] Such was the nature of Hessian diplomacy that it enjoyed diplomatic leverage only in time of war.

The soldier trade also involved substantial risks for the country. No better lesson was provided than by the subsidy treaty William VIII concluded with Great Britain in June 1755. At the time the landgrave hoped it would cement the British guarantee of the *Assekurationsakte*. Given Britain's complete disinterest in a conflict with Prussia and the financial leverage it enjoyed with its Austrian ally, he assumed with considerable justification that there was little likelihood of a war erupting inside Germany; if it broke out at all, it would pit Austria and Great Britain against France and would likely be fought on the Rhine or in France proper. The Anglo-Prussian Westminster Convention that was concluded seven months later and the Diplomatic Revolution that followed it may have been a shock for most of the European world, but for Hesse-Cassel it was a catastrophe. The Seven Years' War became the first conflict fought on its soil in over a century, all the result of a miscalculation that was subsequently compounded by Great Britain's refusal to indemnify the country for more than 1 million of the 20 million taler in war damages that it suffered.

The Seven Years' War might have made the government more cautious and compelled Frederick to reexamine the Protestant alliance, but it inclined no one to reassess the role of the military or mercenary trade in Hesse-Cassel. By the middle of the eighteenth century the *Soldatenhandel*

---

[25] StAMg, 4h)4220: 6 July instruction, 31 July, 3, 10 Aug. 1764 Moser reports; Both and Vogel, *Wilhelm VIII.*, 17.

had transformed policy in ways far more pervasive and permanent than the destruction of the war. The military establishment had become an indispensable factor in economic and fiscal planning. In a European world obsessed with the need to establish a favorable balance of trade, it constituted the Hessian regime's most successful instrument for developing existing natural resources by converting them from raw material to finished product and then exporting them for foreign exchange. Indeed the army benefited from a broad symbiosis that also served a regime concerned with fiscal integrity, as well as the various levels of Hessian society that derived their livelihood from it. Its acceptance was further cemented by the general respect and admiration the profession of arms had attained.

Nowhere was the marriage of cameralism and militarism more evident than in the landgrave himself. Foreign observers routinely attested to his dual obsession with financial and military matters. Moser himself linked the two, explaining to the emperor's ministers that "the landgrave's strongest passion is the military, which is rooted in his love of money and profit."[26] It would appear that his love for the military went beyond purely mercenary interests. His contemporaries marveled at his penchant for drilling his troops every day, not only on Sundays and holidays, but even during bad weather when he moved them into the palace dining hall. In his enthusiasm he personally added a number of "inventions, innovations, and maneuvers" to the Hessian drill protocols, much as he had frequently attended to the finer details of his domestic projects.[27] Once again, however, Frederick never hesitated to learn from the example of his neighbors. Through his agents abroad he closely followed other countries' military innovations just as readily as he had their economic and administrative reforms. Not surprisingly it was the Prussian system that he "literally and minutely imitated ... in every respect." Not unlike an earlier Prussian king he even established an "extraordinarily beautiful" detachment of guards who were at least five foot eleven inches tall and whom he paid twice the regular wage.[28]

[26]HHStA, RK, Kleinere Reichsstände 163: [Sept. 1766] Moser report; RK, Berichte aus dem Reich 81: 9 Feb. 1765 Pergen report; AAE, CP, HC 12: 3 June 1766 Hennenberg mémoire.

[27]PRO, SP 87/45: 19 May 1763 Clavering report; AAE, CP, HC 12: 3 June 1766 Hennenberg mémoire; HHStA, RK, Berichte aus dem Reich 106: 1 Nov. 1771 Neipperg report; John Moore, *A View of Society and Manners in France, Switzerland and Germany*, 2d ed., 2 vols. (Dublin, 1780), 1: 30.

[28]PRO, SP 87/45: 7 Feb., 19 May 1763 Clavering reports; AAE, CP, HC 13: "Observations

Frederick had no difficulty justifying the benefits of his dedication to the army, claiming in the *Pensées* that every prince should also be a soldier because it afforded him the opportunity to get closer to his subjects and to demonstrate his commitment to their welfare.[29] Although it is difficult to find anyone as devoted to the army as he, no one questioned the need for a strong military. With roughly a third of their own sons enrolled in the Hessian army, few bureaucrats would have disagreed with the official who explained that "the very nature of states requires that one of their primary concerns must be to preserve their internal and external security. Part of society must be charged with protecting the rest and it is this component that comprises the military."[30] After he had left Hessian service Knigge was moved to praise the landgrave's close association with the army. For his part Schlieffen would later assert that warfare was basic to the very nature of man and society. Even Mauvillon felt compelled to agree that the large military establishment represented a necessary evil without which the country "would be the poorest land under the sun."[31]

Society as a whole was no less accepting of the military establishment or the *Soldatenhandel*. Throughout the century the estates never protested the foreign deployment of Hessian soldiers, appreciative as they were of the personal and public benefits that accrued from it. Instead they routinely cooperated with the crown in coordinating the revenue it brought into the country with the levying of ordinary tax receipts. The austere physical and cultural environment was doubtless instrumental in their acceptance. As we have seen, the poverty and limited private opportunities open to Hessian nobles compelled them to seek government employment. For those lacking the requisite education, the army was the obvious, and usually the only, choice. As a result more than two-thirds of all Hessian nobles receiving government pay were in the Hessian army, fully 57 percent of all resident members of the *Ritterschaft*.

An army career also constituted a viable and respected career option for bourgeois youths. Though nobles still dominated the highest ranks, the officer corps was evenly split between noble and commoner by a

---

...Hesse Cassel" [1 June 1773]; HHStA, RK, Berichte aus dem Reich 134: 1, 27 Dec. 1785 Trauttmansdorff report.

[29]"Pensées," #6, 11.

[30]StAMg, 4h)4114: Huth pro memoria [1774].

[31]Knigge, *Roman meines Lebens*, 53–4; Martin Ernst von Schlieffen, *Von den Hessen in Amerika, ihrem Fürsten und den Schreyern* (Dessau, 1782), 5; Mauvillon, *Staatskunst*, 136.

system that drew officers from three sources: nobles, who started as pages; burghers, who began as corporals but became officers after a few years; and common soldiers, who rose through the ranks in unusually large numbers. In contrast to the postwar Prussian army, which was 90 percent noble-officered as late as 1806, commoners comprised between 45 and 63 percent of the officers in Frederick's army. Even in the cavalry, a third of all officers commissioned under Frederick were commoners, a figure far higher than under William VIII.[32] In addition, bourgeois officers enjoyed the same social status as did their noble counterparts, ranging from their equal place in the *Rangordnung* to the same seating at the opera and at the landgrave's own table.[33]

For the rural and urban poor the army was, of course, not just a case of career alternatives but often one of survival. It was for this reason that recruiting always went much better during the summer just before harvest as many people enlisted in order to escape starvation.[34] Once enrolled the common soldier received 1.5 taler per month, a sum comparable to that paid by other German armies but rather better than the wages paid to servants or the unskilled within Hesse-Cassel.[35] In addition, military families were exempted from certain obligations, including the payment of income taxes and performance of *Dienst*, while those soldiers who were Lutheran, or even Catholic, were afforded greater religious freedom than their civilian coreligionists.[36]

It would, however, be misleading to suggest that the Hessian poor, or even the social elite, entered the army for merely pecuniary reasons. There was a cultural factor as well. Centuries of struggle against widely feared and hated enemies such as the Catholics and the French had integrated into the Hessian consciousness a general sense of obligation among all social groups that it was everyone's duty to defend the country. Given

---

[32]StAMg, 4h)3429: "Anciennitätsliste der Kavallerieoffiziere" [1776]; Böhme, *Wehrverfassung*, 24. Overall army estimates vary from 44.9 percent (1780) to 56.5 percent (1764) calculated by Pedlow, "Nobility of Hesse-Kassel," 238, to 63 percent (1779) given by Atwood, *The Hessians*, 46.

[33]Pedlow, "Nobility of Hesse-Kassel," 235; Günderode, *Briefe eines Reisenden*, 193; Moore, *Society and Manners*, 25.

[34]Kipping, *Truppen von Hessen-Kassel*, 42.

[35]Redlich, *The German Military Enterpriser and his Work Force*, 2 vols. [*Vierteljahrschrift für Sozial- und Wirtschaftsgeschichte*, 48 (1965)], 2: 239, 242; Inge Auerbach, "Marburger im amerikanischen Unabhängigkeitskrieg," *ZHG*, 87 (1978–9), 322; Schmidt, *Melsungen*, 87. The monthly wage was normally sufficient to purchase a cow (1.3 taler) or two pigs; 2.5 taler could buy an oxen. Losch, *Kasseler Chroniken*, 140.

[36]HLO, 348: 6 Feb. 1766 protocol; StAMg, 5)14721: 13 Mar. 1772 resolution; Heppe, *Kirchengeschichte beider Hessen*, 340.

the hard and generally mean civilian life most people eked out from the soil or in the towns, the austerity and discipline associated with military service required little psychological adjustment from a new recruit. Moreover, the high esteem in which military life and glory were held and the popular mythology that was passed on from father to son guaranteed a certain enthusiasm for army life.[37] The synthesis went beyond a mere garrison state such as Prussia to what one traveler described as "the most militarized society in all Germany," a nation of soldier-subjects that prompted the awestruck Johannes von Müller to exclaim "before I came to Hesse I hardly knew what a military nation was."[38]

In raw numbers Hesse-Cassel clearly was the most heavily militarized state in Europe. With a 12,000-man field army plus another 12,000 militia serving in garrisons, it claimed a truly remarkable soldier to civilian ratio of 1:15, twice Prussia's 1:30. Indeed, the gap between each society's commitment to its military is even greater than that, since Prussia relied heavily on foreign recruits to fill out its ranks, while the Hessian army consisted overwhelmingly of native sons. In comparing the two, Bopp estimated that only one Prussian household in fourteen was represented in the army, compared to one out of every four in Hesse-Cassel.[39]

Yet the differences between Prussia and Hesse-Cassel go beyond the extent of the citizenry's commitment to the military. In his celebrated work on the subject, Otto Büsch has asserted that Prussian state and society were molded to conform with the army's needs.[40] In Hesse-Cassel the military assumed its high profile by virtue of a merger of cameralist and militarist impulses that largely determined the army's role in terms of the country's economic and fiscal needs. Thus, while the Prussian army portrayed by Büsch absorbed excess rural labor to project military might and prosecute Hohenzollern foreign policy, the Hessian military converted its excess population into an instrument of domestic policy.

The Frederician regime's greater commitment to economic and fiscal objectives surfaces in a recruiting system that stressed the enlistment of only those males not needed by the domestic economy. The Canton *Règlement* the landgrave issued in 1762 was designed to curtail the abuses of recruiting officers, whose determination to meet their quotas had often

[37]Günderode, *Briefe eines Reisenden*, 151–2; Atwood, *The Hessians*, 19–20.
[38]Baron de Riesbeck, *Voyage en Allemagne*, 3 (Paris, 1788), 150; Preser, "Über die angeblich nach Amerika verkauften Hessen," *Hessenland*, 2 (1888), 69–70n.
[39]Inge Auerbach, Niklot Klüssendorf, and Fritz Wolff, *Hessen und die amerikanische Revolution* (Marburg, 1976), 6.
[40]Büsch, *Militärsystem und Sozialleben im alten Preussen 1713–1807* (Berlin, 1962).

led them to violate the government's long-standing requirement that they enlist only men aged sixteen to thirty who volunteered and were also economically expendable.[41] Although fewer exemptions were granted from garrison duty, which placed only minimal demands on a militia-man's time, the great majority of Hessian males were not merely excused but explicitly excluded from service in the regular army. Among them were all self-sufficient farmers (those who owned at least thirty *Acker*) and individuals whose net worth exceeded 250 taler, factory workers, artisans, clergymen, civil servants, students, and the servants of the no-bility. In addition any men who were either married or had young children were exempt as long as they had not wed in order to avoid service. Given the high priority the government initially attached to trade and commerce, it also excluded several of the larger towns from the twenty cantons it had established in 1762.[42] Its determination to reverse declining economic productivity right after the war and following the 1771 crop failure also inspired Frederick to spare as many native youths as possible by seeking recruits from neighboring states, and even by impressing unsuspecting foreign vagabonds found on Hessian soil.[43]

Nor did the government overlook the productive potential of those men it did recruit for military service. Since both field and garrison regiments were usually stationed in their home cantons, they were gen-erally able to perform ancillary economic activities for their families, such as sowing and harvesting. For purposes such as these, militia units or-dinarily served only three weeks in the spring (after planting had been completed) and about one-third of all regulars were also furloughed at any given time. The Canton *Règlement* also allowed for the immediate release of soldiers who acquired a farm or business by inheritance or marriage, as well as those who were suddenly needed at home due to the death or infirmity of other working family members. In practice the processing of such discharges was often delayed by recalcitrant com-manding officers or by the need to determine whether a soldier's petition was valid. Beginning in 1773 the *Landräte* facilitated this process by compiling a detailed account of the number and physical fitness of family males, and the size, value, and annual tax liability of the land or business to be worked. Not surprisingly, the government's main concerns were that the soldier's family be spared a loss in productivity that would

[41] Inge Auerbach, Eckhardt G. Franz, and Otto Fröhlich, eds., *Hessische Truppen in Amerika* (*HETRINA*), 4 vols. (Marburg, 1974–6), 3: 29–39.
[42] *HETRINA*, 2: 19; HLO, 740, 1170: 19 Nov. 1773, 23 Sept. 1784.
[43] StAMg, 4h)4048: Frederick to Frankfurt, 21 May 1764, to Mühlhausen, 9 Jan. 1772.

undermine its current living standards and the discharge of its tax and other financial obligations. Once a petition's validity had been established, discharge was automatic.[44]

Of course the interests of the military also assumed a high priority by virtue of its undisputed position as the country's primary export industry. Though it had been originally created as a means of defending the country, the mercenary army had become an end in itself by virtue of its importance to the economy and state finances. The public welfare, which had always been associated with successful economic and fiscal policies, now became tied to the well-being of the military establishment. Government initiatives were closely scrutinized to ensure that they did not have a negative effect on army recruitment. Thus, when he permitted his Schaumburg serfs to purchase their freedom, Frederick limited their eligibility to those who were already exempt from military service. Following the promulgation of the *Hufen-Edikt* the government instructed the *Landräte* to study whether it "has been beneficial or harmful for the country and the military." The subsequent decision to retain it despite popular outcry was reinforced by the widespread expectation that it would increase enlistments among younger sons.[45] Nor was the general population ignorant of the regime's military bias. In successfully petitioning against a trade treaty with neighboring Eichsfeld the Cassel guilds warned the government that the accord would lead to resettlement there, thereby hurting future army enlistments.[46] Having initially employed the army to conserve its native population, the regime now strove to retain these same subjects in order to conserve the army.

The government's determination to organize the military assumed all the forms of societal regimentation that typified the cameralist practice of *Polizei*. The government guaranteed its mastery over its most precious resource by registering all males with the army at the age of seven. Once they had turned sixteen, youths were mustered for review at Eastertime in order to afford the local recruiting officer an opportunity "to get to know" the latest crop of eligible enlistees. Although recruiters were prohibited from forcibly impressing their new acquaintances there is no question that they employed a certain amount of coercion and peer pres-

[44]StAMg, 17e) Bortshausen 3, 4; Damm 3; Dreihausen 16, 18; Elnhausen 32; Fronhausen 48; Gisselberg 7; Heskem 15; Leidenhofen 24; 4h)4088, 4218; 5)5648.
[45]StAMg, 5)3907: KDK reports 1770–86, 5)14743: 29 Jan. 1779 resolution; AAE, CP, HC 14: 21 Nov. 1775 Grais report.
[46]StAMg, 5)6062: 3 Jan. 1770 petition.

sure. Even the Canton *Règlement*, while explicitly reassuring prospective recruits that they could not be forced to enlist, also reminded them in its penultimate paragraph that it was their duty to serve their country if they were truly available.

Prospective soldiers were also subject to other restraints. Not unlike other raw materials they were prohibited from leaving the country to serve in a foreign army. Those who did so were invariably punished upon their return home. Those who remained abroad could rest assured that their parents would be compelled to pay the cost of recruiting a replacement. Meanwhile, the harshest punishment was reserved for those native Hessian *Zubringer* who assisted foreign recruiters, for whom life imprisonment and even corporal punishment were still a possibility.[47] Nor did the regulations placed upon youths necessarily end with their enlistment in the Hessian army. To minimize the chance of an early discharge, unmarried soldiers were forbidden to marry without their commander's approval, a constraint that had the practical effect of encouraging secret marriages and a higher incidence of illegitimate births in garrison towns.[48]

The American enterprise

In maintaining its military apparatus in such a high state of readiness the Hessian government was operating under the assumption that it was just a question of time before it would again market its troops with a friendly power. Frederick's unquestioning acceptance of the system was qualified only by his desire to move cautiously, lest an ill-advised treaty repeat the catastrophe of the Seven Years' War. Although he had begun reducing the army as early as 1762 by furloughing the militia and releasing most of his cavalry horses for plowing, Frederick had remained confident that another conflict would afford new opportunities to employ his forces. Yet, despite these expectations and numerous exploratory talks with the French, Dutch, and British, he was unable to sign any troop subsidy treaties during the first half of the reign.[49]

[47]StAMg, 4h)4218: 1 Apr. 1774 resolution; 4h)3700: 1 May 1781 Wille report, 7 Dec. 1784 GR protocol.
[48]Paul Taylor and Hermann Rebel, "Hessian Peasant Women, Their Families and the Draft: A Social-Historical Interpretation of Four Tales from the Grimm Collection," *Journal of Family History* 6 (1981), 370–1.
[49]StAMg, 4h)4452: Frederick to Bose, 22 Dec. 1762, 4h)3020: 29 Aug. 1767 protocol, 4f)Niederlande 762: Frederick to Oeynhausen, 7 Mar. 1768; AAE, CP, HC 12: 27 May 1766 Hennenberg report; HHStA, RK, Kleinere Reichsstände, 163: "Extract Schreibens ... 18 Oct. 1766."

Great Britain's troubles in the New World finally presented Frederick with what appeared to be a truly golden opportunity. Clearly the timing could not have been better for Hesse-Cassel. A troop convention would offer immediate relief for the dual burdens of rural overpopulation and poverty that had been aggravated by the recent crop failures. It also promised to replenish a *Kriegskasse* that had been depleted by previous deficits and the landgrave's extensive efforts at reform and remedial poor relief. A treaty with Great Britain also offered him the prospect of cementing a previously strained relationship with a traditional ally, without incurring any military danger to the country itself.

Historians have always assumed that the Anglo-Hessian negotiations started sometime in 1775, after the outbreak of hostilities in America. Yet the reports of the French envoy Grais make it clear that secret preliminary discussions began at Hofgeismar during the winter of 1774–5, several months before the first shots were fired at Lexington and Concord. Very little progress was made at the time, both because the British were unwilling to pay the landgrave's price and because Frederick insisted on first consulting with the representatives of the estates before concluding an agreement. Nevertheless, all the major problems were ironed out in the weeks following the action at Bunker Hill. By August the ministry was already confidently predicting the dispatch of about 12,000 troops to America.[50]

Having been humiliated by his allies during peacetime, Frederick was finally in a position to command the respect he had always craved. In his despatches to London the British negotiator William Faucitt reversed years of cynical criticism with compliments of the landgrave's "generosity" and Schlieffen's "great good will." He even resisted the temptation to ridicule either man for wanting to head the Hessian expeditionary force.[51] Indeed, for once the landgrave held all the cards. Unlike the other German princes he was not deep in debt and desperate for British subsidies. Furthermore, having held a 12,000-man regular army in readiness for over a decade, he was now the only ruler who could immediately commit strong forces to crush the Americans before they could organize.[52]

---

[50] AAE, CP, HC 14: 23 June, 7, 19 July, 25 Aug., 6 Sept. 1775 Grais reports.
[51] PRO, SP 81/181: 12, 20 Dec. 1775, 182: 14 Jan., 25 Feb. 1776 Faucitt reports; AAE, CP, HC 14: 25 Oct. 1775 Grais report; Schlieffen, *Einige Betreffnisse und Erlebungen*, 2 vols. (Berlin, 1830–40), 1: 186.
[52] Atwood, *The Hessians*, 26–7; Kapp, *Soldatenhandel*, 55–9.

The treaty Frederick concluded on January 31, 1776, met his most sanguine expectations.[53] Although it did not include the infamous "blood money" clause that was granted the rulers of Hanau, Brunswick, and Waldeck for men wounded and killed, it was easily the most lucrative of all the troop conventions. Since they expected that the quick dispatch of the Hessian forces would end the revolt in one or two campaigns, the British undertook to pay the landgrave twice the rate per soldier agreed on by the other auxiliaries until at least one full year beyond the end of hostilities. They also backdated the treaty by two weeks in order to give the Hessian government a large infusion of cash with which to quicken its recruitment efforts. They even agreed to indemnify Hesse-Cassel with an additional 2.2 million taler for the destruction suffered during the last war. Beyond these considerable financial rewards, the British promised not to break up the Hessian forces or commit them outside North America, a pledge that protected them against the "unhealthy air" of the West Indies or Gibraltar and the possibility of a confrontation with other European powers. As added insurance against another foreign invasion the British also pledged to come to Hesse-Cassel's assistance should it be attacked.

In many respects the country also appeared to be well served by the treaty. Given the *Kriegskasse*'s newfound riches, Frederick anticipated an immediate reduction in the annual tax contribution, a prospect that ensured a positive reception for the treaty in the *Landtag*.[54] The country's steel and textile industries as well as the Carlshafen Company were favored by a major British concession that paid the Hessian government for maintaining the army even after it arrived in America, thereby permitting Frederick to purchase all its provisions and weaponry from Hessian, rather than British, suppliers. As British auxiliaries all Hessian soldiers were to receive the much higher wages paid by His Majesty's service. The British pay scale benefited officers most, especially the 360 noncommissioned officers (58 percent of whom were commoners) who were now promoted from the ranks for service in the expanded army. Nevertheless, the five-taler monthly wage paid to common infantrymen

---

[53]For the text, see Preser, *Soldatenhandel*, 50ff.
[54]Friedrich Münscher is probably right when he states that the initial popular reaction was positive as people anticipated the forthcoming campaign and tax cut, but he offers no documentation. See *Geschichte von Hessen*, 429.

was more than three times their normal wage, an attraction the government immediately emphasized in its recruiting posters.[55]

In sum the January 1776 treaty appeared far safer and better than the last Anglo-Hessian convention concluded twenty years before. It afforded the government considerably more money, much less risk of involvement in a European war, and very little danger of heavy battle casualties. Indeed, Frederick and his ministers appear to have concurred with the British that it was likely to be a short, successful campaign against ill-trained settlers, consisting mainly of skirmishes and two or three years of garrison duty.[56] Once again, however, Frederick's most sanguine expectations were destined to go unfulfilled. Although it was hardly a fiasco on the scale of the 1755 convention, the new Anglo-Hessian treaty soon produced unwelcome and largely unexpected repercussions on a scale comparable to his most ill-fated reforms. As early as March news of the fall of Montreal and Boston filled him with consternation that the Americans might not be the pushovers everyone had expected.[57] More distressing still were developments at home, especially the treaty's effects on the Hessian peasantry and rural economy, as well as on Frederick's own image within the European community.

Frederick's greatest shock doubtless came from the immediate outcry against the *Soldatenhandel*. Nothing in the recent past had suggested so negative a reaction. The letting of auxiliary forces not only had been common practice but had met with the approval of Germany's foremost philosophers and legal scholars. Christian Wolff had, in fact, argued that it was compatible with natural law, while Johann Jacob Moser had approved such pacts so long as they had the consent of the estates. As late as 1773, Friedrich Karl von Moser had judged them permissible, although he does not appear to have advertised his own involvement as a Hessian negotiator.[58] Nonetheless, the Anglo-German troop conventions touched a sensitive nerve among the European intelligentsia. Although Enlightenment thinkers had tolerated warfare as a necessity for

[55]W. Grotefend, "Hessischen Offizierkorps," 3–4; Pedlow, "Nobility of Hesse-Kassel," 233–4; Auerbach, "Amerikanischen Unabhängigkeitskrieg," 322.
[56]AAE, CP, HC 14: 2 Feb., 30 Apr. 1776 Grais reports.
[57]AAE, CP, HC 14: 13 Mar. 1776 Grais report.
[58]Preser, *Soldatenhandel*, 57; Atwood, *The Hessians*, 23, 30–1.

national defense, the involvement in America appeared well beyond the immediate concern of the German princes and their people. Perhaps most important, they saw America as nature's nation, a paradigm for all that they wished to create in a seriously flawed European society. To introduce European armies there was to impose the worst upon the best of all possible worlds.

Although the reaction inside Germany was far from universally critical, Schiller, Herder, Klopstock, and Kant all joined the large number of foreign thinkers who condemned the greed of the German princes. Eventually even Moser felt compelled to join in the public attack on the *Menschenhandel*, even while his father was condemning Great Britain's "disloyal" and "hypocritical" American subjects.[59] The landgrave was probably most distressed by the self-serving personal attacks of Frederick the Great, who used the occasion to posture before the philosophes at his expense, writing Voltaire that the landgrave had "sold his subjects to the English as one sells cattle to be dragged to the slaughter" and publicly announcing that Hessian troops would not be allowed through Prussian territory, later that they would be afforded passage but would be taxed as so many head of cattle. Once again Frederick had been humiliated by the ruler he admired most, by a man who only recently had told him that he himself detested the rebels and would gladly contribute volunteers to their suppression.[60]

Having negotiated only one subsidy treaty, the most favorable of thirty such conventions signed by a Hessian landgrave, Frederick expressed his frustration with the "inundation" of criticism levied against him. He was especially mortified by the damage the attacks inflicted on his carefully nurtured reputation as an enlightened ruler. Within a short while he decided to fight back. Before the end of the year he had commissioned the publication of an expanded version of his *Pensées sur les princes et les ministres* through a Swiss publisher. Its opening words betray the transparency of Frederick's motives, with the intonation that "these are not the thoughts of a typical philosopher; they belong to an enlightened ruler who employs them as a guide for a wise and benevolent government." Indeed, much of the revised text now touched on the numerous reforms he had initiated during his first fifteen years as landgrave. In an apparent attempt to deflect the obvious rejoinder that the book was self-

[59]Horst Dippel, *Germany and the American Revolution 1770–1800* (Chapel Hill, N.C., 1977), 124–9; Atwood, *The Hessians*, 228; Preser, *Soldatenhandel*, 57.
[60]AAE, CP, HC 14: 5 Feb. 1776 Grais report.

serving, Frederick published it anonymously, trusting that its author would be easily identified. Instead, at least one reviewer attributed it to the king of Prussia.

Frederick got a second chance one year later when Mirabeau's *Avis aux Hessois* appeared, with its appeal to Hesse-Cassel's "oppressed slaves" to join the Americans in their struggle "against the arrogant greed of their oppressors."[61] On this occasion he bought up all the available copies, then commissioned Schlieffen to pen a suitable rebuttal. In his *Von den Hessen in Amerika* Schlieffen presented a series of persuasive arguments that reflected his own brilliance as much as they did the regime's positive image of itself.[62] The damage, however, had been done.

Much of the outcry directed against the Hessian monarch focused on the unwillingness of many of his soldiers to fight in the war. Contemporary accounts make it clear that significant though indeterminate numbers of Hessians did desert or emigrate to avoid recruitment.[63] For Frederick, who does not appear to have anticipated this problem, it constituted yet another unwelcome surprise and public embarrassment. But the reasons for desertion are complex and do not support the simple explanation that the Hessian peasant did not want to fight in an unpopular war. The great majority of soldiers who were sent to America were army regulars by choice and generally were willing to go. In fact, some of those who deserted in late 1775, prior to the conclusion of the Anglo-Hessian convention, actually appear to have done so not to avoid the war but only to take advantage of attractive Hanoverian recruitment incentives.[64] Most of the remaining deserters were not so much opposed to fighting a foreign war as they were afraid of the Atlantic crossing, the exaggerated perils of the American wilderness, and the inevitable separation from their families.[65]

---

[61] Mirabeau, *Avis aux Hessois*, 15–16.
[62] The book defends Frederick by stressing his accomplishments and popularity within the country, as well as the treaty's success in halving taxes and increasing the earning power of military families. It also argues that the use of mercenaries, like war itself, was a human, not Hessian, phenomenon that could be traced to antiquity. It justifies involvement in America by citing the country's need to nurture its close ties with Great Britain, and even the possibility of a Hessian succession to the British throne.
[63] AAE, CP, HC, 12 May 1776 Grais report; Kapp, review of "Friedrich II. von Hessen und die neuere Geschichtsschreibung," *HZ*, 42 (1879), 316.
[64] AAE, CP, HC 14: 21 Nov. 1775 Grais report.
[65] Kipping, *Hessian View of America*, 13, 20; King, *Echoes of the American Revolution*, 172.

Meanwhile, there is little question that the American conflict attracted a far greater number of volunteers than were lost to desertion. They included not only a large influx of native and foreign civilians but also deserters from other armies and Hessian militia wanting to transfer from garrison regiments to the expeditionary force. In some instances foreign officers actually resigned their commissions to accept lower-ranking positions in the Hessian service. Their motives varied. Some simply wanted to go to war. Others were attracted by the prospect of enlistment bonuses and higher pay. Yet, by far the greatest number hoped to start a new life in America. The government had realized from the beginning that many of its native and foreign recruits intended to settle in the New World, a prospect it did not discourage among foreigners, so long as they served their full term of duty beforehand.[66] It found much more disturbing the likelihood that the same held true for a considerable number of Hessian recruits. Once again, however, it had only itself to blame for yet another miscalculation. As late as November the government had been counting on the effects of the *Hufen-Edikt* to help with native enlistments, hoping that disinherited younger sons would choose a career in the army as an acceptable alternative to slow starvation in the countryside.[67] Its expectations did not go unfulfilled as large numbers of such youths now flocked to the colors. Yet to its horror many were seeking not a career in the army but merely a one-way ticket to resettlement and a better life in America.

For the moment the government could do little to forestall a massive Hessian resettlement in the New World, if only because it desperately needed all the recruits it could find to meet its commitment to the British. In promising to provide 12,000 men, the landgrave appears to have purposely overcommitted himself, both because he could not resist the awesome monetary temptation offered by the treaty terms and because he hoped to make good the difference by recruiting foreigners. Yet, in his desire to maximize state receipts, he now compounded his original error with a second misstep that intensified the desertion crisis. Having already negotiated and advertised British pay scales for its soldiers, he decided in January to reduce the five-taler monthly wage by half, with the intention of pocketing the rest. Although the government attempted

---

[66]StAMg, 4h)4069: I/II; Kipping, *Truppen von Hessen-Kassel*, 43. As early as August 1775 a large body of French army deserters had arrived in Cassel with their families seeking passage to America. AAE, CP, HC 14: 31 Aug. 1775 Grais report.
[67]AAE, CP, HC 14: 21 Nov. 1775 Grais report.

to compensate for the cut by promising ample pillage in America, its action appears to have dissuaded many prospective recruits from enlisting, while persuading others who had already signed up to desert. The British ultimately compelled Frederick to restore the full five-taler wage, but by then he had already lost the chance to enlist and retain a greater number of new recruits.[68]

If nothing else, this blunder now forced the government to dig even deeper into its existing reserves. In order to raise the full 12,000, the government had expected to send four garrison regiments to America. Since these militia units included a large number of men who were needed by their families or their local community, the government now attempted to pare from them those individuals whose wealth or skills would normally exempt them from the regular army.[69] Such men were generally excused from the expeditionary force. Yet the pressure on local commanders to fill their musters and on the regime to fulfill its treaty commitments prevented them from exempting other, poorer and less skilled soldiers who had originally joined the militia thinking it entailed only three weeks of local service but who now did not want to leave their families to accompany the regular army to America.

As had happened in the past, many soldiers petitioned the regime for discharge, arguing that they were indispensable to their families. An examination of these documents reveals, however, that soldiers who could not satisfy the minimum property or skill qualifications were less likely to secure their release than at any other time during the reign. In desperation some families actually hid their sons shortly before departure or encouraged them to desert. In one tragic case an elderly widower even cut off one of his son's fingers in order to secure his release. Instead, he and his son were jailed, and a few days later he committed suicide.[70] In the end many militiamen simply took their families with them to America. The fact remains, however, that many families that stayed behind did suffer hardships from the sudden removal of their loved ones.[71] Moreover, the emotional impact of the separation exacted its toll on the families of garrison and regular army soldiers alike. It was this anguish that was

---

[68]AAE, CP, HC 14: 26 Jan., 2 Feb. 1776 Grais report.
[69]Garrison commanders were, in fact, explicitly ordered not "to take all of the expendable, but only those who are totally destitute." StAMg, 4h)4066: 9 Jan. 1776 Gen Kriegs Dir protocol; Atwood, *The Hessians*, 44; Kapp review, *HZ*, 315.
[70]AAE, CP, HC 14: 15 Mar. 1776 Grais report.
[71]StAMg, 4h)3700: 23 Mar., 5 Apr. 1776 Schenk report; Atwood, *The Hessians*, 221–4; Kipping, *Hessian View of America*, 7.

most evident to Grais when he reported numerous teenage soldiers weeping as they marched off to war.[72]

Nor did the recruitment problem end with the departure of the expeditionary force. It soon became evident that the government had underestimated not only its ability to meet the original commitment of 12,000 men but also the number of replacements it would later have to send to America. Over the next seven years it was obliged to dispatch an average of a thousand troops each year, bringing the total number of Hessian forces to 19,000 men. In order to spare the country from additional hardship Frederick restricted the recruitment of reinforcements to non-Hessians, to the point of excluding native volunteers.[73] Large numbers of deserters from the armies of neighboring states helped make this arrangement work. In a touch of irony it was the hundreds of Prussian soldiers who enlisted who proved to be the only men whom the landgrave could not march through the dominions of Frederick the Great.[74] Yet foreign recruitment also became increasingly difficult, especially after the disaster at Trenton. As the war progressed Frederick was forced to write a steadily widening circle of twenty or more states seeking permission to recruit on their territory. Meanwhile the five taler in *Handgeld* paid at the beginning of 1776 had to be raised until it had been quadrupled by the spring of 1782.[75] Only in 1782 did the government's recruiting difficulties ease somewhat as the war's impending end attracted a large group of volunteers eager to settle in America.[76]

In their desperation to meet their quotas, recruiters consistently enlisted men who were physically unqualified to serve. As early as 1777 the government found numerous recruits who were over the recently expanded age limit of forty years, including one enlistee who was completely lame and another who was sixty-three and "completely bent over." To weed out the unfit it enlisted medical personnel to examine each recruit.[77] Yet the government itself was obliged to lower the qualifications for foreigners. By 1781 Frederick announced that "for the greater conser-

[72]AAE, CP, HC 14: 10 May 1776 Grais report.
[73]Kipping, *Truppen von Hessen-Kassel*, 29, 39, 44, 78; Atwood, *The Hessians*, 254; StAMg, 4h)4066: 18 Feb. 1777 GD protocol.
[74]Atwood, *The Hessians*, 211; Kapp review, *HZ*, 319; StAMg, 4h)3776, 4069.
[75]StAMg, 4h)4069 I: 5 Dec. 1776 Stockhausen report, 4079, 4295, 4066: 1 Apr. 1782 rescript.
[76]Erich Kaiser, "Nachschub für die hessischen Regimenter in Amerika. Das Rekrutendepot in der Festung Ziegenhain," *ZHG*, 86 (1976-7), 191.
[77]Kipping, *Truppen von Hessen-Kassel*, 42–3; StAMg, 4h)4069 II: 15 Apr. 1777 GD protocol.

vation of our loyal subjects and natives," recruiters could enlist men who were only four feet eleven inches tall, five inches less than the original minimum.[78]

～By all accounts many replacements were not only physically unfit but unsavory as well. In examining one group of foreign recruits one observer went so far as to assert that "it would be good if Germany could be purged of all such men."[79] Indeed, one reason Frederick was able to find so many replacements was because neighboring states were pleased to rid themselves of undesirable social elements through foreign recruiting. His fellow princes were less receptive, however, when his recruiters began employing coercion to meet their quotas. Frederick did require that all recruits be volunteers and routinely responded to diplomatic protests by releasing victims of impressment and punishing those recruiters who had disregarded his orders. Nevertheless, the numerous petitions of neighboring states suggest that, by 1779, desperate Hessian recruiters were regularly abducting foreign subjects traveling through Hesse-Cassel, as well as some living just across the frontier.[80]

These difficulties notwithstanding, the government was able to resolve the replacement problem principally by recruiting foreigners, whether by voluntary or other means.[81] Yet, while the great majority of the 7,000 reinforcements may have been foreigners, the government was ultimately forced to resume recruiting expendable native volunteers.[82] That local recruiters violated even these restrictions is evident from several successful discharge petitions. Many of these latest Hessian recruits were, however, unaware that they could refuse induction and never appealed for their release.[83]

In practice the government also permitted its recruiters to impress loafers, deadbeats, and other ne'er-do-wells so long as their families were amenable. For example, in Marburg the local recruiter regularly resolved

---

[78]StAMg, 4h)4066: 1 Dec. 1781 rescript.

[79]Günderode, *Briefe eines Reisenden*, 173; *Neue Reisebemerkungen*, 2: 131.

[80]StAMg, 4h)4295: [1781] pro memoria, 93)405: 15 Mar. 1779, 25 Feb. 1780 reports, [Feb. 1782] petition, 93)405: 8 Apr. 1779, 13 Mar. 1780 reports, 93)24: 20 Apr. 1781 report; 4f) Fulda 37: 6 Apr. 1779, 20 Mar. 1782 GD protocols.

[81]By 1781 Johannes von Müller would claim, with doubtless exaggeration, that there were no native Hessians among that year's replacements. King, *Echoes of the American Revolution*, 172.

[82]StAMg, 4h)4074: 5 Feb. 1779 circular letter, 17 Feb. 1779 report.

[83]StAMg, 4h)4066: 5 Apr. 1778 Klinkerfus report, 7 Aug. 1778 circular order; 4h)3700: 6 Aug. 1778 Stockhausen report, 25 Aug. 1778 resolution; 4h)4074: 14 Mar. 1779 report.

family problems by offering abusive husbands and disobedient youths service in America as an alternative to jail sentences. One baker's wife even operated a family counseling service that referred her clients to him.[84] Considerations of family welfare did not, however, extend to recruits who volunteered for service, only to disappear at the last minute. In these instances parents who were suspected of encouraging them to desert were arrested and put on bread and water until their sons reappeared.[85]

The dearth of recruits underscores a third problem that was potentially more damaging and permanent than either the embarrassing public outcry or the difficulty in finding troops willing to fight overseas. Furthermore, in this instance alone, the government correctly foresaw the consequences of its actions. As early as July 1775, and again in the days immediately prior to concluding the treaty, Frederick had expressed concern that the dispatch of so many troops overseas might severely depopulate the countryside. It was for this reason that he initially insisted on first consulting with the estates before committing himself to the treaty.[86] In making the final decision to go ahead with it the landgrave balanced – and accurately predicted – the likely positive and negative effects it would have on the country and concluded that the fiscal and economic benefits outweighed the negative consequences it would have in the countryside.

The American venture clearly benefited the state and country in several ways. In fiscal terms the American venture delivered everything Frederick had hoped for, and then some. Although he did not welcome the rebels' successes, the lengthening of the war added considerably to the government's receipts. More than 21 million taler poured into the *Kriegskasse*, leaving it with a net profit of 12.6 million taler. Moreover, on this occasion the British paid their subsidies promptly throughout the war, delivering all but £386,261 by mid–1785.[87] Frederick was able to annuitize the profits by investing them in British and Dutch stocks and by floating loans to foreign governments and princes. One such loan of 1

[84]Auerbach, "Amerikanischen Unabhängigkeitskrieg," 330; StAMg, 17e) Cyriaxweimar 9: 13 Oct. 1780 GD protocol, Langenstein 72: 30 Jan. 1781 Schenk report.
[85]StAMg, 4h)3700: 9, 17 Nov. 1780, 18 Jan., 4 Apr. 1781 reports, 23 Jan., 10 Apr. 1781 resolutions, 4h)4069 II: 13 Feb. 1777.
[86]AAE, CP, HC 14: 19 July 1775, 13 Jan. 1776 Grais reports.
[87]StAMg, 4h)3616: "Extract ... verbliebenen Rückstände" [n.d.]; Sauer, *Finanzgeschäfte*, 31–2.

million taler to nearly bankrupt Waldeck afforded Frederick control over so much of that state's revenue that he was virtually running the country by the end of the reign.[88] By then the annual interest on all of Frederick's investments totaled 260,000 taler, or roughly 30 percent of the country's ordinary tax revenue.

— Hesse-Cassel's commercial economy also benefited as expected. The army's ongoing need for weaponry and munitions returned Schmalkalden's iron industry to profitability after a frustrating decade-long search for new markets.[89] Since the entire army needed new uniforms virtually every year of the war, the country's textile industry was also able to increase production by about 20 percent. In addition, the eventual exclusion of Dutch traders from Britain's American possessions provided Hesse-Cassel with a second and ultimately permanent foothold in the West Indies. By 1782 one government official was estimating that textile exports had risen 250 percent since 1774 to 2 million taler a year.[90]

If the war benefited the iron and textile industries, it rescued the Carlshafen Company from oblivion. Since its establishment the company had been plagued by a variety of shortcomings, including undercapitalization and poor management. Yet the worst problem had been its inability to attract merchants to the upper Weser. Between 1771 and 1777 no fewer than three attempts to conclude a trade agreement with France had foundered on the "great number" of tolls that blocked the river passage between Carlshafen and Bremen.[91] Furthermore, those few foreign merchants who did send their goods up the Weser tended to pass Carlshafen and deliver them to Münden, where they could be sure to load a full cargo for the return voyage. Even Hessian merchants continued to do their business at Münden out of habit, despite the tariff savings Carlshafen offered.[92] With the war in America the company was given exclusive control over the provisioning of the expeditionary force with Hessian goods purchased and shipped by the British. It also provided the

[88]Hermann Bing, *Finanzgeschichte Waldeck-Pyrmonts von der Wende des 18. Jahrhunderts bis zum Jahre 1929* (Corbach, 1929), 36-7; Fritz Wolff, "Absolutismus und Aufklärung in Hessen-Kassel, 1730–1806," in Uwe Schulz, ed., *Die Geschichte Hessens* (Stuttgart, 1983), 142; StAMg, 118)2252: 19 Feb. 1785 extract.
[89]StAMg, 5)4015: [Aug. 1774] KDK report, 26 Aug. 1774 rescript; Brauns, *Kurhessische Gewerbepolitik*, 102.
[90]Dascher, *Textilgewerbe*, 141–2, 151–2, 154; Fox, "Upper Hesse," 29.
[91]StAMg, 4a)91,22: Malet to Frederick, 1 Nov. 1771; 5)6058: 13 Jan. 1774 petition, 14 July 1774 KDK report; 4f) Frankreich 1706: 14 Jan. 1777 mémoire; AAE, CP, HC 13: 5, 15 Feb., 9 Aug. 1774 Verac reports, D'Aiguillon to Verac 5, 10 Mar. 1774.
[92]StAMg, 5)7431: [1783] F. S. Waitz pro memoria.

company with a Trojan horse for smuggling a wide variety of commercial products into New York City at British expense.[93]

As might be expected these positive commercial developments had their greatest impact in the towns, which now interrupted their long-term demographic stagnation with population gains that averaged 4.2 percent during the period 1773–81. Not surprisingly the biggest advances were recorded by textile centers. Hersfeld jumped from 3,046 to 4,016, a 32 percent increase that reflected the wartime employment of as many as 2,000 textile *Hilfsarbeiter*. Meanwhile, Melsungen grew from 2,000 to 2,370 souls, a 19 percent increase that easily compensated for the departure of 107 of its men with the expeditionary force.[94] Even Marburg grew by 15 percent to 5,854. Meanwhile, in Cassel, the war's positive effects were reflected not only by a 10 percent population increase, but also by the stabilization of mortality rates and the sudden reversal in the upward spiral of its poor rolls after 1776.[95]

Of course, some of the war's benefits were felt statewide. Nothing benefited the population at large more than the 50 percent reduction in the Contribution that Frederick decreed in July 1776. By 1783 1.3 million taler in taxes had been remitted by a government that, until recently, had been most concerned by the need to raise taxes in order to fund poor relief. In a gesture typical of the new mood at the *Kriegskasse*, the estates were even invited to keep for their own purposes the overpayments that had been collected in the months before the reduction was declared.[96] As appreciable as this sum was, it was dwarfed by the 9.5 million taler in wages and bonuses paid out directly to soldiers and their families. Individual soldiers actually sent or brought home with them large amounts of money they had accumulated from wages, plunder, and labor performed for colonists at the high American labor rates. At the very least 591,000 taler were sent home through the *Kriegskasse* by 1779, an amount that dovetails with the overall popular estimate of 1 million taler

---

[93]StAMg, 5)13467: Lorentz to Kopp, 16 Feb., 9 July 1777; Dascher, "Karlshafen," 244–5. It is from this illegal intercourse that the Hessian porcelain industry established a popular, postwar market for its products, especially *Steingut*. Ducret, *Porzellanmanufaktur*, 183–5.

[94]"Seelenzahl und Häuser einiger hessischen Orten," *HB*, 2 (1785): 675–6; Heil, *Hersfeld*, 50–1; Schmidt, *Melsungen*, 87.

[95]"Tabelle ... in der Stadt Cassel" *HB*, 2 (1785), 679; Stein, "Waisenhaus in Kassel," 121; StAMg, 5)10597. My thanks to Gerald Soliday for furnishing me with the 1773 population statistics for Cassel and Marburg from StAMg, 49a) Generalia 120.

[96]*HLO*, 870–1: 30 July 1776; StAMg, 5)14796: 1779 Landtagsabschied; 13)Kriegszahlamtsrechnungen, 1776–84.

cited at the end of 1783 by the court architect Simon Louis du Ry.[97] Finally, there were the considerable sums that Frederick put into circulation through increased spending on domestic programs, court patronage, and building projects that he now financed with British subsidies. He himself put this amount at 1.5 million taler in a 1779 address to the estates, but it doubtless rose much higher by the end of the reign.[98]

All this could be interpreted as so much rationalization were it not for the regime's consistency in visualizing the military as a vehicle for employing and exporting its uniformed population. In his published defense of the landgrave, Schlieffen took great pains to justify his involvement in the American war in strictly economic terms. Repeating the standard bromide that a country's wealth was best served by increasing the number of people engaged in agriculture and commerce, he asked

But what becomes of a country where all available land is already cultivated with the result that increasing the number of workers cannot raise appreciably more grain or foodstuffs, and where local and other circumstances over which one has no control do not permit the expansion of industry beyond certain modest limits? What becomes of such an increasingly impoverished people? What can you do with people for whom there is no available work? Might they not be best employed elsewhere, where they can try to support themselves as best they can?[99]

Undeniable as Schlieffen's arguments were, the fact remains that the government overcompensated for the country's excess population by dispatching perhaps 12 percent of its able-bodied male adults overseas.[100] The landgrave's actions may have had minimal effect on the towns, several of which were exempt from the canton system, but they clearly denuded the countryside of too many workers. Although he had remained faithful to the Canton *Règlement* in ordering that new recruits be volunteers, Frederick had violated its spirit by dispatching garrison soldiers who had entered the army in the expectation that they would never be sent far from home. Moreover, while many regular and garrison soldiers sent to America were technically expendable because they were not economically self-sufficient, they were often still indispensable both to their

---

[97] Atwood, *The Hessians*, 249, 251.

[98] StAMg, 5)14739: 16 Apr. 1779 rescript; Kertsen Krüger, "Absolutismus und Stadtentwicklung: Kassel im 18. Jahrhundert," *HJLG*, 28 (1978), 210. Krüger estimates that Frederick reinvested 17.3 million taler, or 81 percent of the treaty proceeds, through civil and military spending.

[99] Schlieffen, *Von den Hessen*, 14–15.

[100] My calculation is based on an estimate of 13,000 native Hessians dispatched to America out of a total male population of about 165,000, less young children, the elderly, and disabled.

families and to the local economy by virtue of the work they performed as laborers. Frederick's calculated sacrifice in dispatching so many troops was further compounded by many youths who left the country to enlist in other German armies because they feared eventual impressment and shipment overseas. That many of these youths were actually exempt from service attests both to their ignorance of the laws and to the willingness of recruiters to violate them.[101] Nor can we ignore the simultaneous influence of the *Hufen-Edikt*, which prompted not only young men to leave the country but women as well.[102]

Indeed, the combined effect of the *Hufen-Edikt* and the greater representation of peasant youths in the army guaranteed that the sudden, government-imposed labor shortage hurt the rural population most. Farmers either were unable to secure adequate labor or were obliged to pay high wages to attract workers from neighboring states. Unfortunately, they could not offset these higher labor costs with higher grain prices due to the prevailing government price ceilings that had been put into effect to protect the urban poor.[103] Many families were able to defray these expenses with money sent by loved ones fighting in America. It appears, however, that some soldiers provided less than others, whereas others sent nothing at all. Hit hardest were those families that owned less than the thirty-*Acker* minimum necessary to secure exemption from military service. Though these families had plots that had always been too small to provide a decent living, they now also lost the labor of male family members who formerly had done the farming and provided supplementary income by working odd jobs. In these families the elderly, women, and children were now expected to assume the burden, with generally unsatisfactory results. In desperation some even petitioned the government to discharge those family members currently serving in America. Yet, even in special circumstances brought on by the death or illness of an adult male family member, the government generally rejected such petitions in view of "the greatest difficulties involved" in shipping soldiers home.[104] Nor were all instances of suffering limited to the countryside. In Marburg, for example, the dispatch of only one hundred of its native

[101]StAMg, 4h)3700: 3 Aug. 1778 Stockhausen report, 17e) Grüningen 28: 22 May 1779 GD protocol.
[102]Taylor and Rebel, "Peasant Women," 374.
[103]StAMg, 5)3542: 26 Jan. 1778 SK report, 5)13446: 15 Jan. 1784 Motz report.
[104]StAMg, 4h)4069 II: 23 Mar., 5 Apr. 1776, 13 Feb. 1777 reports, 5)14739: [1779] pro memoria, 4h)3700: 10 Apr. 1781, 26 Feb. 1782 resolutions, 20 Feb. 1782 Baumbach report.

sons to America forced eighty-two people onto the poor rolls, including thirty soldiers' wives who received insufficient support from their husbands and now had to be supported by the *Wochensteuer*.[105]

As they observed the painful repercussions a number of individuals ranging from *Kammerdirektor* Bopp to Louis XVI predicted that Hesse-Cassel would never gain as much from the war as it had already lost.[106] In its decision to enter the American Revolution the government had certainly sacrificed the agrarian economy and the poor, precisely those two problem areas that until recently had enjoyed the very highest priority. Devised earlier in the century to resolve the problems of overpopulation and the consequent emigration of Hessian youths, the *Soldatenhandel* had suddenly joined with the *Hufen-Edikt* in resurrecting the specter of emigration and replacing the surfeit of overpopulation with the demographic catastrophe of depopulation.

These problems and the need for corrective measures weighed heavily on the *Landtag* when it reconvened at the end of 1778. The deputies never questioned the wisdom of the American venture. They did, however, seek the immediate repeal of the *Hufen-Edikt*, which they now admitted had actually worsened living conditions by collapsing land prices and depopulating the countryside through emigration, army enlistment, and a dropoff in marriages. Yet the regime held firm, tying its defense of the edict to the parallel actions of other states and the need to save at least elder children from ruin. Indeed, though it admitted to the extensive depopulation of the countryside, it argued with considerable justification that demographic decline was inevitable, whether through poverty and starvation or preemptive government action.[107]

It did agree to the *Ritterschaft*'s request that those remaining rural laborers be exempted from service in America, though it had already effectively done this nearly two years earlier by instructing the *Landräte* that recruiters should pay close attention to the "most important cultivation of agriculture." To the dismay of local army commanders, the government also resumed its former practice of discharging soldiers who were needed to farm thirty-*Acker* plots, so long as they were not already

---

[105]For this and similar instances of popular suffering, see Auerbach, "Amerikanischen Unabhängigkeitskrieg," 323–4, 333–4; Atwood, *The Hessians*, 220–4.

[106]Bopp, "Fehler," 38; AAE, CP, HC 14: 1 Mar. Grais report, Louis XVI to Grais, 12 Mar. 1776; Riesbeck, *Voyage en Allemagne*, 150–1.

[107]StAMg, 5)14743: "Desideria ulteriora ... 5," 19 Mar. 1779 GR protocol.

in America.[108] It still insisted, however, that such discharges not be without tangible economic or fiscal benefit. Hence, when Allendorf's *Commissarius Loci* requested the release of a salt hauler who claimed he had been dragged from church into the army, the government first carefully weighed an itemized nine-year account of his hauling tonnage and the possibility that his absence would either decrease salt tax proceeds or increase the import of foreign salt before finally approving the petition.[109] By contrast one *Landrat* was unable to secure a discharge for a soldier who had taken a job teaching school and another who had been compelled to leave school to replace his older brother in the army when the latter was discharged to farm the family plot.[110] In another incident the *Landrat* himself actually ordered the seizure and reinduction of a soldier who had secured a discharge to farm his parents' land only to sell it following his release.[111]

Despite its newfound wealth, the government continued to employ conservative fiscal and mercantile practices and was even unwilling to extend public relief beyond the many remedial measures it had instituted over the past few years. In fact, its sudden riches now led to an immediate and precipitous dropoff in domestic initiatives. During the three years 1773–5, the regime had published an average of eighty-seven new ordinances, a pace higher than at any time during the reign. Over the next six years the average dropped by more than half, to fewer than forty-three. Moreover, only a tiny number of these actually had an economic purpose (five each in 1776, 1777, and 1778, nine in 1779, eight in 1780, and only four in 1781), and all were either of a trivial nature or were merely clarifications of existing laws. By contrast no fewer than thirty-three of the ordinances published in 1775 had dealt with economic problems. Because economic hardship not only continued but actually intensified during this period, these statistics dramatize exactly how important fiscal considerations were in the reforms of the previous quinquennial. Though purely humanitarian incentives had played a part in the many reforms of that period, fiscal motives such as alleviating the costs of

---

[108]StAMg, 4h)4069 II: 11 Apr. 1777 Biedenfeld, 5)14737: "Desiderium speciale der Ritterschaft, 1," 8 Dec. 1778 GR protocol, 5)14739: 16 Apr. 1779 resolution, 17e) Beltershausen 8–9, Brungershausen 4, Dreihausen 11, 13, Hachborn 28, 34, Kirchvers 26–7; 4h)3700: 7 Sept. 1781 resolution.

[109]StAMg, 4h)4068: 9 Feb. Müller petition, 17 Feb. Motz report, 11 Mar. 1777 KDK report.

[110]StAMg, 17e) Dreihausen 11–12: 12 Sept. 1782, 24 Oct. 1783 GD protocols.

[111]StAMg, 17e) Dreihausen 13: 20 Sept. 1783 Schenck rescript.

supporting the poor and increasing individual productivity and income levels had provided the most compelling impetus, an impetus that was simply no longer present after 1775.

The regime did, however, remain concerned over maintaining continuity in the collection of revenues. It was distressed by revelations that, despite the halving of the Contribution, some people were still falling behind on their taxes. A Tax Office report confirmed that the new delinquencies stemmed from a combination of government policies, including high labor costs and collapsing land values caused by the recent depopulation, peasant abuse of Frederick's ban on the seizure of "productive" capital, plus the standard vices of lethargy and wasteful consumption that had been inspired by the recent tax cut.[112] Nevertheless, the government felt that both the tax cut and the recent spate of agrarian and welfare decrees had already given the peasantry sufficient security against poverty. Hence Frederick rejected out of hand the *Landtag's* request for an additional 20 percent cut in the Contribution, retorting that the recent 50 percent reduction was already "without example in history."[113] For the time being, the peasantry was simply going to have to fend for itself and curb those vices that the government felt were principally responsible for its renewed hardships. The landgrave himself was especially adamant, convinced as he was that peasant lethargy and wastefulness had reached new levels following the tax cut.[114]

His resolve was already apparent some months before the estates convened, when he ordered that the land and livestock of tax delinquents be offered at auction at a price equal to the taxes owed.[115] Though he had only recently made it impossible for creditors to collect private debts, Frederick was now making sure that peasants would not shirk their financial obligations to the state. In so doing he realized that he was striking yet another blow against private creditors by forcing them to take a place in line behind the government in seeking payments from indebted farmers. For this reason he kept the new ordinance secret, lest it further discourage private investment in agriculture. Over the next few years the regime studied less hazardous ways of extracting the halved Contribution from its peasants, eventually enlisting the assistance of the

[112] StAMg, 5)3542: 26 Jan. SK report, 21 May 1778 Reg Cas report.
[113] StAMg, 5)14737: 5 Mar. GR protocol.
[114] StAMg, 5)14739: 16 Apr. 1779 Frederician rescript.
[115] StAMg, 5)3542: 26 Jan. SK report, 21 May Reg Cas report, 3 Mar., [Aug.] Frederician rescripts, 17 Aug. 1778 Actum.

Landräte in tax collection to the point of giving them the option of using troops to collect taxes in those instances where they were convinced that tax delinquents actually were able to pay. By 1783 it was instructing tax collectors to distinguish not only between deadbeats and the truly indebted but also between those who had been victimized by bad luck and those who had only themselves to blame for their present predicament.[116] As always, the government had more compassion for the purely unlucky than it did for the undeserving.

The Hessians and America

If the domestic effects of the Anglo-Hessian convention were unexpected and unwelcome, so were the actual military developments in America. The Hessian regime had never expected that the war would be so long or so unsuccessful. In most other respects, however, it fulfilled the regime's earlier sanguine expectations. The Hessians were far from the reluctant warriors pictured by American historiography. There is, in fact, little dispute that they fought better than any other auxiliary force – and probably better than the British themselves – exhibiting the discipline and loyalty to their sovereign that were characteristic of Hessian society as a whole. They were unquestionably better prepared mentally and militarily to confront the rebels than any other auxiliary corps. Unlike the Ansbachers, only half of whom were natives, or the Brunswickers, who counted only 600 natives among their 4,000-man contingent, the original 12,000 Hessian troops dispatched to America were a largely homogeneous force that prided themselves in being *Landeskinder*.[117]

They also compare favorably to the American "citizen army" that opposed them. In many respects the two forces were not much different from each other. Both comprised a combination of social outcasts and the very poor, with almost no tradesmen or landholders. Both also included many "volunteers" who had enlisted because of peer pressure and coercion, as well as former militiamen who had never expected to go to

[116]StAMg, 5)3542: 17 Aug. 1778 Actum, 5)2747: 5 Oct. 1781 KDK report; *HLO*, 1041–2, 1119–20: 8 Jan. 1782, 20 June 1783.
[117]Bernhard A. Uhlendorf, ed., *Revolution in America. Confidential Letters and Journals 1776–1784 of Adjutant General Major Baurmeister of the Hessian Forces* (New Brunswick, N.J., 1957), 22–3; Atwood, *The Hessians*, 215; Kapp, *Soldatenhandel*, 220; Kipping, *Truppen von Hessen-Kassel*, 20–2; Redlich, *The German Military Enterpriser*, 2: 98.

war but who were now obligated to do so. If anything the Hessians were the more representative of the poorer and more militaristic society from which they came. At least in the beginning they also fought much better and with more enthusiasm and were more faithfully and adequately attended to by their own government.[118] Nor did they ever exhibit the kind of opposition to the war that inspired thousands of American Tories. Even the writer Seume, who would later claim that he had been abducted into the Hessian army against his will, confessed that he and his fellow soldiers were "disappointed" following the conclusion of peace because they had hoped to fight "a bloody war" and not a conflict consisting of skirmishes and garrison duty.[119]

Nor were the Hessians easily seduced by the rebels' revolutionary message. Far to the contrary they were clearly more sympathetic to the British. Regardless of whether they were written by common soldiers, noblemen, or bourgeois officers, the large body of diaries and correspondence that survived the war make it clear that the Hessians never sympathized with the constitutional arguments presented by the Americans. Coming as they did from a country where even the average nobleman was poorer than most colonists, they were also appalled by the Americans' unwillingness to pay taxes for British protection against the common French enemy. Most of all they were deeply critical of the hypocrisy of men who could proclaim "freedom" from oppression, yet persecute Tory loyalists and enslave and brutally mistreat a half million African blacks.[120]

The Hessian treatment of blacks demonstrated, in fact, that the two societies were worlds apart in their definition of equality. So appalled were they at the denial of human dignity to slaves that individual Hessian officers tried to purchase or otherwise free blacks from their masters.[121] They also appear to have protected many of the 131 runaways who enlisted in the Hessian army (94 of them as drummers). At their request

---

[118]John Shy, *A People Numerous and Armed* (Oxford, 1976), 29–30, 165-79; Martin and Lender, *A Respectable Army*, 90–1, 101–10.

[119]Margaret Woelfel, "Memoir's [*sic*] of a Hessian Conscript: J. G. Seumes [*sic*] Reluctant Voyage to America," *William & Mary Quarterly*, 5 (1948), 569-70; Max Eelking, *German Allied Troops*, 15.

[120]Dippel, *Germany and the American Revolution*, 78–84; Atwood, *The Hessians*, 159–66, 170; Kipping, *Hessian View of America*, 25–6, 32–5; Losch, "Der Uriasbrief," 102–3.

[121]Marvin L. Brown, ed., *Baroness von Riedesel and the American Revolution: Journal and Correspondence of a Tour of Duty 1776–1783* (Chapel Hill, N.C., 1965), 112–13; Atwood, *The Hessians*, 165–6.

many were actually permitted to return with their units to Germany, where they were honored by being enrolled in the Gardes Regiment.[122]

The view from Cassel was less one-sided, reflecting as it did the clash of new Enlightenment currents with Hesse-Cassel's traditional societal and diplomatic institutions. Like most German intellectuals and the Hessian soldiers themselves, Schlieffen never understood the truly revolutionary nature of the Revolution and continued to conceptualize the American notion of "liberty" in the traditional European terms of the corporate privileges enjoyed by various oligarchies. Hence he concluded that American society was no more free or just than its Hessian counterpart, that history had already proved that the "political freedom for which some states are famous is often as inimical to individual liberty as the most oppressive despotism."[123]

What is truly remarkable is that Schlieffen was actually in a minority among those Cassel intellectuals who expressed their views on the American Revolution. It is a tribute to Frederick's support for intellectual freedom that no fewer than three of his new professors at the *Collegium Carolinum* – Jakob Mauvillon, Christian Wilhelm von Dohm, and Johannes von Müller — openly championed the American side in the war. Thus, in marked contrast to Göttingen, whose prestigious faculty dutifully supported its elector against his rebellious American subjects, Cassel became a center for the expression of pro-American sentiments among German writers.[124] Dohm actually published in translation the first German edition of both *Common Sense* and the Declaration of Independence within months of his arrival in Cassel (1776). As the war dragged on he continued to publicly defend the American position in the strongest terms, predicting at one point that the inevitable American victory would give "greater scope to the Enlightenment, new boldness to the popular consciousness, [and] new life to the spirit of freedom."[125]

---

[122]StAMg, 4h)3793: 12 Apr. 1784 rescript; Elliott Hoffman, "Black Hessians: American Blacks as German Soldiers," *Negro History Bulletin*, 44 (1981), 81–2; Auerbach et al., *Amerikanische Revolution*, 19, 35–6. The deference shown toward the black soldiers appears to have continued under the next landgrave, who became godfather to the son of one of their number.

[123]Schlieffen, *Von den Hessen*, 19–21; Dippel, *Germany and the American Revolution*, 143–8, 347, 361.

[124]Götz von Selle, *Die Georg-August-Universität zu Göttingen 1737–1937* (Göttingen, 1937), 141; Günderode, *Briefe eines Reisenden*, 89; Robert R. Palmer, *The Age of the Democratic Revolution: A Political History of Europe and America, 1760–1800*, 2 vols. (Princeton, 1959–64), 1: 265; Dippel, *Germany and the American Revolution*, 219.

[125]Herbert P. Gallinger, *Die Haltung der deutschen Publizistik zu dem amerikanischen Unabhängigkeitskriege, 1775–1783* (Leipzig, 1900), 19, 53.

Jakob Mauvillon was even more outspoken. Having served since 1771 as the college's professor of military engineering, Mauvillon actually trained Hessian cadets and junior officers who later went off to serve in America. At the same time he was one of the few German intellectuals who comprehended the nature of the American struggle for freedom from the feudal social and mercantile order that was the Old Regime. Though Frederick could have restricted him to writing in his appointed field of military science, he permitted Mauvillon to champion the American cause, just as he later allowed him to pursue his Physiocratic attacks on cameralism and his contemptuous criticism of the Christian religion. It was from his college sanctuary that Mauvillon now criticized British misrule in America, cynically refuting Schlözer's apologies for George III with the assertion that his Hanoverian colleague secretly favored the American cause but was afraid to jeopardize his post at Göttingen. In championing the American notion of popular sovereignty and even suggesting that the German regimes could afford greater enlightenment, he tested to the fullest the landgrave's intention to permit freedom of thought.[126]

Of course, the defense of American freedom against British tyranny did not necessarily constitute a frontal attack on the Frederician regime. What distinguished Hesse-Cassel from the troubled Anglo-American commonwealth were constitutional issues regulating the relations between the crown and its subjects that had already been resolved in Hesse-Cassel. Indeed, whereas Great Britain's need to fund its past and present military commitments had compelled it to increase taxation, initiate unpopular mercantile policies, and circumvent the colonies' established legislative bodies, Frederick had profited from his own military relationship with the British by lowering taxes, investing in economic development, and deferring to existing parliamentary institutions. Despite their constitutional impotence, the *Landstände* were alive and well in Hesse-Cassel, *virtually* representing all segments of the country's population.[127] The legitimacy and popular acceptance of Hessian institutions were not lost

---

[126]Mauvillon, *Staatskunst*, 75–188; Gallinger, *Deutschen Publizistik*, 33–4, 37; Dippel, *Germany and the American Revolution*, 89–90, 94–5. Nor was Frederick's tolerance lost on Mauvillon. Long after the landgrave's death he recalled how "the individual in Hessian service was able to defend those oppressed people against whom his prince had declared himself. Praise be to a government when a man of learning is able to do that without ever having to suffer any ill consequences!" Quoted by Bödeker, "Aufklärungsgesellschaft," 73.

[127]For a more detailed comparison of the two, see Ingrao, "Barbarous Strangers."

on Johannes von Müller. Notwithstanding his own admiration for the Americans' "virtue and enlightenment," Müller concurred with Schlieffen that the success and justness of government depended most on its appropriateness to local conditions. Like so many Hessians, Müller agreed that these institutions met the country's needs, stating at one point in a letter to a Swiss friend, "I find the system good, as good for the Hessians as the Swiss [is] for the Swiss."[128] As the war wound to a close each Hessian soldier would have to make that decision for himself.

With the coming of peace the landgrave was obliged to pay once more for his decision to participate in the American Revolution. The time had arrived for a final reckoning of the human losses the country had suffered during the war. As expected, battlefield casualties were only a tiny fraction of those sustained in conventional European wars. Battles had been few and had involved far smaller units with much less firepower. Only two Hessians had been killed in action at the battle of Long Island, twenty at Trenton, and twenty-two at Redbank, the bloodiest Hessian engagement of the war. If we accept the highest and most recent estimate presented by Atwood, total Hessian battle deaths came to only 535 men. Yet losses from all causes were 4,983, fully one-quarter of all the forces sent to America.[129] As usual, disease proved the greatest enemy of the common soldier. Another was the climate of the southern colonies. Despite Frederick's attempts to keep his forces stationed in the northern colonies, large numbers were sent to Georgia and the Carolinas, where they succumbed to the heat.[130] Great as these losses were, they numbered only about 1,000–1,500 higher than the number of deaths that a like number of Hessian civilians might have sustained over the same period of time.[131]

If anything the loss of nearly 3,000 men to desertion was of greater significance, if only because it suggests a repudiation of Hessian society

[128]Müller to Jacobi, 23 May 1781, *Sämmtliche Werke*, 162; King, *Echoes of the American Revolution*, 166–8.

[129]Atwood, *The Hessians*, 68, 95, 128, 255.

[130]Jungkenn to Knoblauch, 12 Sept. 1781, in Valentine C. Hubbs, ed., *Hessian Journals: Unpublished Documents of the American Revolution* (Columbia, S.C., 1981), 111–12; Kipping, *Hessian View of America*, 19–20, and *Truppen von Hessen-Kassel*, 57.

[131]My estimate assumes that the flow of replacements maintained a constant muster of 12,000 Hessian soldiers and the validity of available civilian mortality rates for Hesse-Darmstadt among men aged sixteen to forty over an eight-year period. Arthur E. Imhof and Helmut Schumacher, "Todesursachen," in Imhof, ed., *Historische Demographie als Sozialgeschichte*, 2 vols. (Darmstadt and Marburg, 1975), 1: 594–5.

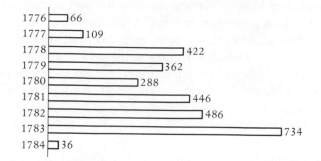

Figure 3. Hessian deserters and missing, 1776–84. These tabulations differ slightly from Atwood's, which total 3,014 (cf. *The Hessians,* p. 256). Source: StAMg, 4h)4294: "Auszug von dem Abgang... des hessischen Corps..." [n.d.]

by its native sons. Clearly this had been the expectation of the Americans, whose sanguine hopes of massive German desertions led them to disseminate leaflets among the auxiliaries immediately after they had landed in the New World.[132] Though he offers no documentation as support, Horst Dippel asserts that German deserters as a group were profoundly affected by exposure to American culture and ideals.[133] Yet surviving accounts give no indication that those soldiers serving with Hessian units either understood or appreciated the American message of freedom and equality, or that they were dissatisfied or disillusioned with their own country or its government. If anything in America made a great impression on them, it was its awesome beauty and potential, and the great wealth of its society, not the country's revolutionary political and social message.

Such an explanation is borne out by the pattern of Hessian desertion (Figure 3). The 2,949 Hessian missing and confirmed deserters listed by the military authorities did not run away at the first opportunity, or on the eve of the first battles. Nor did they desert following exposure to American propaganda and bribes. Even Hessian prisoners of war generally resisted American inducements, choosing to remain interned rather than become settlers or enlist in the Continental Army. Rather, the great bulk of them fought on for several campaigns, choosing to stay in America only as the war was coming to a close and after they had already been

[132]Lyman Butterfield, "Psychological Warfare in 1776: The Jefferson-Franklin Plan to cause Hessian desertions," *Proceedings of the American Philosophical Society,* 94 (1950), 233–41.

[133]Dippel, *Germany and the American Revolution,* 239–40.

demoralized by capture, idleness in garrison duty, or impending defeat.[134] It was only at this point that the soldiers began to turn their attention to the future and to the impending choice between returning home and staying in the New World.

Even if we assume that all of the Hessian missing deserted, the 15.5 percent Hessian attrition rate was low by the standards of European warfare, as well as lower than the rate for the other German contingents, their British allies, or even the American forces.[135] Moreover, if we distinguish between native and foreign-born soldiers, the desertion rate among the landgrave's subjects declines to less than 12 percent, if only because a disproportionately high percentage of those who did desert were non-native recruits who had enlisted, whether in the original expeditionary force or with the replacement units, specifically in order to start a new life following their free passage to America.[136]

Nevertheless, the question remains why approximately 1,600 native Hessians chose to forsake their units and all hope of returning to their homeland. Obviously those soldiers who had originally enlisted in order to gain passage to America were well represented among those who stayed behind. So were youths who subsequently married into settler families. Hessian POWs who had been sent to work as indentured servants also stayed after they were denied release unless they either reimbursed their sponsor for the cumulative costs of food and shelter or agreed to settle permanently in the United States. Their detention stemmed in part from the Americans' determination to retaliate against Hessian efforts to liberate black slaves. Once their fate became known the landgrave purchased the release of thirty-two such detainees.[137] Yet others simply took the

---

[134]Kipping, *Hessian View of America*, 9; Atwood, *The Hessians*, 184–206; Lowell, *The Hessians*, 286-7.

[135]Eelking, *German Allied Troops*, 257; Kapp, *Soldatenhandel*, 217; Martin and Lender, *A Respectable Army*, 132–3.

[136]I derive my estimate from a random sample of 1,465 Hessian soldiers taken from the musters compiled and published by the Hessian Archivschule. My interpolation of these data indicates that, because of the high percentage of non-natives among the 7,000 replacements sent to America, 30 percent or somewhat fewer than 6,000 of the 18,970 men who fought in the Hessian expeditionary force were actually non-Hessian. Non-natives accounted, however, for 47 percent of the deserters listed, making them more than twice as likely to desert as native Hessian soldiers (24.5 versus 11.7 percent). See Auerbach et al., eds., *HETRINA*, 1–4.

[137]"Vaterlandsliebe; oder das Betragen der gefangenen Hessen in Amerika," *HB*, 1 (1784), 67–9; Matthew M. Volm, *The Hessian Prisoners in the American War of Independence and Their Life in Captivity* (Charlottesville, Va., 1937), 11–12; Uhlendorf, *Revolution in America*, 569; Kipping, *Hessian View of America*, 10–11; Auerbach, "Amerikanische Unabhängigkeitskrieg," 326.

path of least resistance and opted to stay in America once they had been confronted with the choice between continued indenture and their instant release as citizens. They too would now be listed as having deserted.

The material inducements offered by Congress to all Hessian soldiers were tempting enough, initially amounting to a cash bounty, instant citizenship, and fifty acres of farmland, but ultimately increased at war's end to 200 acres, a cow, and two pigs. By contrast their future in Hesse-Cassel was almost uniformly bleak. Once again the *Hufen-Edikt* had played an important role. Just as it had originally driven many younger sons to emigrate or enlist in the army, it now posed a potent argument for staying in America. The landgrave himself was aware of the material temptation that settlement in America offered them. As early as 1779 both the *Landtag* and his own ministry had concluded that the edict had been responsible for the bulk of new enlistments and subsequent desertions among native Hessians as disinherited youths decided to "seek a better fate in other parts of the world."[138]

The available evidence supports their judgment. After a soldier had been declared a deserter the military not only seized his disposable wealth but also inventoried his parents' property in order to calculate his portion of the family inheritance, which was then seized on their death. Once the military had confiscated and resold this property, it carefully recorded the proceeds of each transaction. *Kriegskasse* records list the names of 1,279 such soldiers whose property was confiscated and resold between 1777 and 1789 (Figure 4). Unfortunately, this group includes a small but indeterminate number of Hessians who deserted home-based garrisons at various times before 1789. Nevertheless, it presents us with a reasonably accurate profile of what the typical native Hessian soldier stationed in America owned or could expect to inherit in the near future at the moment he deserted. The cumulative picture is one of a Hessian soldiery that was almost uniformly destitute, comprising as it did both disinherited younger sons and elder brothers who were hardly any better off. Over 80 percent owned, or could expect to inherit, property worth less than fifty taler. Of that group nearly half had less than ten taler to their name.

Nor were the remaining 20 percent of this group significantly better off. Land prices fluctuated considerably in Hesse-Cassel, depending on location, soil fertility, and time of purchase. Yet, in order to acquire the

[138]StAMg, 5)14743: "Desideria ulteriora ... 5," 19 Mar. 1779 GR protocol; 304)580: 7 Nov. 1785 Robert votum.

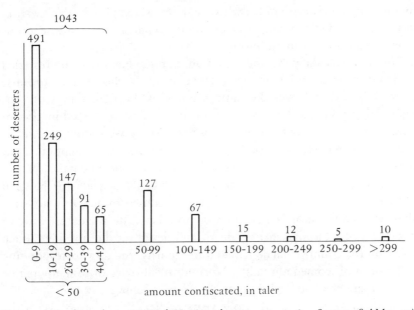

Figure 4. Confiscated property of Hessian deserters, 1777–89. Source: StAMg, 13) Kriegsrechnungen, Kriegszahlamtsrechnungen, 1777–89.

typical twenty- to thirty-*Acker* plot that the government considered minimally sufficient for a subsistence living for a family of four, a peasant usually needed from 800 to 1,000 taler. The *Kriegskasse*'s confiscation records indicate, however, that only 2 of the 1,279 soldiers whose property was auctioned off by the military would have inherited an amount in excess of 700 taler. Even thirty *Acker* of the poorest land, which might have cost as little as 300 taler owing to the depressed prices caused by the *Hufen-Edikt*, were within the means of only ten soldiers, or less than 1 percent of the deserters listed.[139]

The poverty of Hessian deserters assumes an even more dramatic profile when we account for those hundreds of native deserters whose names never appear in the military's record of confiscations because they were likely either completely penniless or had no realistic prospects of inheriting a share of their parents' wealth – such as younger sons disinherited

[139]Both contemporary accounts cited earlier and price statistics compiled by Möker suggest that land values sank by half after the issuance of the *Hufen-Edikt*. While the edict may not have had a depressing effect on larger plots that could be divided among surviving children, the war itself very likely played a role in keeping land values low due to the shortage of farm labor. Möker, *Geschichtliche Entwicklung*, 142, 148; Sakai, *Kurhessische Bauer*, 46n., 172.

by the *Hufen-Edikt* or youths whose parents were still years away from death. This group too had every reason to weigh seriously the generous offers of the American authorities.

Thus it seems likely that the great bulk of those Hessians who resettled in America did so mainly for economic reasons. In choosing the promise of the New World over the hard realities of the Old, they were not repudiating political oppression or social inequality enforced by an unpopular or authoritarian regime – although they were doubtless influenced by the repercussions of the government's own well-intentioned but misconceived attempts to deal with the country's endemic poverty.

The American venture had, of course, had its benefits for Hessian society. In addition, many of the ill effects caused by the war subsided shortly after the army's return from America. The premature loss of perhaps 3,000 Hessian men to death and desertion did not have much effect on the country's male-female ratio, partly due to a corresponding emigration of women abroad.[140] Nor did the absence of so many native sons prevent the country's population from reaching 383,000 by 1781, as opposed to 342,000 just eight years earlier. In any event, with the army's return, the government quickly reintegrated its peasant soldiers into the depressed agrarian labor market.[141] Finally, although the government never intended either the *Hufen-Edikt* or the American venture to spur massive emigration abroad, the fact remains that the resulting demographic adjustment was probably good for the country – and certainly for those who stayed to start a new life in America.

At the same time, however, the American venture constituted just one more example of a bold and carefully conceived measure that had ultimately become laden with largely unexpected and unwelcome consequences: for the peasantry the sudden excesses in recruiting, dearth of available labor, and forced separation of family members; for the soldiers, the usual misfortunes of war, including nearly 5,000 dead and more than 1,000 injured; and for the landgrave himself the crushing of his carefully sculpted image as a sensitive and enlightened ruler. Although he renewed the Anglo-Hessian convention when it came up for renewal in 1779,

---

[140]Fox, "Upper Hesse," 356; Taylor and Rebel, "Peasant Women," 374.
[141]Indeed, at the estates' request the government discharged only foreign recruits in America, thereby transferring all remaining native troops home. StAMg, 5)14739: 1 May 1779 pro memoria; 4h)3793: 29 Sept. 1783 Instructions; Kurt Günther, "Das Truppentagebuch des hessischen Grenadier-Regiments von Bischhausen 1776–1783," *ZHG*, 86 (1976–7), 181; *HLO*, 1101–11: 4 Mar. 1783.

Frederick had learned as his father had in 1757 that the *Soldatenhandel*, like domestic reform, was not without its risks. In the last seven years of his reign he turned down no fewer than five requests for troop conventions, including one from Emperor Joseph II, and two each from his Prussian and Dutch adversaries. The *Kriegskasse* now had the money it needed. The time had come to minimize the price the country would have to pay. Or as Schlieffen explained in rejecting the last of these overtures, "the landgrave is always true to the principle that the good of his country could be compromised by an engagement too hastily entered into."[142]

[142]StAMg, 4h)3617: [Nov. 1784] Jungkenn report, 4e)2679: Schlieffen to Wittorf, 26 Mar., Wittorf to ?, 2 Apr. 1785; Joseph George Rosengarten, "A Defense of the Hessians," *Pennsylvania Magazine of History*, 23 (1899), 163; Losch, *Kurfürst Wilhelm I., Landgraf von Hessen: Ein Fürstenbild aus der Zopfzeit* (Marburg, 1923), 148; Atwood, *The Hessians*, 230.

6

Cassel's golden age

Regardless of their overall opinion of Frederick, historians have hastened to point out that the money from the American venture helped pay for the great building boom that converted Cassel into one of Europe's most beautiful cities and its court into one of Germany's most brilliant. To his detractors it was a self-indulgent waste of the blood money he had received from the British. To his apologists it demonstrated Frederick's commitment to stimulating intellectual and cultural life, as well as Cassel's local economy. The fact is that Frederick had committed himself to rebuilding Cassel during his first decade as landgrave, long before his involvement in the American Revolution. In launching the building program, he was not merely spending excess cash either through senseless extravagance or as a patron of the arts but, rather, was simply succumbing to the inexorable pull of yet another consuming passion that was reinforced and rationalized by the conviction that he was doing it for the good of society.

Like so many of Frederick's policies the beautification of Cassel followed established patterns of princely or government behavior that could be easily justified by Enlightenment ideas. This does not impinge on the sincerity of his commitment to these ideas, but it does illustrate the ease with which initiatives could be launched when they already conformed and could be combined with existing praxis. Since the Renaissance the patronage of a brilliant and cultured court had been as much a part of a prince's world as was his military calling. Although Hessian monarchs could point to considerable advantages to be derived from expenditures on either the military or court patronage, they made those outlays primarily because they enjoyed both and valued the intrinsic worth of each, regardless of the social implications. The cultural ambience in which Frederick grew up guaranteed that both values would survive. His predecessors had already launched extensive building projects that had earned

Cassel a favorable aesthetic reputation before 1760. There is, in fact, no question that he was already a committed lover of both the fine and martial arts in his youth.[1] Hence, during the fiscal crisis of the early 1770s the landgrave maintained a large army because he loved the military, but he could also justify it as a necessary investment in the soldier trade. At the same time he spent much smaller but nevertheless considerable sums of money on the artistic and intellectual life of his residence because it too was his passion, though once again he could clothe it in the value system of the late eighteenth century.

Although Frederick's passions for the military and the arts were well-developed Hessian traditions, it would be a mistake to discount outside influences as well. In his recent book on Württemberg, James Vann points out that the landgrave's brother-in-law Duke Charles Eugene spent to the verge of bankruptcy because he was merely trying to keep up with accepted standards of court extravagance as practiced by his peers.[2] Frederick's own declared intention of making Cassel "one of the most beautiful cities in all Germany" was consistent with the competitive building programs of princes who sought to achieve or maintain a coveted reputation for their residences. It also paralleled his penchant for copying the reforms of other states because they served both his subjects and his own international image. As he explained in his *Pensées*, public works were a "pleasant chore that are also beneficial for one's subjects" because they employed the poor and helped to rehabilitate the economy.[3] Of course, Charles Eugene is almost never characterized as an enlightened monarch. By the standards of the age Frederick *was* "enlightened," but before we give him credit for court patronage, we should be prepared to distinguish between Enlightenment ideas and yet another set of preexisting institutions and values that merely co-opted the language and arguments of the new age.

Building Cassel

Like his reforms Frederick's building programs began immediately after the Seven Years' War. He relied principally on Simon Louis du Ry, a

---

[1] Both and Vogel, *Friedrich II.*, 231.
[2] Vann, *The Making of a State: Württemberg, 1593–1793* (Ithaca, N.Y., 1984).
[3] "Pensées," #26; Josef Friedrich Engelschall, *Johann Heinrich Tischbein, ehemaliger fürstlich hessischer Rath und Hofmaler als Mensch und Künstler* (Nuremberg, 1797), 46.

gifted Huguenot architect who had studied both French classical and Italian architecture at first hand. By 1765 du Ry had already built a new opera house amid the city's war ruins and laid plans for a theater and a long promenade called the Rennbahn for the parading of Frederick's troops. In February of that year the Austrian envoy Pergen was reporting that building projects were the landgrave's favorite extravagance after the army.[4] His decision to expand the city itself evolved within the next couple of years. Two foreign trips, one to Paris (1766), the other to Paris and London (1767), served as the inspirational prelude for the project.

The landgrave welcomed private construction by offering land clearance, a 1,500-taler subsidy and ten years' tax freedom. Nevertheless, he intended to employ principally public funds, a prospect that had occasioned fiscal anxiety and opposition from within the ministry.[5] Government construction concentrated on connecting medieval Cassel to the upper town that Landgrave Charles had built at the beginning of the century for the city's large Huguenot population. To do so Frederick tore down the city walls, arguing that the Seven Years' War had demonstrated that they were of use only to foreign occupiers since no Hessian ruler would ever risk the destruction of his own residence by defending or besieging it.[6] The two focal points of the building program were the huge Friedrichsplatz, which became Germany's largest square, and the Königsstrasse, an elegant street that connected it with its own Königsplatz. Meanwhile, high above the city Frederick expended additional sums in converting the modest Schloss Weissenstein into a great palace equipped with a French garden and numerous Chinese and classical Greek motifs.[7]

Always one to get involved personally with his projects, the landgrave's concern for aesthetics led him to work hand in hand with du Ry in virtually rebuilding his residence. Under their supervision armies of laborers straightened and paved the city's streets, lining them with sidewalks, streetlights, and trees. In order to ensure structural soundness and aesthetic appeal he required that all planned construction, including the renovation of existing buildings, be approved beforehand. In the process he ordered and paid for the rebuilding of well over a hundred private

---

[4]HHStA, RK, Berichte aus dem Reich 81: 9 Feb. 1765 Pergen report.
[5]*HLO*, 396–7: 10 Feb. 1767; AAE, CP, HC 13: 12 Jan. 1783 Aigremont report.
[6]Piderit, *Residenz-stadt Cassel*, 289.
[7]Karl Paetow, *Klassizismus und Romantik auf Wilhelmshöhe* (Cassel, 1929), 16–17, 37, 45. Frederick also employed the French architect Cuvilliés in completing the renovation of a second palace, Schloss Wilhelmstal, which was located five miles outside the city.

dwellings, making them conform to a long list of aesthetic and architectural specifications.[8] As usual he never hesitated to institute ideas gleaned from his foreign travels. His recent trips to Paris inspired a decree ordering shopkeepers to post and illuminate storefront signs for easier recognition. He also decided to enhance the elegance of over a hundred of the city's *Gassen* by converting them into *Strassen*, a process he assisted with numerous names of his own devising.[9] Subsequent excursions to Paris, Brussels, and Düsseldorf harvested a new crop of ideas ranging from the use of small, less expensive taxi coaches and the introduction of house-to-house postal delivery to such trivialities as the regulation of carriage traffic at the opera and the employment of gold letters on all store signs for easier recognition.[10]

The finished product brought universal acclaim from travelers and natives alike. Georg Forster spoke for the multitude of awestruck travelers when he told his father in 1778 that "never was a city more beautiful than Cassel." Indeed, the city's popularity among travelers is reflected by the doubling in the number of "finer" *Gasthäuser* from thirteen (1764) to twenty-six (1784).[11] The beautified city complemented the brilliant court and cultural life that surrounded the landgrave. As early as 1772 an Austrian diplomat had noted the "total entertainment" available at court, remarking that, with "opera, comedy, concerts, *parforce* hunting, games, [etc.] each day has its work and play." With the resumption of British subsidies expenditures surged, averaging over 40,000 taler annually just for theatrical and musical productions. The favorite among these, operetta, employed a very good staff of Parisian and Italian performers in the staging of seventy different productions a year.[12]

[8]Berge, "Friedrich II.," 284–5; *HLO*, 1139–45: 9 Jan. 1784.
[9]StAMg, 5)13448: Frederick's notes [n.d.].
[10]StAMg, 5)1582: "Punkte, welche auf gnädigst befehl ..." [1781], 4a)90,21: "Articles pour introduire ..." For a thorough account of the rebuilding of Cassel, see Hans-Kurt Boehlke, *Simon Louis du Ry* (Kassel, 1981); Piderit, *Residenz-stadt Cassel*, 286–93; Heidelbach, *Kassel*, 164–71, 200.
[11]Forster to father, 8 Dec. 1778, Hettner, *Briefwechsel*, 178; Brunner, *Residenzstadt Cassel*, 290.
[12]HHStA, RK, Kleinere Reichsstände, 163: Bödiger to Benzel, 18 June 1772; Berge, "Friedrich II.," 288. With the singular exception of Charles Eugene, who was doubtless accustomed to yet higher levels of extravagance, both the court and city received universally enthusiastic reviews from visitors. Uhland, *Carl Eugen*, 133–4. For their observations (with the approximate date in brackets), see Vehse, *Deutschen Höfe*, 167 [1768]; Knigge, *Roman meines Lebens*, I, Pt. 1: 48–9, 55 [1769]; *Briefe eines Iungen Reisenden*, 82–3, 102 [1771]; Moore, *Society and Manners*, 24, 41 [1779]; Johann Bernoulli, ed., *Sammlung kurzer Reisebeschreibungen*, 3, 9 (Berlin, 1781–3), 3: 137–63 [1781], 9: 153–9 [1777]; *Neue Reisebemerkungen*, 2: 101, 132–3 [1782]; Johann Matthias Hassencamp, *Briefe*

The question remains, who benefited from the landgrave's patronage? Clearly the general population profited indirectly through increased employment and consumption. Though he did resort to the customary device of levying a tax to provide permanent support for street maintenance, Frederick bore virtually all building and court costs himself. Outlays for construction amounted to about 1 million taler, a not insignificant amount for a city of 20,000 people. While he initially used convicts and troops to tear down the town walls, he ultimately employed large numbers of Cassel's swollen population of itinerants and poor, despite the opposition of Cassel's construction guilds. Even after the work had been largely completed, he continued to devise ways of employing the indigent in city services.[13]

Yet, it doubtless helped Cassel's elite even more. Not only were they the focus of court life, but they also were among the chief recipients of the 350,000 taler in building subsidies Frederick awarded. Even the pattern of construction symbolized the integration of all privileged social elements – court, civil, and military officials, artists and academics, cadet princes, and *Ritterschaft Landtag* deputies – into the Hessian establishment. One long row of twelve elegant townhouses that had been built along the Königsstrasse and Königsplatz with the help of government subsidies actually housed members of each group. Nor was the significance of this integration lost on their owners. When in 1772 Jungkenn's debts obliged him to sell the palatial home that du Ry had built for him, the Hessian *Ritterschaft* quickly purchased it for the princely sum of 45,000 taler, even though it was currently very hard pressed for funds and had no particular need or projected use for the building. When he learned of the purchase one cost-conscious nobleman exclaimed that "either the *Ritterschaft*'s heads must be spinning or the joy over the great acquisition of a *Landständisches Palais* ... must have clouded their vision."[14] In fact, its value lay solely in its location at the center of power, a privilege for which the estates need not pay: With characteristic gen-

eines Reisenden von Pyrmont (Frankfurt, 1783) 49, 51–2 [1783]; Gottlob Friedrich Krebel, *Die vornehmsten europäischen Reisen* ... 1 (Hamburg, 1783), 282, 285 [1783]; Günderode, *Briefe eines Reisenden*, 26–7, 197 [1781]; Riesbeck, *Voyage en Allemagne*, 149 [1783].
[13]Berge lists 170,000 for razing the town walls, 350,000 in subsidies, and 15,000–20,000 taler annually in construction costs. "Friedrich II.," 278–9, 287; Heidelbach, *Kassel*, 171; StAMg, 4a)90,21: "Articles pour introduire ..."
[14]Freiherrlich Riedeselsches Archiv, Lauterbach, 64)225: Rantzau to Riedesel, 12 Sept. 1772.

erosity Frederick soon granted them what amounted to an interest-free loan for the entire amount.[15]

Although he had already committed himself to considerable expenditures for his court and building projects long before 1776, the resumption of British subsidies permitted Frederick to enlarge the scope of each. The same could be said of his patronage of Cassel's academic life and institutions. Once again the primary beneficiary was the *Collegium Carolinum*. Having expanded its faculty from seven to nineteen, Frederick had not hired anyone else since "discovering" the fiscal crisis in 1771. Armed with an expanded budget that soon reached 40,000 taler, he now made seven new appointments in the next seven years, principally by attracting scholars from nearby Göttingen.

Although none of these men had reached the pinnacle of his career, several were beginning to establish major reputations that blossomed during their tenure in Cassel. Thus Christian Wilhelm von Dohm's translations of Paine and Jefferson, together with his multivolume *Materialen zur Statistik und neuesten Staatengeschichte* helped launch his distinguished career as a political theorist. The naturalist Georg Forster had just published his celebrated eyewitness account of Cook's second voyage when Schlieffen recruited him in 1778 while in London negotiating with the British government. His greater notoriety as a German Jacobin still lay in the future. Johannes von Müller had only begun to make his mark as a historian and political commentator with the publication of the first volume of his Swiss history in 1780, one year prior to his appointment. It was only after he came to Cassel in 1779 that Thomas Sömmerring's research earned him recognition as Germany's foremost anatomist, a reputation he complemented by working in telegraphy and engineering Germany's first successful balloon flight from Cassel in 1784.[16] Indeed, Dohm, Forster, and Sömmerring were still only in their mid-twenties when they arrived in Cassel.

For Frederick's new recruits Cassel was not without certain professional attractions, not the least of these being incumbent faculty like

---

[15]As late as 1785 the estates had not paid either interest or principal on the 45,000 taler, which had been lent at a rate of 2.5 percent. StAMg, 5)14794: 1772 Landtagsabschied; 12) Kriegszahlamtsrechnungen 1772, 1785. In the end the building was never used for conclaves and was ultimately rented out to guests. Ledderhose, *Kleine Schriften*, 1: 114.
[16]W. Haberling, *German Medicine* (New York, 1978), 57–8; Käthe Heinemann, "Blütezeit der Medizin," 92; Hermann Schelenz, "Kassel, Goethe, und Luftschiffahrt," *Hessenland*, 25 (1911), 2–3.

Mauvillon, Raspe, and Stein, who joined them in forming a formidable constellation of gifted scholars. Dohm, for example, was drawn in part by the presence of his fellow political economist Mauvillon, whereas Sömmerring was enticed by his close friendship with Forster, with whom he now maintained a joint household. Yet the most magnetic figure of all was probably Schlieffen, the man who actually recruited most of them. Though he lacked a university education, this remarkable intellectual had acquired an extensive knowledge of the classics while still in the Prussian army, a specialty that impressed not only Frederick but men like Forster, who admiringly dubbed him the "Maecenas of Cassel" for his knowledge and support of the arts. Indeed, Schlieffen befriended all of the new appointees, catering to their professional needs, even reading and critiquing their work to the point of appending thirty-six pages of footnotes to one passage of Müller's Swiss history.[17]

Frederick enhanced the attractiveness of the new positions by affording each scholar ample resources for his research and an unusually broad degree of intellectual freedom. No one profited more then Sömmerring, who enjoyed considerable latitude as director of both the menagerie and a new anatomical theater just built by du Ry. To meet the good doctor's needs Frederick issued special orders that kept him supplied with the unclaimed bodies of all accident victims, *Findelhaus* interns, and even the animal carcasses scavenged from his own table. He also later established a small colony of African blacks for Sömmerring's research in comparative anatomy.[18] Dohm also benefited from the landgrave's resources by beginning his tenure with a lengthy, fully paid sabbatical tour of the German southwest. Upon his return to Cassel he was required to give only a one-hour lecture each day, a schedule that prompted him to declare that "I have as much independence and leisure as anyone can demand once he has sold his freedom to a prince." Meanwhile, Frederick not only permitted Dohm to spend much of his time supporting the American cause but also allowed him to write Prussian propaganda during the War of Bavarian Succession despite his own declaration of neutrality.[19] Nor was Müller less impressed by the landgrave's willingness to support the highly critical history of the papacy that he began during

[17]Forster to Jacobi, 17 Dec. 1778, Hettner, *Briefwechsel*, 186; Henking, *Johannes von Müller*, 27–39, 55; Koenig, "Althessische Silhouetten," 51–2.
[18]*HLO*, 989–90: 10 Dec. 1779; Heinemann, "Blütezeit der Medizin," 89–94; Koenig, "Althessische Silhouetten," 46.
[19]Dambacher, *Christian Wilhelm von Dohm*, 13–14, 141–2.

his stay in Cassel. Before the end of his first full year at the college he would write home to one of his countrymen, "I would like to ask all Switzerland whether it is possible to have more personal freedom than I enjoy here."[20]

In return for the many amenities he afforded them, Frederick intended to employ the expanded college faculty as the cutting edge of his attempt to better educate his court and make it one of Germany's leading cultural and literary centers. Hence the arrival of new faculty permitted him to formalize the ongoing instruction of young army officers and cadets with the establishment of a military academy, or *Kadettenkorps*, in 1778. It also provided him with the means to form no fewer than four new societies and institutions of learning. One of these was somewhat standard fare for a major residence that Frederick had already discussed in his *Pensées*. The Academy of Fine Arts (*Malerei- Bildhauer- und Baukunst-Akademie*) was a training school run by du Ry, Tischbein, and the eminent sculptor Nahl that attracted seventy students in its first year.[21]

The *Société des Antiquités* was different. Though sustained in its operations by British subsidies, it was the inspiration of a six-month tour of Italy that Frederick had taken with du Ry during the winter of 1776-7. Having brought back a trove of ancient and Renaissance art, the landgrave decided to establish a society for the study of ancient civilization modeled after Bologna's prestigious *Instituto di Scienze*. The landgrave took his society seriously. He scheduled fortnightly meetings, sponsoring over a hundred lectures by the end of the reign, including eleven that he delivered himself on ancient art and literature. He even decreed Germany's first ancient artifacts law requiring people to deliver any archaeological discoveries to the state in return for full reimbursement and a reward.[22] Frederick's society ranked with only three sister institutions in Bologna, Rome, and London – all of which now graciously made him an honorary member. Honorary members were, in fact, a precious commodity in the landgrave's society. While he stocked its active membership with college faculty and high civil and army officers, he took great pride in including numerous foreign luminaries such as Herder, Heyne, Lessing, Wieland,

[20]King, *Echoes of the American Revolution*, 167; Henking, *Johannes von Müller*, 39–40. For a similar remark in a 19 July 1781 letter to Dohm, see Müller, *Sämmtliche Werke*, 118.
[21]"Pensées," #5; *HLO*, 971–3: 22 May 1779; "Nachricht von der fürstl. hessischen Akademie der Malerei- Bildhauer- und Baukunst zu Cassel," *HB*, 1 (1784), 401–12; Heidelbach, *Kassel*, 182.
[22]Heidelbach, *Kassel* 180; *HLO*, 1015: 22 Dec. 1780.

Voltaire, d'Alembert, and Casanova on its membership list, doubtless because their willingness to serve honored him as much as it did them. Indeed, after Voltaire's death in 1778 Frederick even created a category for recently deceased members for inclusion in the *Staats- und Adresskalender.*

Another source of both princely pride and devotion was the Continent's first public museum, the Fridericianum. The landgrave had laid the plans for the building in 1767 – immediately after returning from his tour of London and the British Museum – placing it in the dominant position at the center of the Friedrichsplatz. Though construction began in 1769, it was still unfinished when he returned from Italy eight years later, thereby enabling du Ry to redesign its interior after the *Instituto di Scienze.*[23] In the spirit of the age the Fridericianum attempted to present an exhaustive portrait of the universe in all its complexity, to be an "aesthetic encyclopaedia" to visitors. Like the British Museum it combined books and art, housing the Academy of Fine Arts, Matsko's Mathematical and Mechanical Institute, Forster's collection of rocks, minerals, and fossils, and the landgrave's own library and priceless *Münzkabinett* of rare coins and medallions.[24]

Frederick spared little effort or cash in building up these holdings. On one occasion he employed Moser to acquire coins while on a secret mission to Vienna. On another he selected Raspe for sensitive diplomatic negotiations with Paderborn so that he could purchase 900 manuscripts from its monastic repositories.[25] Indeed, though he was unsuccessful in an attempt to buy Voltaire's library, he still managed to nearly triple his own holdings to 38,000 volumes by the end of the reign.[26] Once they had been moved to the Fridericianum all collections were open to the public, a service that impelled the landgrave to levy a piddling but predictable tax on the bureaucrats, students, and book merchants whose interests they served.[27] It is, however, unlikely that anyone used it as often as Frederick, who reputedly visited it straight from the parade

[23] Both and Vogel, *Friedrich II.,* 239–42.
[24] Karl-Hermann Wegner, "Gründung und Einrichtung des Museums Fridericianum in Kassel. Seine Bedeutung für die Kulturgeschichte der Aufklärung," *Hessische Heimat,* 27 (1977), 154–64; Hanno Beck, "Vulkanisten und Neptunisten in Hessen," *Berichte zur deutschen Landeskunde,* 27 (1961), 93–4.
[25] StAMg, Moser to Frederick, 26 Feb. 1783; Carswell, *The Prospector,* 70, 75–6, 78–9.
[26] Gallatin to Frederick, 29 July, 19 Sept. 1778, Stengel, "Briefe Voltaire's," 217; Wilhelm Hopf, *Die Landesbibliothek Kassel 1580–1930* (Marburg, 1930), 44, 50.
[27] Hopf, *Landesbibliothek Kassel,* 41.

ground virtually every morning at ten, and frequently in the afternoon as well.[28]

For a time the combination of the city's beauty and the concentration and activities of its college faculty helped make Cassel a significant cultural center in the heart of north central Germany. Just as Frederick had attracted many academics to Cassel, so they now received visitors in turn. The retired Klopstock visited from his home in Hamburg, Herder from his court pastorate at Bückeburg. The young Goethe made several trips to see his friends Forster and Sömmerring, staying whenever possible in his favorite accommodations along the elegant Königsstrasse. Dalberg visited Dohm on a number of occasions. Above all, the city became a favorite excursion for the faculty and students of nearby Göttingen, with over 200 of them visiting on a single occasion during 1781.[29] Indeed, during the years of the American Revolution, Cassel's professoriate was part of a matrix of German intellectuals living within a 100-mile radius of the city, a group that included Lessing at Brunswick, Dalberg at Erfurt, Jacobi at Düsseldorf, Moser at Darmstadt, Schlözer and Heyne at Göttingen, Goethe, Wieland, and, eventually, Herder and Knigge at Weimar.

One of Cassel's most remarkable features within this matrix of German cultural centers was that it was, in many respects, not German at all but French. Much of the the city looked French, thanks to du Ry's and Frederick's preference for the French classical style. His three great "squares" – the Rennbahn, Königsplatz, and Friedrichsplatz – were all modeled after French cities. Even the water cascadé he built high above the city at Weissenstein was widely regarded as the best Versailles imitation in Germany.[30] With their French and Italian performers, the theater and opera were anything but German. Virtually all of the plays they produced were French, written by the likes of Molière, Racine, Voltaire, Rousseau, and numerous less distinguished figures. French operas were also the rule, though Gluck's reform opera *Alceste* became a favorite after its premiere in 1781.[31] French was not only Frederick's language of preference but also the official language of the *Kadettenkorps*, the

[28]Günderode, *Briefe eines Reisenden*, 217, 219, 220.
[29]Edward Schröder, "Goethes Beziehungen zu Kassel und zu hessischen Persönlichkeiten," *ZHG*, 52 (1919), 24–5; Dambacher, *Christian Wilhelm von Dohm*, 16; Bernoulli, *Reisebeschreibungen*, 3: 160; Both and Vogel, *Friedrich II.*, 245–8.
[30]Carswell, *The Prospector*, 48.
[31]Heidelbach, *Kassel*, 190.

Société des Antiquités, and even the inner administration and catalog system of the princely library. It was a measure of the court's French influence that one of Cassel's German-language newspapers and some of the merchants who serviced the court began advertising in French. Many Cassel natives even hired Huguenot tutors to teach them the language.[32]

The French influence was reinforced by a number of prominent individuals. The French envoy enjoyed a high profile at court, as did a number of lesser French luminaries whom Frederick had brought to Cassel on the recommendations of Voltaire and Madame Gallatin.[33] One of the first to come was Jacques Mallet du Pan, the future apologist for Louis XVI, whom Frederick initially hired to write a history of Hesse. The most notable was Pierre Louis, marquis de Luchet, a widely published author whom the landgrave showered with a variety of posts, making him among other things head librarian, permanent secretary of the Antiquity Society, and even vice-president of the Commerce College. As one of Luchet's colleagues at the Fridericianum observed, "It is the custom of our German princes to have at least one learned Frenchman, and he who can have no Voltaire satisfies himself with a Luchet."[34]

The limits of patronage

The court's French ambience symbolized to a certain extent the artificiality of Frederick's creation. His grandiose designs for the residence were, in fact, not altogether unlike his other, more ambitious initiatives in domestic or even foreign policy in that they reached beyond the structural realities of Hessian society. Given his considerable zeal and financial resources, Frederick had once again eschewed conservative policies that would arouse few protests in favor of launching bold initiatives that promised glamorous results but often led immediately to unpleasant side effects, while seldom bringing lasting change.

Frederick's most notable misstep was his reliance on imported foreign talent. Just as Cassel attracted legions of beggars and vagabonds from elsewhere in Germany, so it had become a Mecca for charlatans, alchemists, rogue nobles, unscrupulous entrepreneurs, and other assorted ad-

---

[32]Münscher, *Geschichte von Hessen,* 432; Casparson, *Kurze Geschichte sämmtlicher hessen-casselischen französischen Colonien vom Jahr 1685* (Cassel, 1785), 76.
[33]*Neue Reisebemerkungen,* 2: 133; AAE, CP, HC 14: 21 May 1776 Grais report; Günderode, *Briefe eines Reisenden,* 246, 249.
[34]Both and Vogel, *Friedrich II.,* 84.

venturers who sought to capitalize on the easy opportunities the landgrave's ample cash flow seemed to promise. The Italians were probably the least trusted group of foreign courtiers, especially after the founder of the state lottery, the appropriately named Francesco Sinistrario, was caught embezzling 70,000 taler of its proceeds. In the end, even the French element of Cassel's Golden Age proved to be of a somewhat baser mettle. Notwithstanding the honors Frederick bestowed on them, they generally tended to be intellectual mediocrities who had failed to make a mark for themselves in their native country. None was more overrated than Luchet, whom Schlieffen exposed as "certainly no *savant* but only a writer of wide but superficial knowledge who was pleasant enough but unreliable, like many of his countrymen." In a letter to his father Forster cynically betrayed the widespread conviction that Cassel had become a dumping ground for France's failed writers, asking "if you know a Frenchman who can glibly utter nonsense and has a high forehead, send him here and within a short time he will be highly respected."[35] If the court's German denizens were disappointed by the intellectual limits of their French colleagues, they were angered by their cultural arrogance. As a group they made little attempt to learn German, capitalizing on the landgrave's own preference for their native tongue. Luchet's ignorance of all the Germanic tongues was especially galling since he was director of a princely library that was composed of works written almost exclusively in those languages. Moreover, he compounded the problem by replacing the Fridericianum's simple but effective catalog with a French system that consigned all German books – nearly the entire collection – to a tiny catalog classification that made individual books virtually impossible to locate. To correct Luchet's mistake Frederick was eventually compelled to use troops to return the books to their former positions, regrettably at some cost to the volumes themselves. By the end of the reign a definite reaction had set in against the French cultural tyranny. Even Schlieffen, who had routinely spoken and written in French, began urging the exclusive use of German, at one point pressing Müller to purge all non-German terms and cognates from his Swiss history, a policy he himself practiced in drafting his own unreadable autobiography.[36]

Frederick's efforts to make Cassel a cultural and intellectual center were limited not only by the muted brilliance of his French luminaries

[35] 19 Sept. 1782, Henking, *Briefwechsel*, 290–1; Both and Vogel, *Friedrich II.*, 84.
[36] Carl Scherer, "Martin Ernst von Schlieffen, sein Leben und sein Verhältniss zur Sprachreinigung," *Hessenland*, 5 (1891), 254–5, 282.

but also by his inability to retain his most gifted German faculty. Part of the problem stemmed from the high cost of living at court. Despite respectable annual salaries of about 500 taler, Mauvillon, Forster, Sömmerring, and Müller all succumbed within a short time of their arrival to the extravagant tastes and life-style the court promoted. Although Frederick actually advanced additional funds to help some of them, their growing indebtedness was a major reason behind each man's decision to move on.[37] Among the college's veteran faculty, Raspe was lucky to be able to leave at all. Having fallen deeply in debt over the past decade, he used his position as curator of Frederick's *Münzkabinett* to embezzle 3,000–5,000 taler in precious coins. When discovered he fled to England, from where he would achieve instant fame by publishing the *Adventures of Baron Munchausen*, that delightful collection of tall tales that he had filched from the brother of the Hessian *Landrat* for Schaumburg.[38]

Yet the most difficult problem in retaining the college's gifted faculty was not Cassel's high living costs but its limited potential as a cultural center. Frederick's attempt to use his professors to effect a Hessian Renaissance in the sciences, arts, and humanities was essentially limited to the small, captive audience that resided at court. He was not wholly unsuccessful in attaining these goals. For example, the achievements of the *Kadettenkorps* in combining the teaching of military science with such subjects as history and foreign languages were not lost on one traveler who was struck by how well educated the military officers at court were.[39] On the other hand, there was only so much that the bevy of formal instruction, public lectures, and learned societies could accomplish.

In departing Cassel back in 1772 Mallet had been openly contemptuous of the cultural backwardness of the court, expressing his "boredom" with its "slight taste for *belles lettres*." In reporting these remarks Frederick had explained to Voltaire that Mallet had come to Cassel seeking French muses but had found only German ones instead.[40] Yet one decade later it remained a view shared even by the Germans themselves. Not-

---

[37] Jochen Hoffmann, *Jakob Mauvillon. Ein Offizier und Schriftsteller im Zeitalter der bürgerlichen Emanzipationsbewegung* (Berlin, 1981), 46–7, 51, 53; Schelenz, *Collegium Carolinum*, 79–80; Henking, *Johannes von Müller*, 56; Kersten, *Forster*, 115.

[38] Carswell, *The Prospector*, 78–84, 91. He also translated most of Forster's account of Cook's voyage into English while staying as a guest in Forster's London home.

[39] "Kurzgefasste Beschreibung des hochfürstlich hessischen Kadettenkorps zu Cassel," *HB*, 2 (1785), 373–4, 377, 384–5; *Neue Reisebemerkungen*, 134.

[40] StAMg, 4a)91,44: Frederick to Voltaire, 6 Oct. 1772.

withstanding his enchantment with Cassel's beauty and his friendship with Forster and Sömmerring, Goethe was unimpressed with the court as a whole, saying that its "learned court [had] the erudition of only one side of a very large page."[41] Forster was particularly jaded, telling Jacobi that "nobody reads here in Cassel. I cannot get a book to see or read unless I buy one." It was a sign of his disillusionment that he eventually rented a house in nearby Göttingen.[42]

If the faculty had a limited impact on the court, it had even less on the burghers themselves. Foreign observers were struck by the diffidence with which the city's austere Calvinist population treated the cultural and intellectual life offered by the court. Public attendance at operatic and theatrical events was so minimal that, by 1782, Frederick was obliged to provide the theater with 90,000 taler just to service the interest on its debts.[43] The faculty's publications were no better received. The *Mémoires* of the *Société des Antiquités* expired in 1780, after having produced just one volume for want of a sufficient readership. The *Hessische Beiträge zur Gelehrsamkeit und Kunst*, a humanities and public affairs journal modeled after Nicolai's *Allgemeine Deutsche Bibliothek* and Bibra's *Journal von und für Deutschland*, lasted but two years despite a rich variety of essays written by several college and foreign contributors. Even the college itself failed to gain popularity with the burghers, who continued to send their children directly to the country's two full-fledged universities or to nearby Göttingen and Giessen. Despite Frederick's continuing efforts to increase enrollments by strengthening the college's curriculum and offering additional fellowships, it remained in Schlieffen's words "an accursed mediocrity" whose courses were either too advanced or too elementary for the sons of local citizens – and totally without challenge for its prestigious faculty.[44]

Given these realities it was inevitable that the college's more prominent faculty would move on to better opportunities. Although he was compelled to flee, Raspe would have likely voluntarily left Cassel earlier than 1777, except for his fear that his successor at the *Münzkabinett* would

---

[41] The pun emerges only in English translation. Schröder, "Goethes Beziehungen zu Kassel," 30.

[42] Vehse, *Deutschen Höfe*, 173; Kersten, *Forster*, 83, 134.

[43] Moore, *Society and Manners*, 34; Günderode, *Briefe eines Reisenden*, 194; Berge, "Friedrich II.," 289.

[44] *HLO*, 714–26, 740–8: 17 Sept., 23 Nov. 1773; Hartwig, "Mitteilungen aus der Geschichte des Collegium Carolinum in Cassel," *ZHG*, 41 (1908), 89; Dersch, "Universität Marburg," 168.

discover his crime. The next to depart was Dohm, who left for Berlin in 1779, after just three years in Cassel. Müller returned to his native Switzerland in 1783 after just two years, to be followed one year later by the departures of Sömmerring for Mainz and Forster for Vilna, each after four years at the college. Although financial difficulties mandated each man's departure, Müller also cited Germany's unfavorable weather and intellectual climate, writing that "the military pervades everything" and that "while there are some wonderful things, there is generally little taste, little true love of letters." It was in fitting contrast that the German-born Mauvillon left for Brunswick early in 1785 because he would be able to combine active service as an officer in the regular army with a faculty position in that city's own *Collegium Carolinum*.[45]

Perhaps the most damning criticism that can be made of Frederick's patronage of the arts and sciences is that he concentrated so heavily on Cassel itself, while virtually ignoring the Hessian hinterland. There are several reasons for this, not the least of which were the egocentrism and elitism of the court itself, and the greater reputation that a glamorous residence afforded the landgrave. In addition, however, his relative neglect of the countryside was a function of his more immediate awareness of the conditions and needs of his residence. In a regime that was more responsive than creative, his consciousness was usually circumscribed by the information he received from the countryside. Under such circumstances, Cassel was always going to reap the greatest benefits of governmental concern so long as the country was content to languish in relative obscurity. Finally, in Frederick's defense, the fact remains that there was always greater feasibility in launching progressive initiatives in Cassel than in the Hessian hinterland, where there was often a much poorer chance that they would succeed, or even be welcomed and appreciated.

Each of these factors surfaced in the government's handling of education outside Cassel during the second half of the reign. Frederick was certainly handicapped in his attempts to improve primary education outside Cassel, both by the constraints placed on him by the *Assekurationsakte* and by the countryside's own meager resources. He did not fail, however, from want of trying. During 1778 he began pressuring the Consistory to address the "pitiful state" of public instruction, complain-

[45]Karl Schib, *Johannes von Müller 1752–1809* (Constance, 1967), 116; Henking, *Johannes von Müller*, 55–6; Carswell, *The Prospector*, 63; Hoffmann, *Mauvillon*, 48–51.

ing that country schools were not teaching their students how to read or write. His appeal reflected new, utilitarian trends in public education during the 1770s that stressed the need to teach the masses the "three R's" in order to enhance their potential as productive workers and socially responsible citizens.[46] It was also persuasive. The Consistory promptly responded by carrying out his request for the examination and exclusion of incompetent teachers from the classroom.[47]

To replace them with qualified instructors Frederick personally founded the *Lyceum Fridericianum* in Cassel during the following year. Although he also intended it to serve as a vocational school, his primary goal was to establish the country's first institution specifically designed for the training of public-school teachers. Once again his initiative was hardly an act of creative genius but was instead closely modeled after Fulda's establishment of teacher-training seminaries five years earlier. Yet its curriculum reflected his long-standing commitment to the new learning. Hence all its students – whether they be vocational or teacher trainees – were required to receive a liberal education that was delivered in French and included literature, history, foreign languages, and natural science. Meanwhile, all student teachers were awarded a full fellowship and favored by ordinances requiring provincial clergymen to list all teaching openings with the government and afford *Lyceum* graduates the right of first refusal.[48] The curriculum also reflected Frederick's growing concern for the agrarian economy: Teacher trainees were routinely instructed in numerous agricultural techniques for dissemination in the countryside.

The *Lyceum* was clearly a positive step in the direction of public education and enlightenment. Its establishment also demonstrates that the landgrave was responsive to the problems of the Hessian hinterland despite the partiality and greater sensitivity he showed his residence. Of course, with its Königsstrasse address the *Lyceum* constituted yet one more institution centered in Cassel in the very shadow of Frederick's court. Moreover, with its modest enrollment of about a dozen teacher trainees, it hardly satisfied the needs of the hundreds of inadequately

---

[46]Payne, *Philosophes and the People*, 99–111; Chisick, *The Limits of Reform in the Enlightenment: Attitudes toward the Education of the Lower Classes in Eighteenth-Century France* (Princeton, 1981), 183, 238–40.

[47]StAMg, 5)16049: Frederician memorandum, 3 Apr. 1778 GR protocol.

[48]*HLO*, 991–6: Dec. 1779; Heinrich Theodor Kimpel, *Geschichte des hessischen Volksschulwesens* (Kassel, 1906), 329–32; W——, "Vom höheren Unterrichtswesen in Hessen unter Landgraf Friedrich II. (1760–1785)," *Hessenland*, 13 (1899), 202.

staffed country schools. The *Landtag* recognized this when it next met in 1785 and voted supplementary funds to boost enrollments. Yet no one disputed the government's decision not to open additional teacher seminaries in the countryside because everyone realized – as the *Lyceum*'s directors were obliged to admit – that the Hessian hinterland did not have the necessary instructional staff to "spread enlightenment among the lower classes."[49]

Of course, Frederick had no such excuse when it came to university education. To his credit he continued his earlier efforts "to create a better future" for the universities and approached the representatives of the *Landtag* for advice on how to revive them.[50] Nevertheless, neither Marburg nor Rinteln ever benefited from the high fiscal priority he afforded the *Collegium Carolinum*. Instead he concentrated on increasing his control over the university curriculum and strengthening the thrust of the "new learning" in the arts and sciences. This commitment surfaced in decrees directing the library to increase its purchase of "important works" in the natural sciences, and in a stern reminder that he would not tolerate faculty who rejected those "mathematical, pure philosophical, and historical sciences that have lifted us out of barbarism, that we have our current Enlightenment to thank for, and that we must instill in the hearts and souls of our young people."[51] Subsequent reforms regulated everything from the curriculum to faculty vacations and outside income and even led to the removal of Marburg's aged president following the discovery that he was ignoring new government guidelines.[52] In a move that paralleled his efforts in Cassel Frederick started two new medical journals at Marburg, as well as literary societies at each university expressly for the propagation of Enlightenment ideas.[53]

Unfortunately, what was missing from these initiatives was strong financial backing. The government funded almost no new appointments during the second half of the reign. There were now several more professors at the *Collegium Carolinum* than at Marburg, whose staff remained at seventeen. Notwithstanding progressive curriculum reforms that required medical students to take fourteen courses in the discipline,

[49]Kimpel, *Volksschulwesens*; Berge, "Friedrich II.," 240.
[50]StAMg, 5)7851: 2 Aug. 1776 resolution.
[51]StAMg, 5)7864: 22 Sept. 1775 resolution and rescript; Hermelink and Kaehler, *Philipps-Universität*, 420.
[52]HLO, 1063–6: 21 June 1782; StAMg, 5)8077: 1 Apr. 1783 Frederician memorandum and rescript; 5)7835: 28 Apr. 1783 Selchow proposal.
[53]Dersch, "Universität Marburg," 174; 5)8215: 23 Aug. 1774 rescript.

there remained only two faculty qualified to teach them. By contrast, the *Collegium Carolinum* had eighteen faculty qualified to teach medicine but not a single student enrolled in its medical program.[54] Nor was the library any better funded. Its holdings had more than tripled since 1768 from 5,000 to 18,000 volumes, but most of the increase stemmed from a single bequest of 8,000 books from the estate of a deceased faculty member. New purchases were still limited to the proceeds from the 3-taler fines levied on rowdy students, good for about 100 taler per year, as opposed to the *Collegium*'s 400-taler book budget, the unlimited spending for the 38,000-volume princely library housed in the Fridericianum, or Göttingen's 4,000-taler allowance for its 80,000-volume collection. A woeful shortage of books on science was complemented by an acute shortage of scientific instruments. Whereas Cassel's anatomical theater boasted Germany's finest collection, Marburg was without a single microscope. Indeed, long-standing requests from both Hessian universities for surgical equipment, an anatomical theater, and a botanical garden had gone unmet, even as they were being fulfilled fifty miles away.[55]

There is, of course, some question whether greater funding could have rescued either Hessian university from the stagnating enrollments that were a problem elsewhere in Germany. Certainly Rinteln's prospects of ever making a significant contribution had long since passed, as Fleckenbühl made clear when he dismissed one petition by asking, "How much money does the university bring into the country?" Nevertheless, Frederick refused to make the one move that promised to effectively minimize the enrollment crisis. In 1776 he did raise to three years the minimum residency requirement for all native university students.[56] Yet, in the previous year, Schlieffen had proposed the more radical step of transplanting both universities to Cassel, where they could be merged with the *Collegium Carolinum*, thereby forming a major institution of adequate size and facilities. The landgrave immediately embraced the idea, reflecting sanguinely on the competition it would give nearby Göttingen.[57] When he presented the plan at the next *Landtag* the deputies not only

[54]StAMg, 5)15444: "Über die Verbesserung des Collegii ... " [19 Jan. 1784].
[55]Hermelink and Kaehler, *Philipps-Universität*, 365, 417–18; Both and Vogel, *Friedrich II.*, 70; Dersch, "Universität Marburg," 185; StAMg, 5)7835: 28 Apr. 1783 Selchow proposal; Schormann, *Academia Ernestina*, 246–7, 250, 254.
[56]StAMg, 5)7783: 19 Nov. 1776 Actum Reg Cas.
[57]StAMg, 5)7851: "Gedancken um die Universität Marburg zu verlegen nacher Cassel" [1775].

gave their approval but even voted moving allowances for the university faculty. Nevertheless, the project foundered on Marburg's intense opposition. Although the landgrave promised to compensate it with a significantly larger garrison, the town fathers continued to fear the worst for the city's already stagnant economy. Meanwhile, the faculty and administration objected for a number of reasons, not the least of which was the negative effect Cassel's attractions and higher costs would have on the students themselves.[58]

Although the plan for a university at Cassel was now dead, the possibility of a merging of institutions resurfaced in 1784 – but with an important twist. Disgusted with tiny enrollments, the *Collegium Carolinum* faculty proposed its own transfer to Marburg. Indeed, when Frederick solicited the views of thirteen faculty members, all but one endorsed the idea, among them Stein, Sömmerring, Forster, and the philosopher Tiedemann, who complained that he had not seen a student in six months. Yet their *votae* went for naught. Two weeks later the landgrave vetoed the petition.[59] For Frederick the college's role was simply indispensable to the educational and cultural needs of his court and to the proper functioning of such institutions as the *Accouchir- und Findelhaus* and the recently completed *Charité* hospital. With his decision the interests of Cassel, its court, and its ruler had won out over those of the country as a whole.

In addition to patronage of the arts and education, Cassel ultimately served both as the focus and showplace for Frederick's advocacy of religious toleration. Once again the scope and success of the landgrave's initiatives were limited by existing structures and values, in this instance by the intent of the *Assekurationsakte* and the expectations of his subjects that he would act no differently than a Protestant prince. Such parameters were still readily apparent at midreign. Frederick's decision during 1770 to erect a Catholic church next to the Fridericianum for his personal use generated a certain uneasiness among the people of Cassel, even though he was careful to observe the conditions of the *Assekurationsakte* by giving it a simple interior and an inconspicuous facade. Nor did he allay

[58]StAMg, 5)7815: Hombergk to Schlieffen, 18 Oct. 1775; Dersch, "Universität Marburg," 170.
[59]StAMg, 5)2902: [13 Feb.] faculty votae, 27 Feb. 1784 resolution, 5)15444: 27 Feb. 1784 GR protocol.

these fears by suggesting to his ministers that a certain confessional sym-
metry might be gained by erecting Cassel's first synagogue on the other
side of the Fridericianum.[60] Muted murmurs of discontent were also
evident two years later when Cologne's Papal Nuncio visited the landgrave at his summer residence at Hofgeismar and when he briefly enter-
tained the notion of choosing a Catholic princess for his second
marriage.[61]

Yet times were changing, a fact that the landgrave himself celebrated
following the completion of his *Elizabethkirche* in November 1776. Although Frederick was already on his way to Italy at the time, he wor-
shipped there regularly following his return in April 1777. He postponed
the consecration seven months, however, until the first Sunday in November 1777 so that it would fall on the fourth anniversary of Frederick
the Great's consecration of Berlin's first Catholic church (itself the anniversary of Brandenburg's suppression of Roman Catholicism in 1539).
The landgrave never forgot that he was acting on a European stage – or
that his famous namesake was its greatest performer. It was testimony
to the growing toleration of his faith that many non-Catholics, including
the Calvinist landgravine, sometimes joined him at mass, if only to enjoy
the music played at high mass.[62]

The consecration of the *Elizabethkirche* afforded Frederick his greatest
opportunity to celebrate his and his country's emerging triumph over
religious intolerance. Indeed, during the closing years of the reign, he
began to acquire some latitude in giving expression to his own deeply
held feelings toward religious toleration. He never would have been able
to play even a limited role in confessional matters had he not first earned
the trust of his subjects over the first two decades of the reign. He also
benefited greatly, however, from the trends toward secularization, religious relativism, and toleration that became evident within the Hessian
elite during the course of the 1770s. Although men like Mauvillon and
Knigge were exceptional in the virulence of their attacks on Christianity,
the country's academics were in the forefront of these developments.
Marburg's theology faculty was already dominated by those who espoused the equal justification of the different Christian faiths; the the-

[60]Rudolf Hallo, "Kasseler Synagogengeschichte," in Hallo, ed., *Geschichte der jüdischen
Gemeinde Kassel* (Cassel, 1931), 21.
[61]HHStA, RK, KR 163: Bödiger to Benzel, 18 June 1772; Gustav Berthold Volz, "Prinzessin
Philippine von Schwedt," *Hohenzollern-Jahrbuch*, 15 (1911), 289.
[62]Günderode, *Briefe eines Reisenden*, 83–4.

gy professor Karl Wilhelm Robert, who was a leading force in Marburg's Masonic Lodge and the university's representative in the 1785 *Landtag*, even took the unusual step of switching to the philosophy faculty because of his deistic beliefs and greater interest in teaching Kantian philosophy. In Cassel, the country's chief censor and head of the faculty at the *Collegium Carolinum*, Wilhelm Johann Casparson, openly rejected the doctrine of original sin and human depravity.[63] Meanwhile, the *Hessische Beiträge* reflected the views of the *Collegium Carolinum* faculty by publishing a regular feature on toleration in Hesse-Cassel in which it praised individual instances of accommodation between the two Protestant faiths as a triumph of *Aufklärung* and Christian love, and expressed the "hope that these new instances of toleration – a hithero generally unknown phenomenon – will be received favorably within the land."[64] Frederick's ministers would not have permitted these developments had they not shared some of these convictions. Indeed the Consistory itself demonstrated that toleration was neither limited to the academic world nor reserved for Protestants when, beginning in 1774, it began to admit Catholic immigrants to Cassel and other towns, granting them guild membership and even *Bürgerrecht* providing they agreed to raise their children Protestant.[65] In the same year the Cassel *Regierung* mandated greater integration of Lutheran and Calvinist school children, declaring that "language and science are neither Reformed nor Lutheran."[66]

That the Hessian intelligentsia and regime were committed to change was most evident in their handling of the reactionary theologian J. R. A. Piderit (1720–91). Piderit's career was punctuated by a string of controversies that stemmed from his own intolerance of religious diversity and fervent opposition to the influence of Enlightenment ideas on Christianity. In 1751, as a professor of theology at Marburg, he penned treatises on indulgences and the keys to heaven that so angered the archbishop-elector of Mainz that Landgrave William VIII felt obliged to suppress them.[67] By 1766 he had become so outspoken in his opposition to the teaching of *Aufklärungstheologie* that he was transferred from Marburg to the

---

[63] Hermelink and Kaehler, *Philipps-Universität*, 406; Maurer, *Aufklärung*, 18–21; Strieder et al., *Gelehrten, Schriftsteller, und Künstler Geschichte*, 2: 134, 137.
[64] "Toleranzfälle aus dem casselischen Nieder-Hessen," *HB*, 2 (1785), 149–51, 526–7.
[65] StAMg, 5)10292, 10294–5.
[66] StAMg, 5)2846: 5 May 1774 Act Reg Cas; Berge, "Innenpolitik," 241.
[67] Koenig, "Althessische Silhouetten," 26–7.

Collegium Carolinum, where he was instantly ostracized by the rest of the college faculty. Within a year he had published two new tracts championing divine revelation, one of which bore the title "Whether the Christian Religion Is the Offspring of a Whore or the Daughter of Heaven Cannot Be Determined Through Human Reason Alone." These works so alienated the Consistory that he was removed from the college theology faculty and restricted to teaching philosophy and Eastern languages. In a college that permitted the military scientist Mauvillon to indulge in criticism of the country's religion, system of political economy, and closest ally, Piderit was told that he would be summarily dismissed if he published outside his new teaching fields.[68]

But Piderit was not to be stopped. In 1775 he dispatched another diatribe to the *Corpus Evangelicorum* that called for the suppression of the "Socinian and naturalist innovations" of men like Casparson before they destroyed Christianity. The college was deeply embarrassed by Piderit's latest effort and by his personal attack on Casparson, informing the Consistory that it "will win the *Collegium Carolinum* few accolades." For the moment the Consistory stopped short of removing Piderit, apparently because it feared that he would avenge himself by vilifying the college and Hessian university system in his future publications. Within a short time, however, the treatise had aroused such a storm of rebuke in the other Protestant states that Piderit felt compelled to publish and send a second, 168-page rebuttal to the *Corpus Evangelicorum*.[69] Although the Consistory now ordered his dismissal, Piderit saved himself one more time by appealing to Frederick on behalf of his large family. At the landgrave's request the Consistory relented, albeit with the understanding that the next time Piderit published he would not only perish, but land in prison.[70]

Frederick's intervention in the Piderit affair was, of course, only incidental. Nevertheless, by the end of the decade, he was able to capitalize not only on the growing acceptance of religious relativism and toleration within Hesse but also on the growing trend toward government control of public education. Thus he was ultimately able to exclude the Consistory from the *Collegium Carolinum* as well as from his own creations, the *Kadettenkorps* and *Lyceum Fridericianum*. Moreover, in instituting

---

[68]StAMg, 5)2633: 7 Apr. 1767 Consistory Resolution.
[69]StAMg, 5)2633: 11 Mar. 1775 college report, 17 Mar. 1775 GR protocol, 29 Aug. 1776 Act Cas Consistory, 20 Sept. resolution.
[70]StAMg, 5)2633: Piderit to Frederick 2, 7 Oct. 1776.

competency exams and giving precedence in school posts to *Lyceum* graduates, the landgrave successfully overrode the opposition of the provincial clergy.[71] He also used his influence to make several gestures on behalf of greater religious toleration. By 1781 he had opened all three institutions as well as the university at Marburg to Catholics. He also awarded Catholic cadets full religious observance at the *Kadettenkorps*, a privilege he also intended to grant in his plans for a multiconfessional girls' school.[72]

Even more remarkable, however, were those developments that did not meet the public eye. By 1780 the trust between Frederick and his ministers had grown to the point that he was regularly and actively participating in the resolution of such religious questions as the establishment of a Protestant *Fräuleinstift*, the admission of Catholic immigrants, and the Marburg theology faculty's publication rights for a new catechism. He also enjoyed sufficient freedom of action to recruit a colony of Mennonites, whom he valued for their "stoic, honorable, austere, and industrious nature," even though they did not conform to the state religion.[73] He was even able to overrule the Consistory when it attempted to suppress an article by Sömmerring that contradicted the biblical descent of blacks from the Moorish king.[74]

In the end the trend toward greater religious toleration and Frederick's own gradual integration into confessional policymaking did little to expand the rights of the country's most persecuted minority. To be sure Hesse's Jews made some gains during Frederick's reign. Although the ministry quickly rejected his suggestion of a synagogue on the Friedrichsplatz, it did permit him to offer Cassel's Jews a temple elsewhere in the city, even as it was ordering the expulsion of their coreligionists from the countryside. The 1770s also witnessed the admission of Jews to such institutions as the *Collegium Carolinum* and the university at Marburg. Indeed, by 1781 the Cassel *Regierung* was able to assure the landgrave that most property and educational restrictions had been repealed or were no longer enforced.[75]

[71]Kimpel, *Volksschulwesens*, 328, 331; [Merck], "Merkwürdigkeiten von Cassel," 217.
[72]StAMg, 17II)1159: 11 Oct. 1781 Gutachten Cas Reg; 4a)90,21: "Articles pour introduire …à Cassel" n.d. [1781?]; "Kadettenkorps," 386.
[73]StAMg, 5)13302: 24 Jan. 1782 rescript; 5)2633: Piderit to Frederick, 19 Feb. 1782.
[74]StAMg, 40)24 Cassel 52: Wittorf to Frederick, 11 Sept. 1780, 17II)420: 8 Aug. 1782 Pfeiffer petition; 5)10292; Schelenz, "Collegium Carolinum," 79; Heinemann, "Blütezeit der Medizin," 90–1.
[75]StAMg, 17II)1159: 11 Oct. 1781 Gutachten Cas Reg.

Nevertheless, meaningful change was unlikely so long as the ruling and academic elite were convinced that the Jews' intrinsic character posed a threat to the livelihood and welfare of the Christian population. Hence the government remained committed to the retention of trade restrictions in order to protect the guilds and Christian peasantry. Even the heightened consciousness aroused by Lessing's *Nathan der Weise* (1779), Dohm's *Über die bürgerliche Verbesserung der Juden* (1781), and Joseph II's Toleration Patent (1781) had only a limited impact on events in Cassel. Writing in the *Hessische Beiträge*, Professor Runde accepted the argument of the recently departed Dohm that only the removal of all forms of persecution could correct the Jews' "depraved national character" and enable them to become "better people and more useful citizens."[76] Nevertheless, Georg Forster likely spoke for the majority of Dohm's former colleagues at the *Collegium Carolinum* in welcoming his notion of reform through integration, but expressing the doubt that there were currently any good Jews like Nathan the Wise.[77] Nor did Frederick receive any encouragement from the Cassel *Regierung* when he suggested that they emulate the emperor by eliminating all remaining Jewish dress, residency, legal, and property restrictions so that "by their labor they will become useful to the state."[78] Notwithstanding the attractiveness of Frederick's goal, the fact remained that here, as elsewhere, public gestures and declarations on behalf of the highest ideals could make only limited headway in the face of existing circumstances, institutions, and values.

[76]Runde, "Verbesserung der Juden," 57–65.
[77]Gordon, "Georg Forster und die Juden," 240–1, 253.
[78]StAMg, 17II)1159: 22 Sept. 1781 resolution.

7

The final years

The American enterprise had afforded Frederick the luxury of indulging his passions for the military and for the patronage of the artistic and intellectual life of his residence. Yet, despite the glitter of Cassel and the British gold that helped build it, a host of economic and social problems remained. Some of the latest difficulties stemmed from the economic dislocation of the war in America and from a recurrence of poor weather and subsequent crop failures. For the most part, however, the Frederician regime spent its last years addressing the residual, unresolved problems of the previous two decades, many of which had been aggravated by those government ordinances that had attempted to deal with them. With the war coming to an end, the government now introduced a final flurry of domestic initiatives, publishing over 250 new ordinances over the last four years of the reign.

As had been the case during previous crises, new developments and past failures in domestic reform prompted the regime to revise its assumptions and adopt new strategies. Above all the ministry had come to realize that further commercial-industrial expansion was limited by the existence of inflexible economic structures. Its disillusionment was already becoming evident as far back as 1775, when the General Directory convened to discuss the future of its industrial policy. The assembled ministers went far beyond their long-standing opposition to monopolies by expressing their growing dissatisfaction with the government's commercial projects and their theoretical acceptance of the principle of free trade. It was a measure of their change in direction that one minister could proclaim confidently "that freedom is the life and soul of commerce is an all-too-well-known truth to have to discuss here."[1]

At the same time, however, they acknowledged that free trade was

[1] StAMg, 5)13443: 2 Jan. Schlieffen report, 7 Jan. Bose, Rosey, 9 Jan. 1775 Wittorf votae.

impossible to attain in the existing environment. The tariff walls of the German states posed the most insurmountable obstacle by denying Hessian access to other markets, while failing to protect native industries adequately against the illegal importation of foreign products across its own porous frontier. Even without trade barriers they saw no way of overcoming the lead other German states enjoyed in creating superior products, or of compensating for the lack of skilled native workers who could make them and consumers with money enough to purchase them. Wittorf summed up the general disillusionment with the idea that the government could create a commercial-industrial base, complaining, "How can we convert and refine our raw materials when we have neither skilled nor well-to-do subjects? We no longer live in a time when hard work and industriousness [alone] stand to gain much."[2]

Not even the sudden stimulus provided by the war in America could divert the ministry from its judgment that there were definite limits to what it could accomplish for the country's urban economy. As the opposing armies converged for their final encounter at Yorktown the regime was, in fact, sifting through a rash of personal tragedies that were linked to the continuing difficulties of its state-supported industries. During 1781 it was necessary to grant an emergency loan to one entrepreneur to prevent his creditors from seizing his house and evicting his family.[3] It was not so lenient with a second entrepreneur, a clothing manufacturer named Scharff, whom it had earlier pressured into expanding his operations to manufacture uniforms for the army in America. When the uniforms proved too shoddy to use, he was fired and died destitute soon thereafter. Scharff's death came amidst a number of suicides by government-subsidized entrepreneurs. Among them, the cotton manufacturer Benedikt Niggeler had run the largest and most expensive state-subsidized mill but took his own life in 1783 after repeated government loans had failed to save him from his creditors. Following his death the government needed two years and a promise of additional subsidies before anyone would agree to take over the mill.[4] Yet the most sensational demise was that of Johann Jacob Uckermann, the architect of Frederick's mercantile system, who had assured the landgrave at the start of the reign that

[2]StAMg, 5)13443: 2 Jan. Schlieffen report, 7 Jan. Rosey, 9 Jan. Wittorf, 17 Jan. Wille votae.
[3]StAMg, 5)3016: 30 Oct. 1781 KDK report.
[4]Dascher, *Textilgewerbe*, 60, 62–3, 92; StAMg, 5)6146: 25 Oct. 1784 KDK report; 5)6146: 1 Apr. 1785 GD protocol.

commerce and industry would "make the country rich and populous" but who now stood 500,000 taler in debt.[5] Charged with having swindled his associates, he died mysteriously during 1781 after having been kidnapped by his creditors.

The catharsis within the ministry was now complete. With the war and the economic boom it had created winding to a close, it was inclined to support only established industries that had already proved that they could overcome the obstacles to commercial success. Notwithstanding the fate of men like Scharff and Niggeler, it was still willing to assist the textile enterprises, but imported "luxury" industries were now viewed with more suspicion than ever. This view was especially evident in the War and Domains Board's rejection of a petition by a Strasbourg entrepreneur named Ferrier who was seeking 100,000 taler to start an international trade center in Cassel. In its final report the board roundly criticized state-supported enterprises and monopolies, arguing that they compelled the taxpaying poor to support decadent "foreign luxuries" that were good "only for ostentation and amusement, rather than for [satisfying] hunger and thirst." Citing such examples as Sweden, Brunswick, and Fulda, it pointed out that many states had foolishly launched projects unsuitable for their own circumstances, thereby wasting valuable resources that could have been more wisely spent on native industries or in the development of agriculture.[6]

For the rest of the reign the War and Domains Board operated under the conviction that the few successes wrought by government subsidies had been easily outweighed by the huge amounts of money "wasted" in subsidizing unprofitable operations. It was a measure of both its skepticism and its determination to stem the flow of red ink that it now undertook to review all new petitions with the "utmost caution." By 1782 it had devised definite procedures that examined not only each petitioner's experience and expertise but also his ability to muster sufficient capital to make his enterprise work. For the first time it favored natives over foreigners, who were now also expected to demonstrate that they intended to settle permanently in Hesse-Cassel.[7]

To a certain extent the Board was also motivated by its longtime concern to preserve current revenue sources. Thus when the Cassel theater

---

[5]StAMg, 5)737: Uckermann to Frederick, 18 Mar. 1766.
[6]StAMg, 5)3481: 27 Sept. 1781 KDK report.
[7]StAMg, 5)6082: "Berichte des Commerz-Kollegiums ... 1782–1784"; 5)2703: 26 Sept. 1785 KDK report.

inspector, Moretti, proposed building a chandelier factory at Weissenstein, it delayed his petition for eight months in order to study the operation's likely effects on revenue from import tariffs on chandeliers.[8] Similarly, when the Commerce College urged it to relax the 50 percent duty on coffee because of its depressing effect on the Cassel fair, the Board refused, arguing that it could not afford to lose the 15,000 taler in revenue. The Commerce College could hardly have been surprised by its refusal, having already noted in its petition that "it is well known how reluctant the *Kammerkasse* is to lose revenue."[9]

Nevertheless, despite their own disillusionment and declarations against previous mercantile policy, both the War and Domains Board and the ministry as a whole were unwilling to abandon completely the previous course. They remained committed to the already large numbers of established entrepreneurs whose concerns were facing collapse. So long as these men continued to apply themselves they were generally able to renew their privileges and receive additional funds in order to preserve existing levels of employment and production against foreign imports. A case in point was the state porcelain factory, which had increased sales dramatically with its new American markets but was still operating at only 40 percent of the volume needed to break even. Time and again the government decided to shut the operation down, only to reverse itself on the eve of the closing.[10]

Part of the reason for the government's indecision was Frederick's own reluctance to give up hope, both because he was more optimistic about the long-term prospects of government-subsidized industrial development and because he was less concerned about the losses they incurred against his enormous wealth. He continued to invest heavily in new textile enterprises, approving at least forty-two out of forty-five petitions submitted during the last decade of the reign.[11] In addition he usually approved the proposals of those few entrepreneurs who had successfully completed previous projects and was equally forthcoming to those petitioners who could obtain the backing of court figures. The successes of other governments also continued to inspire imitation, as they had throughout his reign. Following a trip to Paris in 1781 he and Luchet advocated the introduction of a French-style tobacco monopoly, arguing that it would

[8]StAMg, 5)6152: 9 Feb. KDK report, 20 Feb. resolution, 8 Oct. 1784 GD protocol.
[9]StAMg, 5)4039: 18 Nov. 1783 Comm Coll report, Nov. 1783 KDK report.
[10]Ducret, *Porzellanmanufaktur*, 157, 187–8, 217.
[11]Dascher, *Textilgewerbe*, 188–231; StAMg, 5)3424, 5)6347.

generate considerable employment for Cassel and revenue for the state. They even promised Ferrier 100,000 taler to head the project just eleven months after denying him the same amount of money for a trade center.[12] Yet, at least in this instance, the War and Domains Board was able to dissuade the landgrave by warning that the creation of a tobacco monopoly would violate a long-standing pledge to the diet, while actually reducing state revenue.[13]

Of course, if the price was right even the War and Domains Board could be seduced into supporting a new entrepreneur. Thus it put aside its previous concern for the morally corrupting and economically debilitating influence of chocolate by establishing a hot chocolate factory, having been assured by the petitioner that his product was so good that people would purchase the government's product instead of the smuggled chocolate being consumed throughout the country. As the government's latest industrial enterprise, it was immediately favored with a total ban on the import of foreign chocolates, one of a dozen protective bans or tariffs instituted during 1783–4 to nurture the country's new or foundering industries.[14]

Though the government was unable to bring itself to discontinue its industrial policy, its growing disillusionment had paved the way for its acceptance of agriculture as the primary source of the country's wealth. Admittedly the evolution in its position stemmed principally from its own difficulties with industrial policy and with the crop failures of the past decade. Its stance was reinforced, however, by the growing acceptance of Physiocratic thought throughout Germany in the aftermath of the great subsistence crisis of the early 1770s.

The signs of its triumph were especially evident in Hessian academic circles. For his part, Mauvillon played a major role in introducing Physiocratic ideas, first by translating Turgot and Raynal into German, then by promoting wider discussion with his own *Sammlung von Aufsätzen* during 1776–7. As he had hoped, his good friend Dohm responded to the challenge with an essay of his own in which he disputed the Physiocratic assertion that all wealth stemmed from agriculture. What followed

---

[12]StAMg, 5)1582: "Extrait du Journal de Paris ..." [1781], 5)3481: 5 Aug. 1782 KDK report; 5)3678: 26 Feb. 1785 KDK report.
[13]StAMg, 5)3678: "Raisons qui s'opposent a l'Etablissement de l'administration de la France pour le tabac dans la Hesse" [18 Nov. 1784], 18 Oct. 1784, 26 Feb. 1785 KDK reports, 28 Nov. 1784 Comm Coll report, 4 Mar. 1785 resolution.
[14]StAMg, 5)6315: 7 July 1783 Comm Coll report; *HLO*, 1125–6: 7 Aug. 1783.

was Germany's most celebrated debate between the virtues of commercial-industrial mercantilism and Physiocracy, one that consumed the interest of the entire German press but remained focused in Hesse-Cassel after the appearance of Rinteln Professor Karl Gottfried Fürstenau's *Apologie des physiokratischen Systems* (1779) and Mauvillon's better-known *Physiokratische Briefe an den Herrn Professor Dohm* (1780). Actually, despite his defense of trade and industry, even Dohm remained an advocate of agrarian development, having only recently urged Frederick to give all government officials formal instruction in agricultural methods.[15]

Meanwhile his colleagues at the *Hessische Beiträge* and the Agrarian Society responded by sponsoring a spate of new articles that reflected the heightened profile agriculture had assumed in Germany's journal literature. Some followed the growing trend to employ scientific methods, such as one prize essay that established the maximum number of days the average peasant could afford to perform *Dienst* (36) by calculating exactly how many days would be consumed by winter and bad weather (141), the performance of various chores (94.5), and actual work on his crops (93.5). Virtually all focused on the need to eliminate obligatory labor service, which was blamed for everything from the peasantry's lack of enlightenment to lagging agricultural productivity. It was in keeping with their judgment that the Agrarian Society informed the government during 1782 that Hessian agricultural productivity would never improve significantly unless manorial obligations were eliminated.[16]

By then the government was in total agreement that something had to be done. Although the landgrave and many private *Grundherrn* had already replaced obligatory labor service with wage labor, it was still being performed in many communities. To its dismay the War and Domains Board had also learned during the previous year that many laws and regulations designed to remove the worst abuses of labor service were being ignored locally. By 1783 a series of visitations and detailed reports from each of the *Landräte* had laid bare the extensiveness of the abuses. Though Frederick had tightly restricted *Wald- und Jagddienst*

---

[15]StAMg, 5)13302: 20 Feb. 1778 report. For more on the debate, see Hoffmann, *Mauvillon*, 64, 124, 178, 187–8; Folkert Hensmann, *Staat und Absolutismus im Denken der Physiokraten* (Frankfurt, 1976), 289.

[16]"Vertheilung der Bauergüter," 443–5; Fürstenau, "Verwandlung der Domänen," 503–6, 513–16; Lerch, *Hessische Agrargeschichte*, 156; Gerland, *Gesellschaft für Ackerbau*, 262.

two decades ago, they were still being levied indiscriminately, sometimes consuming three to four days of labor in a given week. Peasants were still being called away from their own sowing and harvesting in order to perform labor service ten years after the practice had been outlawed. In some instances labor service obligations had actually increased, in some cases to as much as six days per week.[17]

Nor were the peasants cheerfully accepting these burdens. The village of Caldern reported in 1781 that its peasants were trying "every way possible" not just to reduce their labor service obligations but to eliminate them totally. One *Landrat* estimated that at least 200 cases of *Handdienst* were being litigated before the courts of his district and that each instance in which a peasant won an exemption from labor service only made those who were still *dienstpflichtig* more unhappy.[18]

Once it had learned the extent of its failure to ameliorate the abuses of labor service, the government considered whether to eliminate it altogether. During the summer of 1783 it conferred with the *Landräte* over possible solutions. Though these ten men were themselves major landowners in their districts, they were generally enthusiastic about the prospects of eliminating labor service altogether. *Landrat* Johann Carl von Stockhausen, whose exposition of labor service abuses in the Diemel Valley had filled five separate reports totaling sixty-two pages, spoke for the whole in stating that "the burden of all the labor services levied on the general peasantry is all too great" and advocating their abolition. Eight of the ten endorsed a project first put forward in 1776 by the prominent *Landrat* and *Landtag* deputy Friedrich Moritz von Schenck zu Schweinsberg that called for the commutation of labor service into a money payment, with the landlord then hiring the peasant as a free laborer. Some of the *Landräte* had, in fact, already supervised the voluntary conversion of some labor services to the point of lending government funds to peasants in order to help them commute their obligations. Yet they made it clear that they were too weak and isolated to carry on the work without the benefit of a "basic and comprehensively executed project to convert labor service into cash."[19]

[17]StAMg, 17e) Caldern 26: [Aug. 1781] petition, 40)7 Generalia 43: 15 Aug., 10 Sept. 1782, 2 Mar. 1783 visitation protocols, *Landräte* reports, June–Aug. 1783; 5)13446: 15 Jan. 1784 Motz report.
[18]StAMg, 17e) Allna 16: 10 June 1777, 17e) Caldern 26: 4 Sept. 1781 Schenck reports.
[19]StAMg, 40)7 Generalia 43: 20 Aug. 1783 Stockhausen, 4 Mar. 1784 Baumbach reports, 340) Stockhausen 75: Mar. 1784 Pappenheim/Stockhausen reports.

In justifying their recommendation they reiterated the standard view that labor service depressed peasant living standards and that conversion would make up for any financial losses incurred by the nobility by increasing overall productivity on demesne lands. Indeed, while no one was likely to dispute Schenck's own description of commutation "as the best fate the subjects can have," there was considerably more comfort to be derived from the prediction of one *Landrat* that it would "be equally advantageous for both the landlord and subject."[20]

They did not, however, claim that it would be easy to implement. Although he heartily endorsed conversion, the Fulda Valley *Landrat* Wilhelm Ludwig von Baumbach predicted that everyone would have to work "from morning to night" to ensure an orderly and fair conversion of labor service.[21] The Werra Valley *Landrat* and two-time *Landtag* deputy Wilhelm Friedrich von Keudell was even less sanguine, predicting opposition from Landgrave Constantin of Hesse-Rotenburg, many of whose estates were located in his district. For this reason he became the sole *Landrat* actually to reject cash conversion in favor of an alternative proposal that Schenck had made during 1779 that retained labor service but divided it up more equitably among the peasantry, thereby minimizing the actual physical burden as well as the intense jealousies that arose between those who were exempt and those who were *dienstpflichtig*.[22]

Keudell filed his recommendation with the War and Domains Board in July 1784, the last of the ten *Landräte* to do so. Yet, once it had studied the legal obstacles involved in decreeing *Dienst* reform in the *Quart*, the board accepted his proposal.[23] The government had chosen the relative safety of a conservative half step to a more aggressive initiative that might arouse internal opposition. Only the strong reaction of Baumbach saved the conversion scheme, mainly by pointing out that Keudell's proposal was itself "thoroughly infeasible" since it would require a new *Dienstregister* that would incur not only the opposition of Landgrave Constantin's officials but also the hostility of all those peasants throughout Hesse-Cassel who had previously been *dienstfrei*. Instead he successfully urged the board to commission a pilot conversion project, arguing that this would not violate Constantin's autonomy and would be welcomed by his officials, who Baumbach pointed out were equally

---

[20] StAMg, 40)7 Generalia 43: 30 June Schenck, 26 July 1783 Eschwege reports.
[21] StAMg, 24 Apr. 1783 Baumbach report.
[22] StAMg, 1 July 1784 Biesenrodt report.
[23] StAMg, 40)7 Generalia 43: 25 Sept. 1784 Kleinhans report; 3 Aug. 1784 KDK resolution.

dissatisfied with the oppressiveness of labor service. By the beginning of 1785 a limited conversion program had been set up in the Diemel Valley.[24] After more than two decades of *Dienst* reform the regime was inching ever closer to its final abolition but still had not taken the final step.

If the government was dissatisfied with its previous policies and the current performance of the Hessian economy, it had also become disillusioned with its decade-old program of poor relief. To be sure the *Wochensteuer* had proved at least a qualified success. Financial support for the *Armenkasse* and welfare institutions had grown significantly, doubling in Cassel itself. Unfortunately the number of people in need of assistance had increased as well. Despite the employment of indigent workers during the building boom, Cassel's poor rolls had actually continued to creep up from the height of the famine, reaching a high of 845 in 1785. Admittedly part of the problem may have been Cassel's increasing attractiveness to immigrants in the wake of the Anglo-Hessian Convention and the employment prospects offered by the landgrave's building projects. In addition, the tapering off of construction in the late 1770s may have returned a large number of people to the poor rolls. At 4–5 percent of the overall population, Cassel's poor rolls were, in any event, smaller than those of other major cities such as Hamburg (10 percent), Munich (11 percent), Berlin (15 percent), or Cologne (25 percent).[25] Nevertheless, the sight of "mobs of beggars" going from door to door in an otherwise beautiful and prosperous city distressed the landgrave, who had assumed that the poor-relief system had resolved the problem. It also caught the attention of foreign travelers like Günderode, whose otherwise positive account of the city took note of the large number of beggars amid the splendor of their surroundings.[26] It is not unlikely that Frederick's remonstrances before the *Polizeikommission* during 1782 about the failure of the newly created *Quartierkommissare* were partly influenced by his embarrassment at reading Günderode's recently published book.[27]

A decade earlier the government had blamed the epidemic of beggars on the agrarian crisis and the niggardliness of Cassel's burghers. The

---

[24]StAMg, 40)7 Generalia 43: 3 Jan. Baumbach report, KDK to Kriegs Coll, 15 Jan., 26 Sept. 1785 extract, 4 Mar. 1786 KDK report.
[25]Uhlhorn, *Christliche Liebesthätigkeit*, 3: 279.
[26]Petersdorff, "Aufzeichnungen des badischen Stadtvikarius Rinck über seine Studienreise in den Jahren 1783 und 1784," *Mitt* (1896); Günderode, *Briefe eines Reisenden*, 45.
[27]StAMg, 5)1088: 18 Dec. 1782 Pol Comm report.

Wochensteuer and Cassel's new prosperity had presumably removed both of these causes. Now it was convinced that the real problem was that the poor were abusing the system of relief. Published studies of the beggary problem by Casparson and others indicated that as many as 90 percent of the people on the poor rolls were actually capable of working but had opted to live off the public dole instead. At least one study also charged that many of these *Müssiggänger* supplemented public relief both by collecting alms from autonomous private charities and by going door to door as beggars.[28]

At Casparson's urging, the government initiated two corrective measures. First it instituted a three-tiered system of poor relief similar to one that had been used in Schmalkalden over the past fifteen years.[29] Although it awarded full support to those indigent who were truly disabled and half pension to the partly disabled, it required all other poor people to work. For that purpose the government now established an *Arbeitshaus* to teach its inmates a trade and instill in them the work ethic necessary to escape the poor rolls. In Casparson's view the new system promised "to afford sympathy to the deserving and to help those who need the education, opportunity or energy to begin work."[30] In short, it represented the perfect compromise between the government's competing desires to help the needy, while redirecting everyone else off the public dole and toward a productive life. Modeled after the workhouse in nearby Fulda, the government's latest solution to the city's chronic poverty was operating by the end of 1784 and housed about 200 inmates.[31]

The government's disillusionment with the abuse of its decade-old system of public welfare extended beyond the poor rolls into the increasingly crowded corridors of the *Accouchir- und Findelhaus*. Here too it had hoped that the *Wochensteuer* and the other reforms of the previous decade would meet the facility's future needs. In 1777 Frederick had even moved it to a bigger and more attractive building that he termed the "gem of its neighborhood" on the right bank of the Fulda. The facility's

---

[28]B——, "Ueber einige Hindernisse, welche einer gänzlichen zwekmäsigen Armen-Verpflegung in teutschen Hauptstädten noch im Wege stehen mögten, und über Mittel sie zu heben," *HB* 2 (1785), 680–2; Casparson, *Abhandlung von der Verhütung des Bettelns in einer Haupt- und Residenzstadt* (Cassel, 1783).

[29]*HLO*, 434–6: 27 May 1767.

[30]StAMg, 5)1088: 17 June 1783 Pol Comm report.

[31]StAMg, 5)1088: 21 Feb. 1783 resolution, 17 June 1783 Pol Comm report; Eckel, "Kasseler Werkhaus." The Police Commission had actually been studying the possibility of a workhouse as early as 1774, following the establishment of one in Berlin. StAMg, 5)13461: 19 Aug. 1774 report.

growing popularity had, however, quickly rendered both its share of the *Wochensteuer* and its larger accommodations inadequate.[32] Within a year the *Accouchirhaus* had become so overcrowded that Stein was compelled to entrust the overload to three black market operations that were run for profit by Cassel housewives without benefit of adequate facilities or trained midwives.[33] By these and other means Stein and his staff of nine midwives had managed to hold mortality at the *Accouchirhaus* to under 2 percent of mothers and about 9 percent of newborns, despite an increase from 100 boarders in 1770 to 237 a decade later. As had been the case in the past, the *Findelhaus* had been less fortunate. In 1781 a government study indicated that only a third of its foundlings lived long enough to move on to the equally overcrowded orphanage.[34] Although the government regularly advanced emergency funds and food and even transferred some newborns to rental housing, one official was probably right when he observed that "the only way this [foundling] home ever keeps from going under is that the children keep dying and fewer wet nurses are needed."[35]

The government was, of course, not primarily responsible for the high mortality rates at the *Findelhaus*. Many of the foundlings were already seriously ill or undernourished before they were deposited in its turnstile. Nor was it at fault for the chronic overcrowding. In addition to the hard economic realities that normally obtained in Hesse-Cassel, the facility had been caught in a dramatic, Europe-wide surge in illegitimate births during the second half of the century. In fact, the biggest problem it confronted was its own success in meeting society's needs, success that prompted the abuse of its services by the people it helped. According to Stein, many unwed mothers actually returned to the *Accouchirhaus* two or three times instead of learning from their first mistake. Since their own governments offered no such facility, wayward girls from neighboring states also availed themselves of its offer of free and anonymous care – with one Hanoverian girl making the trip to Cassel no fewer than seven times.[36] Furthermore, married couples who were either unable or unwilling to care for their youngest children began dropping off their one-

[32] StAMg, 5)10846: 3 Sept. 1781 KDK report, 5)13618: 3 June 1774 rescript, Motz to Frederick, 22 Apr. 1782.
[33] StAMg, 5)1213: 19 May 1779 Pol Comm report.
[34] Stein, "Waisenhaus in Kassel," 102, 111–12, 117–18.
[35] StAMg, 5)10852: 27 Apr. 1774 pro memoria, 40)24 Cassel 52–3: 7 Dec. 1781 GD protocol.
[36] Stein, "Waisenhaus in Kassel," 109, 112; StAMg, 5)1213: 27 Apr. 1779 KDK report.

and two-year-olds, literally stuffing them into a turnstile designed to accommodate only newborns.[37]

Although some parents returned to pick up their children once their situation or resolve had improved, the government was understandably disturbed by these and other abuses. Originally intended to save lives, the *Findelhaus* was unwittingly increasing the number of orphaned children by affording irresponsible parents an easy alternative to child care; given the home's high mortality rate, it was very possibly decreasing the likelihood that they would survive infancy. To forestall these abuses the government was compelled to sacrifice the anonymity that had helped make the facility so popular. The turnstile at the foundling home initially was locked after dark and ultimately was closed down altogether. In addition, unwed mothers were made to present an *Ausweis* from their local authorities proving that they were both Hessian and indigent, and the officials themselves were admonished to use the utmost care in certifying that girls were truly poor because "almost all pregnant girls want to deliver at our expense."[38]

The government's continuing difficulties with its economic and welfare programs afford some indication of the uneven success of its domestic policies. Its active concern had clearly helped the country recover from the devastation of the Seven Years' War and the crop failures of the preceding decade. Yet after a quarter century of devising new programs and strategies to promote wealth and protect living standards, the Frederician regime was still groping for better ways of achieving its goals. The perceptions prevalent at the close of the reign were as pessimistic as at any time since Frederick's succession.

With the conclusion of peace in America the urban economy had quickly slipped back into the economic doldrums from which the war had rescued it. Military orders had returned to their more modest prewar levels and the Carlshafen Company's illicit trade with America had trailed off considerably in the wake of renewed Dutch and domestic American competition. By 1784, 65 of Eschwege's 114 textile guild masters were again without work.[39] As he looked to the horizon one official was already

---

[37]StAMg, 5)10847: 29 Jan. 1765 GR protocol; Günderode, *Briefe eines Reisenden*, 134. Once again both the London and Paris homes experienced the same problem of married parents dropping off their unwanted children. See Delasselle, "Abandoned Children," 73; Hoffer and Hull, *Murdering Mothers*, 140.

[38]*HLO*, 1051–2: 4 Mar. 1782.

[39]Dascher, "Karlshafen," 250, and *Textilgewerbe*, 121.

predicting further losses as New England's textile makers attempted to penetrate European markets without the burden of British mercantile regulations.[40] By the beginning of 1785 the country's merchants were reporting that trade was decreasing "day by day." When Frederick's last diet convened that autumn, the deputies decried the "steep decline" of the urban economy, the towns declaring that "it is apparent that Hessian commerce is currently of no special significance and that the residence is particularly depressed." Despite having registered steady gains over the past decade, the Cassel fairs were still attracting only a small number of foreign merchants, reflecting the government's failure to find foreign markets for Hessian goods.[41]

The picture in the countryside was only marginally better. Although the conclusion of peace had returned thousands of peasant soldiers to the land, it had also brought the restoration of the full Contribution in May 1784.[42] Moreover, after several good harvests at the beginning of the decade, unfavorable weather had led to back-to-back crop failures in 1784 and 1785. Distressed officials reported that peasants were once again in danger of being forced into bankruptcy and onto the poor rolls. So many began resorting to brigandage that the government was soon compelled to employ cavalry patrols along the country's highways.[43] Conditions were especially bad in the Diemel Valley, where peasants who had for years dreaded the approach of government officials lest they demand tax payments now welcomed them with open arms in the hope that they might have something to *give* them. With peasants selling off their household goods to pay their debts, several crown officials urged the regime to restore the halved contribution and even to extend the urban system of poor relief to the countryside.[44] The estates were quick to second both requests, claiming that begging had become "so great that every other person has his hand out."[45]

To meet the latest crisis the War and Domains Board acted with its customary haste, instructing the *Landräte* to forgive all uncollectible

[40]StAMg, 5)13446: 15 Jan. 1784 Motz report.

[41]StAMg, 73)273: "Desiderium commune 1mum"; 5)3678: 26 Feb. 1785 KDK report, 5)14744: "Desiderium Speciale," 10 Dec. 1785.

[42]StAMg, 40)7 Generalia 43: 3 Jan. Baumbach report, KDK to Kriegs Coll, 15 Jan., 26 Sept. 1785 extract, 4 Mar. 1786 KDK report.

[43]*Neue Bemerkungen*, 3: 59.

[44]StAMg, 5)13446: 15 Jan. 1784 Motz report, 340) Stockhausen 75: Mar. 1784 Stock-hausen/Pappenheim report.

[45]StAMg, 5)14746: "Desiderium commune XXXIIdum" [n.d.]; 304)580: 21 Feb. 1786 petition.

taxes, plus 50 percent of those arrears that it deemed collectible. It also approved their request to pay off the debts of peasants who were threatened with bankruptcy, with the sole stipulation that assistance be extended only to "responsible" peasants who might benefit from a second chance. It refused, however, to restore the halved Contribution. Drawing from its wartime experience with the tax cut of 1776, the board justified its refusal with the observation that "the subjects seldom benefit by such a remission of taxes. More often they become less able to pay their taxes, having for the most part become accustomed to an easier life-style that they are reluctant to give up thereafter."[46]

Enlightened absolutism under Frederick II: the balance sheet

What had gone wrong? After a quarter of a century of its constant attention, during which it benefited from the cooperation and assistance of the estates and its own awesome financial resources, the government still found itself in a state of flux, continually altering its strategies, and reacting to the latest crisis rather than preempting it with effective programs. To a great extent it was the victim of structural factors beyond its control. Despite some limited successes its remedial efforts on behalf of industry were doomed to failure by a lack of consumer spending that stemmed from the country's endemic poverty, by commercial inexperience that invariably begot inferior goods, by the chronically poor roads of the country's hilly terrain, and by Germany's confusing multitude of competing states, debased currencies, and trade barriers. Notwithstanding all its attempts and initial optimism, Hesse-Cassel was fated to be an essentially agrarian society, at least in the eighteenth century, if not the twentieth.

The government's record in agriculture had, in fact, been more positive. Its initiatives had been instrumental in boosting agricultural productivity and in hastening the country's recovery from the Seven Years' War and the crop failures of 1770–1. Yet the Hessian countryside was also constrained by inflexible realities that limited economic expansion: the vested interests of *Grundherrn* whose own fragile circumstances were also a source of concern to the government, the resistance to change of a stubbornly traditional and ignorant peasantry, the excess of people and dearth

---

[46]StAMg, 5)2703: 26 Sept. 1785 KDK report.

of arable land. Indeed, over the course of the reign increased agricultural
output sustained a remarkable 40 percent population increase that simply
consumed these gains and exacerbated the country's land shortage.[47]

In addition to these structural limits was the government's own failure
to foresee or measure correctly all the consequences of its own initiatives.
Despite the most careful planning and consideration, many seemingly
innocuous reforms boomeranged on the regime and the people it was
trying to assist, often bringing unwelcome side effects that intensified the
problem it sought to correct. After a quarter century of unpleasant sur-
prises, this had become evident both to Frederick's own officials and to
the deputies of the Hessian *Landtag*. In describing peasant hardships in
the Diemel Valley at the beginning of 1784, the *Polizeikommissar* L. G.
Motz offered a review of the government's record that constitutes a
stinging critique of its own counterproductive measures, including peasant legal aid, staple price controls, the *Hufen-Edikt*, the four-year debt
moratorium, the American expedition, and such industrial policies as
monopolies and textile concessions.[48] In another report the new finance
minister Fleckenbühl condemned the tax farming system that, in a decade
of mismanagement, had duplicated all the abuses of the Prussian *Régie*
without yielding any of its fiscal advantages.[49]

The estates had a long list of their own when they convened in September 1785. Though conceding that many problems stemmed from
unfavorable circumstances such as trade barriers and poor weather, the
deputies declared that despite Frederick's "best intentions . . . some of his
programs have not only failed to have the desired effect but, as experience
has shown, have considerably worsened the problem."[50] In addition to
abolishing the Hessian *Régie*, they now sought the repeal of many of the
government's commercial regulations, concessions, and incentives, as well
as Cassel's *Zahlenlotto* and even its system of *Landräte* and *Commis-*

[47]This estimate assumes an immediate postwar population base of 275,000, against hard
figures of 382,797 in 1781 and 393,472 in 1789. StAMg, 5)10597: "Menschen und
Viehverzeichnis de anno 1781"; Hildebrand, *Statistische Mitteilungen*, 1.
[48]Writing on the eve of the 1784 crop failure, Motz warned of the effect that the staple
price controls instituted after the famine were having on peasant living standards, agricultural production, and ultimately, on state tax revenue derived from agriculture. In a
pitch for free trade he urged the government to follow the lead of Grand Duke Peter
Leopold of Tuscany in freeing the grain trade and increasing granary storage capacity in
order to enable peasants to store their grain in times of plenty in expectation of better
prices. StAMg, 5)13446: 15 Jan. 1784 Motz report.
[49]StAMg, 5)13462: "Ohnmassgebliche Gedancken über die Verpachtungen . . ." [1784].
[50]StAMg, 73)273: "Desiderium commune 1mum."

sarius Loci.[51] Nor was that all. It was fitting that, in a government where the estates participated in the drafting of new projects, they should bear their share of the responsibility for the missteps of the past two decades by seeking the repeal of several ordinances of their own devising. The withdrawal of the *Hufen-Edikt* that they had urged in 1764 was high on their list of gravamens, as it had been in 1778. The *Landtag* had also changed its mind about the expulsion of the Jews from the countryside. By 1785 it had become clear that the relocation had deprived not only Jewish farmers of their livelihood but also many noble landlords of their labor supply and the Christian peasantry of certain indispensable services. It had also compelled the cities to support great numbers of newly impoverished Jews and to tolerate increased competition with Christian merchants. Hence the diet now requested that members of the *Ritterschaft* be allowed to invite individual families back to the countryside.[52]

It was also having serious second thoughts about *Steuerrectification*. In a sense the new cadastre is a metaphor for the essence of Frederician statecraft, replete as it was with its good intentions, its sensitivity to the *Landtag* and each of the groups it represented, and, ultimately, its unfulfilled expectations and unwelcome side effects. No other program embraced as much of the reign and as many components of the ruling elite as did the *Steuerrectification* project. In resuming the undertaking at the behest of the 1764 *Landtag* Frederick had doubled annual spending on rectification in an attempt to satisfy its request that all work be completed before it met again in 1778.[53] Instead the surveys were plagued by lengthy delays. Many districts had to be redone either because of registration errors or because they had been completed so long ago that they were already outdated.[54]

Other, more serious problems had arisen as well. The estates and government had expected that rectification would effect only minor changes in the country's tax obligations. There was indeed little difference in the assessment for the country as a whole. Yet rural areas tended

[51] StAMg, 5)14745: "Desideria … 14, 18, 89, 93, 99" [1785–6]; 5)14746: Desiderium commune XXIIdum, 13 Jan. 1786.

[52] StAMg, 5)14743: "Desideria ulteriora … 6," 15 Apr. 1779 KDK report; 304)580: Desiderium commune XXXI, 3 Mar. 1786. The demographic impact had been greatest in non-*Quart* cities, whose Jewish populations had nearly doubled by 1776. "Von der Judenaufnahme in den hess. cassel. Landen," *HB*, 2 (1785), 292.

[53] StAMg, 304)576: 6 May 1772 minutes of 1772 diet; 304)578, Fasc. III: 24 Dec. 1778 Gen Kriegs Comm extract.

[54] StAMg, 40)19 Generalia 33: 26 Jan. 1777 Wackenitz votum, 304)578, Fasc. III: 23 Dec. 1778 F. W. von Schenck votum, "Histoire des Rectifications-Wesens" [24 Dec. 1778].

toward much higher liabilities and urban areas toward lower ones, reflecting in part the overall demographic and economic trends of the past century and the effects of the Seven Years' War. As a result there were considerable jumps in tax assessment, with some communities being liable for twice the previous amount. The affected communities launched immediate protests and were generally joined by other, unsurveyed communities that feared the same fate.[55] For obvious reasons depressed towns like Marburg continued to press for rectification of the "inequities and injustices" of the outdated cadastre.[56] Nevertheless many of the *Ritterschaft*, which had conscientiously pushed for rectification for a half century because it would be more equitable, now backed off in horror once it was clear that their communities stood to owe more.

By 1778 the government had also lost much of its enthusiasm for the new cadastre. Rectification costs had risen to more than 9,000 taler per year, bringing the overall bill since 1727 to 241,239 taler, "a grievous burden" far out of proportion to the government's original expectations.[57] Given their frustration with the need to correct and update so many districts, many officials in the Tax Office were positively enthusiastic about the prospects of abandoning the whole project. It was with that very idea in mind that Wittorf canvassed the estates when they convened in 1778.[58]

The *Landtag* reluctantly decided to complete the project, thereby setting off a stampede of nervous communities that now volunteered to "assist" in the final surveys. In response, Frederick obligingly transferred a number of officials from other chores, warning them repeatedly that all funding would be irrevocably cut off by the end of 1779, whether they were finished or not.[59] In fact, as the diet met again in 1785, the bill had risen to 293,151 taler, eighty-three districts were still undone, and the Tax Office was estimating that they would be finished "in three years at the most." Amid muted expressions of support for the cadastre's equity, the deputies satisfied themselves with repeated attacks on the

[55]StAMg, 5)3542: 26 Jan. 1778 SK report, 21 May 1778 Reg Cas report; 304)578, Fasc. III: 23 Dec. 1778 Buttlar votum, "Extract ... fortgeführten balance des Rectifications-Ab- und Zu-gangs," Jan. 1779.
[56]StAMg, 304)578, Fasc. III: 3 Jan. 1779 Hombergk petition.
[57]StAMg, 5)14737: 24 Dec. 1778 Gen Kriegs Comm report, 304)578, Fasc. III: 24 Dec. 1778 Christ. von Eschwege votum.
[58]StAMg, 304)578, Fasc. III: 20 Dec. 1778 Kay pro memoria, 12 Dec. 1778 Wittorf proposition.
[59]StAMg, 5)3787 II: 4 Sept., 15 Oct. 1782, 26 Aug. 1783 reports; 5)14737: 8 Dec. 1778 Frederician rescript, 23 Apr. 1779 resolution; 4h)4088: 28 May 1784.

costly delays and raised assessments, claiming that rectification had clearly become "more of a burden than a benefit" to the country.⁶⁰

Throughout the cadastre nightmare, Frederick could console himself with the thought that *Steuerrectification*, like the *Hufen-Edikt* and the expulsion of the Jews, was a mistake that he had made at the behest of his subjects. In most instances the government showed itself willing to adjust to such missteps, periodically revising its approach to address the needs and requests of various segments of the population. Thus, though he died shortly after the estates had convened, his successor effected several changes in course by readmitting the Jews to the countryside, emasculating the *Hufen-Edikt*, phasing out the *Landräte* and *Commissarius Loci*, and eliminating outright the *Zahlenlotto* and the tax farms. On his own initiative he also abruptly discontinued Frederick's industrial policy, thereby completing the conversion to an economic policy based on his ministers' conviction that agriculture was "the only source of true wealth."⁶¹

Yet if the landgrave and his ministers had bent over backward to appease the diet's sensitivities, there was never any noticeable evolution in the arbitrary behavior of those officials who carried out its policies at the local level. Rather there existed in the provinces a certain bureaucratic despotism that was perhaps the most unpopular aspect of the Frederician regime.

Much of this petty tyranny can be blamed on the arbitrary restrictiveness of the mercantilist component of cameralist teaching, as it sought to increase national wealth virtually regardless of the human cost. The siege mentality and sense of competition it inspired vis-à-vis neighboring states impregnated everything with economic significance, often with unfortunate effects on the freedom of individual Hessians and their communities. Thus the government's unwillingness to allow journeymen to spend a *Wanderjahre* studying their craft in other states because they might emigrate or export Hessian money abroad, or its restrictions on foreign study in order to strengthen enrollments at Marburg and Rinteln

⁶⁰StAMg, 73)273: Desiderium commune Xmum, 10 Dec. 1785, 304)578: 5 Jan. 1786 SK report, 304)580: "Extract der General SteuerRectification ... Kosten" [1785], 27 Feb. 1786 pro memoria.
⁶¹StAMg, 5)14746: 30 Mar. 1786 Act Reg Cas. He also ended Cassel's Golden Age by unceremoniously expelling the French and other foreigners from Cassel, and transferring the *Collegium Carolinum*, the anatomical theater, and even the *Accouchir- und Findelhaus* to Marburg.

in their competition with nearby Göttingen. It was this same principle that led the Rinteln *Regierung* to grant an exclusive concession to a group of native musicians who "mit seiner Music das publicum mehr belästigte als belustigte," while banning an excellent troupe from Prague because it feared they would take Hessian money out of the country. The foreigners were ultimately permitted to perform, but only after they had promised the landgrave himself they would spend a lot of their own money in town.[62]

A second contributing factor was the cameralist penchant for efficiency, organization, and uniformity that relentlessly ironed out each of the wrinkles that gave early modern society so much of its distinctiveness. Thus the government methodically sacrificed the autonomy of individual corporations, effectively merging Marburg's Lutheran Metropolitan with Cassel's Consistory, introducing mandatory instruction in German into the country's Huguenot communities, placing the towns under the oversight of numerous crown officials, and regularly overriding the privileges of the universities of Marburg and Rinteln. Through a dozen different *Verzeichnisse* it inventoried every form of life and wealth in Hesse-Cassel. No wonder that the *Landtag* complained that the *Inventarisationen* of deceased poor farmers' wealth was gobbling up most of what was left in probate fees or that the *Landräte* were fining people for filing their *Viehverzeichnis* after the deadline.[63]

Much of the blame can be attributed to that enthusiasm for the government's corrective powers that extended beyond Frederick down to those overzealous local officials whose faith in the efficacy of government constituted the perfect counterpoise to their disdain for the folly of the common people. The protests against officious bureaucrats came from all levels. The towns complained of "constant confrontations" with *Commissarius Loci* who they claimed knew little about local conditions, of Tax Office officials who had arrogated the oversight of their finances, and of *Polizeikommissare* who were forcing local preachers to announce new ordinances from their pulpits on Sundays.[64]

---

[62]StAMg, 5)420: 27 Apr. 1780 mayoral petition and rescript Reg Rinteln, 5)3540: 28 Apr. 1780 petition, 30 June 1780 Frederician resolution.
[63]StAMg, 73)273: Desiderium Commune XXImum, 14 Jan. 1786, 5)14747: Ritterschaftliches Desiderium speciale XIVtum.
[64]StAMg, 5)14747: Desiderium speciale XXImum [1785], 5)14745: entry 73, 5)10015: Kopp to Pol Comm Rinteln, 7 June 1774.

When they were not praising the *Landräte* for their assistance to the peasantry, country districts were remonstrating against them for their constant meddling. The *Ritterschaft* objected to their arbitrary, sometimes uncivil, intercession in seigneurial and manorial matters.[65] The peasants objected to regulations that left no leeway for local conditions or exceptional circumstances, such as fire laws enforced by the *Landräte* that compelled them to petition Cassel before they could put a straw roof on a barn because of a lack of slate.[66] Small towns protested their enforcement of anticrime policies that required maintaining a night watch that cost more than all losses from crime. On occasion even the government was nonplussed by the hyperactive conscience of its *Landräte* and other officials. Such was the case in 1778 when the Schaumburg *Landrat* Wilhelm Werner von Münchhausen pressed for the establishment of a local commission to supervise and enforce the fidelity of all women whose husbands were off fighting in America. The ministry replied curtly that this was not the role of government.[67] By then, however, the conscientiousness of *Landräte* like Münchhausen had generated sufficient ill feeling that the estates had begun to argue that they could no longer justify the 10,000-taler expense of paying their salaries.[68]

Such was the cost of the Hessian variety of enlightened absolutism: limited results, unexpected side effects, the unwelcome intrusion of government into people's lives. But if the Frederician regime sometimes disappointed and frustrated government officials and irritated the people it was designed to help, it also had its strengths. It was unquestionably benevolent in intent, consultative in practice – far more so than the ossified French or radical Austrian models – and reasonably successful in its results. Sufficiently benevolent, consultative, and successful, it would seem that it never discredited itself or alienated its subjects. There is, for example, no evidence to support Karl Wegert's provocative suggestion that the failures and intrusions of "enlightened" governments somehow destabilized them, causing a "crisis of confidence" that helped open the way to popular discontent. Rather *Polizeikommisar* Motz was doubtless

[65]StAMg, 5)14747: Ritterschaftliches Desiderium speciale XIVtum [1785].
[66]StAMg, 17e) Lohra 18: 12 Jan. 1776 petition, 17e) Elnhausen 38: 5 July 1781 Schenck report, 28: 11 Sept. 1784 petition.
[67]StAMg, 5)816: 8 Jan. 1778 report, 10 Feb. 1778 resolution.
[68]StAMg, 5)14743: 22 Mar. 1779 pro memoria.

closer to the truth when he conceded amid all the bad tidings of his January 1784 report that the landgrave's "subjects love our gentle ruler with all their heart."[69]

In fact, the negative reports at the end of the reign can be misleading. To some degree the estates doubtless magnified their accounts of the country's plight in order to minimize their own tax burden. At the very least they were written under the impact of the latest recession in the Hessian economy and were not presented as an overview of the entire reign. Furthermore, if the estates' and bureaucrats' reports tended to stress the shortcomings of government policy, that was because it was their responsibility to tell the landgrave what was wrong and needed correction, just as it was his desire to uncover bad news that prompted him to consult each of them regularly. It was a great strength of the Frederician regime that it sought information about society's and the state's ills and that most of its reforms originated as reactions to specific problems that had been brought to its attention.

Even while they were delivering bad news to Frederick, his officials also had a number of positive developments to report. Motz's otherwise dismal survey demonstrated an appreciation for the government's achievements, especially in the fields of judicial and penal reform, education, and agriculture. In his defense of the landgrave in the European press, Schlieffen had no difficulty enumerating the government's accomplishments in creating colonies, schools, hospitals, the *Accouchir- und Findelhaus*, the Fridericianum with its library and observatories, together with much of Cassel itself. Notwithstanding his ultimate disappointment with Cassel's intellectual ambience, Johannes von Müller could still write to a friend that "the landgrave is extremely kind and full of the best wishes. Many foreigners are unjustified in their judgment. The landgrave's state flourishes."[70]

One must retain a certain amount of skepticism when weighing the testimony of court figures such as Schlieffen or Müller. Nevertheless, in its enthusiasm and unanimity the testimony from Cassel compares favorably with the evaluations of other court observers in Paris, Vienna, or London. Foreign visitors to Hesse-Cassel were no less given to praise. Their journals and travelogues attested to Frederick's accomplishments in promoting economic development, education, and justice ("adminis-

---

[69]Karl H. Wegert, "Patrimonial Rule, Popular Self-Interest, and Jacobinism, 1763–1800," *JMH* 53 (1981) 459, 466; StAMg, 5)13446: 15 Jan. 1784 Motz report.
[70]Schlieffen, *Von den Hessen*, 9–11; Preser, "Verkauften Hessen," 69–70.

tered promptly without regard to a person's station") at the end of the reign, much as they had at the beginning.[71] Foreign academics were no less impressed. From his office in Weimar in 1783 Wieland wrote in his *Deutsche Merkur* that "there are some princes in the world who are richer and more powerful, and broader and fatter like our own [Carl August], but there is certainly none better, more honorable and by whom you will be less harassed and restricted." Though he felt his court in Stuttgart was more glamorous than Cassel's, Duke Charles Eugene had no difficulty conceding during a visit in 1784 that the landgrave himself was "full of good qualities." Goethe was somewhat more charitable, linking Cassel and Stuttgart as the two most outstanding examples of what princes could do for the arts.[72] Certainly Georg Forster appreciated Frederick's contribution in the arts and humanities. When he received word of Frederick's death he wrote to his friend Sömmerring, speaking wistfully of the "old days" in Cassel, of his discussions with the "good old landgrave," and even of the French culture and comedy. With Frederick's death, reflected Forster, "it is all for the better that we are no longer in Cassel."[73]

Aside from the testimony of contemporaries, there is a certain amount of quantitative evidence to support the conclusion that, despite its limits, failures, and costs, the Frederician regime succeeded in improving the quality of life of most Hessians. One indication is the dramatic population increase its agrarian policies helped to sustain – even though increasing crop yields ultimately translated into a greater number of mouths to feed. For the first time even the cities registered modest population gains, at least during the years of the American Revolution. The record of urban economic development is in fact not uniformly dismal, especially if we forget the heights to which the government aspired and remember only the depths from which it came. Even without the stimulation provided by the American Revolution, the increase in textile exports to an annual level of 800,000 taler by 1774 was a considerable accomplishment. Just

[71] *Neue Reisebemerkungen*, 2: 135; Hassencamp, *Reisenden von Pyrmont*, 57–8; Günderode, *Briefe eines Reisenden*.
[72] Vehse, *Deutschen Höfe*, 168; Uhland, *Carl Eugen*, 133; Staatliche Kunstsammlungen Kassel, *Aufklärung & Klassizismus*, 11.
[73] Forster to Sömmerring, 1 Dec. 1785, 19 Mar. 1786, Hettner, *Briefwechsel*, 251, 289, 291. For negative comments it is necessary to rely on the British, hence George III's judgment that "the death of the landgrave of Hesse Cassel certainly cannot be looked upon ... by his country but as a fortunate event"; to Carmarthen, 12 Nov. 1785; A. Aspinall, *The Later Correspondence of George III*, 1 (Cambridge, 1962), 192.

two years after Frederick's death Schlözer would describe the country's textile industry – not its army – as the "Hessian Peru and East Indies."[74]

Nor should we dismiss some of Frederick's own projects, such as the Cassel fair. Although both the *Landtag* and Commerce College were disappointed at the meager number of foreigners it attracted, more than 550 merchants did participate in 1785, representing a steady and appreciable increase over previous years.[75] Similarly, the landgrave's near doubling of the number of industrial firms in Cassel between 1764 (forty-nine) and 1784 (eighty-nine) is not totally negated by the failure of many of them to turn a profit, especially since the shortfall was so easily met from the *Kriegskasse*'s existing cash reserves. Ottfried Dascher informs us that, at the very least, Frederick's decision to recruit foreign entrepreneurs in the 1760s and then replace them with native ones in the 1780s helped to prepare the country for subsequent industrialization.[76]

Aside from the testimony provided by rural population growth, it is much more difficult to present reliable evidence on agricultural advances or on the mood of the Hessian peasantry during Frederick's reign. Statistical evidence is simply unavailable or imprecise. Nor did the peasants themselves leave behind any written indications by which we can judge their fate or their mood. Instead, we are obliged to deduce the overall success of Frederick's policies by the total absence of popular unrest, the common soldier's strong performance in the American Revolution, and the positive observations and judgments of government and foreign officials. It is, however, plausible to assume that, despite the drawbacks of some government programs, many initiatives such as the Fire Insurance Fund, the General Deposit and Assistance Fund, the new health code, the reductions in taxation and labor service, and the new farming techniques promoted by the *Landräte* and the Agrarian Society could have only benefited the Hessian peasant. It is also worth noting that Frederick left his successors with the means to continue all of his programs. Through judicious investment and a few more troop conventions concluded by his successor, the 10-million-taler surplus he had left in the *Kriegskasse* was, by 1805, earning 950,000 taler annually in interest, a sum that matches the level of government expenditure under Frederick.[77]

---

[74]Dascher, *Textilgewerbe*, 1.
[75]StAMg, 5)4039: 13 Oct. 1785 Comm Coll report.
[76]Dascher, *Textilgewerbe*, 111–12; Brunner, *Residenzstadt Cassel*, 290.
[77]Sauer, *Finanzgeschäfte*, 24, 45.

Whereas we can only surmise the landgrave's popularity with the mass of his subjects, two personal developments in the closing years of his reign attest further to his success in earning the esteem of the country's elite. Over a five-month span beginning in October 1782 all three of his sons returned to Cassel for the first time in almost three decades for tearful reunions with their father. Eyewitnesses claim that even the soldiers of the Guards Regiment wept when Frederick awarded his eldest son a generalship in a parade-ground ceremony. The landgrave subsequently admitted the future William IX to the center of the government and even gave him 500,000 taler with which to pay off Hanau's state debt.[78]

The following summer it was the estates' turn to pay homage. For nearly a decade they had been closely supervising the sculpting of the memorial they had voted in 1774. Finally, on the occasion of his sixty-third birthday, on August 14, 1783, they unveiled Johann August Nahl's fifteen-foot-tall marble likeness of the landgrave in the center of the new Friedrichsplatz. The statue was presented in a gala ceremony in the presence of Cassel's magistrates and assembled burgher regiments, the representatives of the government, the universities, and the estates. In making the presentation to a cheering crowd, Baron Riedesel, the hereditary *Erbmarschall* of the Hessian *Ritterschaft*, enumerated Frederick's accomplishments in lowering taxes, promoting education, and reviving commerce and agriculture.[79] Riedesel also might have thanked the landgrave for never seeking repayment of principal or interest on the 20,000-taler loan that had paid for the memorial.[80]

Sustained as it was by *Kriegskasse* funds acquired through the soldier trade, the memorial project symbolized the symbiosis between the estates and a regime that both earned and reaped their praise. It also provides eloquent testimony to the popularity of Frederick's regime as measured against the harshest standards. The late eighteenth century was a period when parliamentary bodies tended to pay homage to their rulers at the beginning of a reign rather than at the end, by which time they were

---

[78]HHStA, RK Berichte 134: 7 Oct. 1785 Trauttmansdorff report; Losch, *Wilhelm I.*, 140–1, 146–7.

[79]Georg Ludwig Riedesel, Freyherrn zu Eisenbach, *Eine Rede bey der Weihung der Ehrensäule Friedrichs des Zweiten* (Cassel, 1783), 4, 7; K. Schwarzkopf, "Die kasseler Chronik des Johann Justus Escherich," *Hessenland*, 21 (1907), 37; Piderit, *Residenzstadt Cassel*, 314–15.

[80]By 1785, 8,400 taler in unpaid interest had accrued on the 3 percent loan. StAMg, 12) Kriegszahlamtsrechnungen, 1785.

often in opposition. The Hessian estates demonstrated their genuine appreciation of Frederick twenty-three years after he had succeeded to the throne in a country alienated by his rejection of his wife and Calvinist faith. His relationship with the estates suggests that what has come to be called enlightened despotism was actually compatible with the privileged classes, so long as it was not too enlightened or too despotic. By consulting with the estates and never threatening existing constitutional arrangements and guarantees he disarmed their deepest suspicions. At the same time he earned their cooperation and often their active participation in devising a comprehensive program of domestic reform, principally by limiting himself to projects that always stopped short of radical change that might threaten vested interests.

It would be wrong if we concluded this study with the judgment that Frederick was somehow an exceptional monarch in anything but circumstances. Rather, he was typical of those rulers of his generation who had been influenced by the spirit of Enlightenment thought. Though he doubtless enjoyed the epithet "philosopher-king" that fills the letters he received from the likes of Voltaire and Madame Gallatin, he was not a creative or critical thinker. But then again, exceptional intelligence was neither a characteristic of nor a prerequisite for the enlightened princes of Frederick's generation. What was far more essential was his ability – with an occasional assist from his ministers – to sense just how far he could go. The only things truly exceptional about the Frederician regime were the circumstances in which it functioned: his minority religion, the enormous wealth he derived from the *Soldatenhandel* that allowed him to fund more (though not necessarily different) reforms than most of his contemporaries, and the cooperation of the estates that stemmed both from the discretion his Catholicism required and the mild fiscal demands his wealth permitted him to make on them.

Though he may have initiated more reforms than most princes, few of them were truly revolutionary or challenged the established structures, values, and nature of the Old Regime. In introducing Enlightenment ideas he merely alloyed them with the existing framework of Hessian society to the extent that they were compatible with it, a process that strengthened rather than undermined the overall structure. Although he attempted to minimize their shortcomings, he never abolished the guilds, the complex system of tithes and labor service, or price controls, even though he recognized their flaws, because he did not wish to do violence to any segment of the population, whether it be the petty bourgeoisie, the land-holding nobility, or the urban poor. It was this intention somehow to serve the interests of all social groups – including the *Ritterschaft*, the peasantry, and the various groups in between – that led him to initiate so many reforms, while preventing him from doing anything radical. The consultative nature of the government helped establish these parameters. Insofar as it did give people a voice by affording them input in the making of policy, his regime – like all representative governments in all ages – mortgaged its ability to make sweeping changes on behalf of greater social justice. Indeed, the Hessian experience under Frederick does little to undermine the notion that no government enjoying an extended period of foreign and domestic peace ever effects radical change.

In large part his reforms were also limited by competing forces such as cameralism. Hence the contemporary cameralist emphasis on population growth led him to grant the country's scarce fallow land to foreign colonists rather than to younger native children whom he had just disinherited in the *Hufen-Edikt*. Though he spent large sums of money on domestic projects, the cameralist emphasis on fiscal integrity led him to create new user taxes to make his projects self-sufficient, rather than continue to fund them from his own extensive cash reserves. If at times it appears that the Frederician regime was greedy, it is worth pointing out that its exaggerated concern for fiscal considerations stemmed not from Frederick's venality or from a uniquely Hessian mentality tied to the soldier trade but from cameralist principles that had taken hold everywhere in Germany. It was, in fact, German cameralism rather than militarism that largely determined the destiny of the Hessian army. It is true that Frederick emulated Prussia in many ways. Yet, unlike Prussia, Hesse-Cassel was not a mercenary army with a state but, rather, a mercenary state with an army.

Other studies have shown that enlightened government elsewhere in Europe was also limited in what it could do to effect basic changes in the nature of the Old Regime. In those instances the prospects for reform were immediately obstructed by the active opposition of conservative forces or by competing military and fiscal needs that received a higher priority at the expense of domestic social and economic programs. The Hessian experience demonstrates that, even when these obstacles did not exist, enlightened absolutism was still doomed to limited results, not because the government was insincere but because established values, institutions, and overall structures precluded real change. Frederick II clearly enjoyed the constitutional and financial means to attempt a lot more than he did. Nevertheless, in launching many expensive remedial programs that alleviated the symptoms of socioeconomic dysfunction, he never resolved the problems themselves. Industrial programs were doomed by an excess of trade barriers and a dearth of markets, domestic or foreign. The attempt to alleviate overpopulation in the countryside through a new *Hufen-Edikt* was without hope of success in the absence of an industrial economy capable of absorbing the excess supply of labor. Rural antipoverty ordinances such as the antiforeclosure law could never do more than mitigate the suffering of a country of tiny farms and poor soil.

Of course, monarchs like Frederick tried nonetheless, cheered on by the leading minds of the Age of Reason. In their optimism, the philosophes and their princely cohorts failed to recognize that natural law had never bestowed on government the ability to change meaningfully existing institutions by planned, rational thought in a fashion simultaneously advantageous to all parts of society.

final thought ⇒
last 2 paragraphs = ending result thesis.

Bibliography

Archival sources

Archives des Affaires Etrangères, Paris
  Correspondance Politique
    Hesse-Cassel
Freiherrlich Riedeselsches Archiv, Lauterbach
  64: Landständische und hessisch Ritterschaftliche Sachen
Gräflich von Bocholtz-Asseburg'sches Archiv, Münster
  A: Akte 668
Haus- Hof- und Staatsarchiv, Vienna
  Reichskanzlei
    Berichte aus dem Reich
    Kleinere Reichsstände
Hessisches Staatsarchiv, Marburg
  4: Politische Akten nach Landgraf Philipp
    a) Fürstliche Personalia
    e) Kaiser, Reichs- und Kreissachen
    f) Staatenabteilung
    h) Kriegssachen
  5: Geheimer Rat
  11: Militärkabinett
    Mass- und Rangierbücher
  12: Kriegsministerium
    Kriegszahlamt
  13: Kriegsrechnungswesen
    Kriegsetat
    Kriegsrechnungen
  17: Landgräflich Hessische Regierung Kassel
    d) Familienrepositur
    e) Ortsreposituren
    II) Herrschaftliche Repositur (1708–1821)
  40 b) Hessische Kammer
     7 Dienstsachen
    19 Zehntsachen
    24 Consistorialia

34 Militaria
36 Zunft- und Manufactur-Sachen
73: Landstände (Acc. 1898/6)
90: Reichsabtei Fulda
Auswärtige Angelegenheiten
93: Reichsabtei Fulda
Militaria
118: Waldeck, Kabinett
304: Stiftsarchiv Kaufungen
340: Familienarchive
H: Handschriften
Murhard'sche Bibliothek der Stadt- und Landesbibliothek, Kassel
8° Ms. Hass. 16ᵃ
The Public Record Office, London
Kew: PRO 30
FO 31
Chancery Lane:
PRO 30
SP 81–87
William L. Clements Library, Ann Arbor
Jungkenn Correspondence

Published sources

STATISTICAL AND PROSOPOGRAPHICAL MATERIAL

Auerbach, Inge, Eckhardt G. Franz, and Otto Fröhlich, eds. *Hessische Truppen im amerikanischen Unabhängigkeitskrieg (HETRINA)*, 1–4 (Marburg, 1974–84).

Buttlar-Elberberg, Rudolf von. *Stammbuch der althessischen Ritterschaft* (Wolfhagen, 1888).

Erler, Georg. *Die jüngere Matrikel der Universität Leipzig 1559–1809*, 3 (Leipzig, 1909).
Die Matrikel der Albertus-Universität zu Königsberg in Preussen, 2–3 (Leipzig, 1911–12).

Frank, Karl Friedrich von. *Standeserhebungen und Gnadenakte für das deutsche Reich und die österreichischen Erblande bis 1806*, 5 vols. (Schloss Senftenegg, 1967–74).

Friedländer, Ernst. *Ältere Universitätsmatrikeln der Universität Frankfurt a. O.*, 2 (Leipzig, 1888).

Fürstlich hessen-casselscher Staats- und Adresskalender, 1–22 (Cassel, 1764–85).

Habicht, Max Eberhard. *Suchbuch für die Marburger Universitäts-Matrikel von 1653–1830* (Darmstadt, 1927).

Hildebrand, Bruno. *Statistische Mitteilungen über die volkswirtschaftlichen Zustände Kurhessens* (Berlin, 1853).

Hintzelmann, Paul, ed. *Die Matrikel der Universität Heidelberg*, 4, 7 (Heidelberg, 1903–16).

Jantke, Fritz. *Matrikel der Martin-Luther-Universität Halle-Wittenberg*, 3 (Halle, 1960).

Keyser, Erich, ed. *Hessisches Städtebuch* (Stuttgart, 1957).

Köhler, Otto. *Die Matrikel der Universität Jena*, 3 (Weimar, 1969–81).

Mundhenke, Herbert. *Die Matrikel der Universität Helmstedt 1685–1810* (Hildesheim, 1979).

Praetorius, Otfried, and Friedrich Knöpp. *Die Matrikel der Universität Giessen*, 2 (Neustadt an der Aisch, 1957).

Reimer, Heinrich, ed. *Historisches Ortslexikon für Kurhessen* (Marburg, 1974).

Selle, Götz von, ed. *Die Matrikel der Georg-August-Universität zu Göttingen, 1734–1837* (Hildesheim, 1937).

Strieder, Friedrich Wilhelm, et al. *Grundlage zu einer hessischen Gelehrten, Schriftsteller und Künstler Geschichte vom 16. Jahrhundert bis auf gegenwärtigen Zeiten*, 21 vols. (Cassel, 1781–1863).

Wagner, Karl. *Register zur Matrikel der Universität Erlangen 1743–1843* (Munich and Leipzig, 1918).

Wiegand, Fritz. *Namenverzeichnis zur allgemeinen Studentenmatrikel der ehemaligen Universität Erfurt für die Zeit von 1637 bis 1816, [Beiträge zur Geschichte der Universität Erfurt (1392–1816), 9–10 (1962–3)]*.

Woringer, August, ed. *Die Studenten der Universität zu Rinteln* (Leipzig, 1939).

CORRESPONDENCE, JOURNALS, AND TRAVELOGUES

Allgemeine deutsche Bibliothek, 49 (Berlin and Stettin, 1782).

Apelblad, Jonas. *Beschreibung seiner Reise durch Ober- und Niedersachsen und Hessen* (Berlin and Leipzig, 1785).

Aspinall, A. *The Later Correspondence of George III*, 1 (Cambridge, 1962).

Bemerkungen eines Reisenden durch Deutschland, Frankreich, England und Holland in Briefen an seine Freunde, 1 (Altenburg, 1775).

Bernoulli, Johann, ed. *Sammlung kurzer Reisebeschreibungen*, 1, 3, 9 (Berlin, 1781–3).

Beschreibung der schönsten Städte der Welt (1572).

Briefe eines iungen Reisenden durch Liefland, Kurland, und Deutschland, 2 (Erlangen, 1777).

Brown, Marvin L., ed. *Baroness von Riedesel and the American Revolution. Journal and Correspondence of a Tour of Duty 1776–1783* (Chapel Hill, 1965).

Büsching, Anton Friedrich. *Neue Erdbeschreibung*, Pt. 3: 1 (Hamburg, 1779).

Curtius, M. C. *Die Geschichte und Statistik der weltlichen kurfürstlichen und altfürstlicher Häuser in Deutschland* (Marburg, 1780).

Dielhelm, Johann Hermann. *Antiquarius der Neckar-Main-Mosel und Lahnströme oder ausführliche Beschreibung dieser vier in den Rheinstrom einfallenden Flüssen*, 1 (Frankfurt, 1781).

Donne, W. Bodham. *The Correspondence of King George the Third with Lord North 1768 to 1783*, 2 vols. (New York, 1971).

Donovan, Frank, ed. *The Benjamin Franklin Papers* (New York, 1962).

Erdmannsdörffer, B., ed. *Politische Correspondenz Karl Friedrichs von Baden 1783–1806*, 1 (Heidelberg, 1888).

Gatterer, Johann Christian, ed., *Allgemeine historische Bibliothek von Mitglieder des königlichen Instituts der historischen Wissenschaften zu Göttingen*, 8 (Halle, 1768).

Göttingische Anzeigen von Gelehrten Sachen, 1 (Göttingen, 1781).

Günderode, Friedrich Justinian Freiherr von. *Briefe eines Reisenden über den gegenwärtigen Zustand von Cassel mit aller Freiheit geschildert* (Frankfurt and Leipzig, 1781).

Halem, G. A. *Blicke auf einem Theil Deutschlands, der Schweiz und Frankreichs bey einer Reise vom Jahre 1790* (Hamburg, 1791).

Hassencamp, Johann Matthias. *Briefe eines Reisenden von Pyrmont* (Frankfurt, 1783).

[Heinzmann, Johann Georg]. *Beobachtungen und Anmerkungen auf Reisen durch Deutschland* (Leipzig, 1788).

Hettner, Hermann, ed.. *Georg Forster's Briefwechsel mit S. Th. Sömmerring* (Brunswick, 1877).

Hubbs, Valentine C., ed. *Hessian Journals: Unpublished Documents of the American Revolution* (Columbia, S.C., 1981).

Krebel, Gottlob Friedrich. *Die vornehmsten europäischen Reisen...* 1 (Hamburg, 1783).

Losch, Philipp. *Zwei kasseler Chroniken des achtzehnten Jahrhunderts* (Cassel, 1904).

Mead, William. *The Grand Tour in the Eighteenth Century* (New York, 1914).

[Merck, Johann Heinrich]. "Über einige Merwürdigkeiten von Cassel," *Der teutsche Merkur* (1780), 216–7.

Moore, John. *A View of Society and Manners in France, Switzerland, and Germany*, 2 (2nd ed.: Dublin, 1780).

Müller, Johannes von. *Sämmtliche Werke*, 16 (Tübingen, 1814).

Neue Reisebemerkungen in und über Deutschland, 2–4 (Halle, 1786–7).

Petersdorff. "Aufzeichnungen des badischen Stadtvikarius Rinck über seine Studienreise in den Jahren 1783 und 1784," *Mitt* (1896), 47.

Pottle, Frederick A. *Boswell on the Grand Tour: Germany and Switzerland 1764* (New York, 1953).

Riesbeck, Baron de. *Voyage en Allemagne*, 3 (Paris, 1788).

Schlözer, A. L. *Briefwechsel meist historischen und politischen Inhalts*, 3 (Göttingen, 1778).

Schmincke, Friedrich Christoph. *Versuch einer genauen und umständlichen Beschreibung der hochfürstlichen-hessischen Residenz- und Hauptstadt Cassel* (Cassel, 1767).

Schwarzkopf, K. "Die kasseler Chronik des Johann Justus Escherich," *Hessenland*, 21 (1907), 13–16, 37–8, 54–5.

[Sneedorf, F.]. *Briefe eines reisenden Dänen, geschrieben im Jahr 1791 und 1792 während seiner Reise durch einen Theil Deutschlands, der Schweiz und Frankreich* (Züllichau, 1793).

Stengel, Edmund. "Ungedruckte Briefe Voltaire's an ... den Landgrafen von Hessen-Kassel nebst Auszügen aus dem Briefwechsel der Madame de Gallatin an den Landgrafen," *Zeitschrift für neufranzösische Sprache und Literatur*, 1 (1879), 7 (1885), 71–96, 173–218.

Uhland, Robert, ed. *Herzog Carl Eugen von Württemberg: Tagebücher seiner Rayssen* (Tübingen, 1968).

Uhlendorf, Bernhard A., ed. *Revolution in America. Confidential Letters and Journals 1776–1784 of Adjutant General Major Baurmeister of the Hessian Forces* (New Brunswick, N.J., 1957).

Willebrandt, Johann Peter. *Historische Berichte und practische Anmerkungen auf Reisen in Deutschland* (Frankfurt and Leipzig, 1758).

PUBLIC AFFAIRS, LITERATURE, AND COMMENTARY

Asseburg, Achatz Ferdinand von der. *Denkwürdigkeiten* (Berlin, 1842).

B——. "Ueber einige Hindernisse, welche einer gänzlichen zwekmäsigen Armen-Verpflegung in teutschen Hauptstädten noch im Wege stehen mögten, und über Mittel sie zu heben," *HB*, 2 (1785).

Bopp, Heinrich Christian Ernst. "Fehler, Missbräuche, und Verbesserungen in Hessen!" handwritten, Murhard'sche Bibliothek, Kassel. 8° Ms. Hass. 16a.

Busch, D. "Ueber den Kaffee," *HB*, 1 (1784).

Canngiesser, Leonhard H. L. G. von. *Collectionis notabiliorum Decisionum supremi tribunalis appellationum Hasso-Cassellani*, 1 (Cassel, 1768).

Casparson, Wilhelm Johann. *Abhandlung von der Verhütung des Bettelns in einer Haupt- und Residenzstadt* (Cassel, 1783).

Aeltern und Vormündern eine Anstalt bekannt, in welcher junge Manns-Personen von Stand und Range sollen erzogen werden (Cassel, 1764).

Kurze Geschichte sämmtlicher hessen-casselischen französischen Colonien vom Jahr 1685 (Cassel, 1785).

"Ueber das schädliche Betteln der sogennanten Passanten oder Vagabunden," *HB*, 1 (1784).

Wie kann der Landmann seine Dorfwege ohne Kosten des Staats und seine eigne Ueberlast zu seinem Nutzen verbessern? (Cassel, 1822).

"Casselische Armenverpflegungs- und Werkhausanstalt," *HB*, 2 (1785).

Casselische Polizey- und Commercien-Zeitung (Cassel, 1760–85).

Dohm, Christian Wilhelm von. *Denkwürdigkeiten meiner Zeit*, 3 (Hanover, 1817).

"Einfälle eines Kameralisten," *HB*, 1–2 (1784–5).

Friedrich II. von Hessen. "Pensées diverses sur les princes," *Hessische Blätter*, 16 (1882).

Fürstenau, [Karl Gottfried]. "Zweifel gegen die Verwandlung der Domainen in Bauergüter," *HB*, 2 (1785).

"In wie weit ist es rathsam, durch die Landpolizei der Veräuserung und Vertheilung der Bauergüter Schranken zu setzen?" *HB*, 2 (1785).

Justi, Johann Heinrich Gottlob von. "Ueber die von den Deisten vorgegebene Unnöthigkeit der christlichen Offenbarungslehre," *HB*, 2 (1785).

Karl, Prinz von Hessen. *Mémoires de mon temps, dictés par S. A. le Landgrave Charles, prince de Hesse* (Copenhagen, 1861).

Knigge, Adolph Freiherr. *Der Roman meines Lebens*, 2 vols. (Liechtenstein, 1978).

Kopp, Ulrich Friedrich. "Von den Landräten," in [G. H.] von Berg, ed., *Hessen-Casselischen teutsches Staatsmagazin* (1796).

Kopp, Ulrich Friedrich, and Carl Friedrich Wittich. *Handbuch zur Kenntnis der hessen-casselischen Landes-Verfassung und Rechte*, 7 vols. (Cassel, 1796–1808).

"Kurze Nachricht von den Beschäftigungen der Gelehrten in Rinteln in einem Schreiben an Herrn ** in Cassel," *HB*, 1 (1784).

"Kurzgefasste Beschreibung des hochfürstlich hessischen Kadettenkorps zu Cassel," *HB*, 2 (1785).

Ledderhose, C. W. *Kleine Schriften*, 1 (Marburg, 1787).

Mauvillon, Jakob. *Das einzige System der christlichen Religion* (Berlin, 1787).

Physiokratische Briefe an den Herrn Professor Dohm (Brunswick, 1780).

Sammlung von Aufsätzen über Gegenstände aus der Staatskunst, Staatswirthschaft und neuesten Staaten Geschichte, 1 (Leipzig, 1776).

Mirabeau, Gabriel Riquetti, comte de. *Avis aux Hessois et autres peuples de l'Allemagne vendus par leurs Princes à l'Angleterre* (Cleves, 1777).

Mönch, K. "Medizinischer Aberglaube," *HB*, 1 (1784).

"Nachricht von der Entstehung, dem Zunehmen und dem jezigen Zustand der Bibliothek bei der Universität zu Marburg," *HB*, 2 (1785).

"Nachricht von der furstl. hessischen Akademie der Malerei- Bildhauer- und Baukunst zu Cassel," *HB*, 1 (1784), 401–12.

"Nachricht von öffentlichen Gesellschaften zu Beförderung der Gelehrsamkeit und Künste in den hess. casselischen Landen," *HB*, 2 (1785).

Neubert, Johann Christian. "Wichtiger Beitrag zu Verbesserung der Feuerlöschungs-Anstalten," *HB*, 1 (1784).

Riedesel, Georg Ludwig von, Freiherr zu Eisenbach. *Eine Rede bey der Weihung der Ehrensäule Friedrichs des Zweiten* (Cassel, 1783).

Empfindungen getreuer Unterthanen für ihren geliebten Fürsten (Cassel, 1783).

Runde, Justus Friedrich. "Über die bürgerliche Verbesserung der Juden," *HB*, 1 (1784).

Sammlung fürstlich hessischer Landesordnungen, 6 (Cassel, 1785).

Schlieffen, Martin Ernst von. *Einige Betreffnisse und Erlebungen*, 1 (Berlin, 1830).

Von den Hessen in Amerika, ihrem Fürsten und den Schreyern (Dessau, 1782).
Schmincke, [Friedrich Christoph]. *Personalia des Landgrafen Friedrich II. von Hessen-Cassel* (Cassel, 1785).
Schneider, Ludwig. "Ueber die Frage: Ist der Vorwurf gegründet, dass der übermäsige Kartoffelbau den Verfall des Ackerbaus und den Ruin der Mühlen nach sich ziehe?" *HB*, 1 (1784).
Schröder, Theodor Wilhelm. "Geschichte einer epidemischen Krankheit, welche Anno 1784. in verschiedenen Gegenden des Hessenlandes grassirt hat," *HB*, 2 (1785).
"Seelenzahl und Häuser einiger hessischen Orten," *HB*, 2 (1785).
"Tabelle von den Getauften, Begrabenen und Geehlichten in der Stadt Cassel, von den Jahren 1765 bis 85," *HB*, 2 (1785).
Tiedemann, Dietrich. "Etwas zur Schande der Menschheit," *HB*, 2 (1785).
"Toleranzfälle aus dem casselischen Nieder-Hessen," *HB*, 2 (1785).
Varnhagen, Johann Adolph Theodor Ludwig. "Versuch einer Beantwortung der Frage: Ist der Vorwurf, dass das übermässige Kartoffelpflanzen den Verfall des Ackerbaues und den Ruin der Mühlen nach sich ziehet, gegründet," *HB*, 1 (1784).
"Vaterlandsliebe; oder das Betragen der gefangenen Hessen in Amerika," *HB*, 1 (1784).
"Von der Judenaufnahme in den hess. cassel. Landen," *HB*, 2 (1785).
Wittorf, Julius Jürgen von. "Kurz gefasste Beschreibung meines Lebenslaufs im dienst der fürstlichen Hauses Hessen-Cassell," StAMg, 340) Wittorf.

Secondary material

Adams, Henry. *The Life of Albert Gallatin* (New York, 1943).
Alden, John R. *The American Revolution, 1775–1783* (New York, 1954).
Allgemeine Deutsche Biographie, 44 vols. (Leipzig, 1875–1900).
Anderson, M. S. *Europe in the Eighteenth Century* (London, 1961).
Aretin, Karl Otmar Freiherr von, ed. *Der aufgeklärte Absolutismus* (Cologne, 1974).
Armbrust, L. *Geschichte der Stadt Melsungen* (Cassel, 1905).
Atwood, Rodney. *The Hessians: Mercenaries from Hessen-Kassel in the American Revolution* (Cambridge, 1980).
Auerbach, Inge. "Marburger im amerikanischen Unabhängigkeitskrieg," *ZHG*, 87 (1978–9), 321–35.
Auerbach, Inge, Niklot Klüssendorf, and Fritz Wolff. *Hessen und die amerikanische Revolution* (Marburg, 1976).
"Aus den Tagen der althessischen Gesellschaft des Ackerbaues," *Hessenland*, 25 (1911), 171–3, 193–5.
Bachmann, Karl. *Geschichte der Kirchenzucht in Kurhessen* (Marburg, 1910).
Bähr, Otto. *Der Hessische Wald: Eine Darstellung der in dem vormaligen Kurfürstentum Hessen am Walde bestehenden Rechtsverhältnisse* (Cassel, 1879).
Balde, Joachim H., and Leopold Biermer. *Medizin in Kassel* (Cassel, 1973).
Baumbach, August von. *Geschichte der zur althessischen Ritterschaft gehörenden Familie von Baumbach* (Marburg, 1886).
Baumbach, Karl von. "Geschichte der Familie von Baumbach-Nentershausen vom 18. Jahrhundert bis zur Mitte des 19. Jahrhunderts," typescript (1948), StAMg, Adelsarchiv.
Becher, Ursula A. J. *Politische Gesellschaft. Studien zur Genese bürgerlicher Öffentlichkeit in Deutschland* (Göttingen, 1978).
Beck, Hanno. "Vulkanisten und Neptunisten in Hessen," *Berichte zur deutschen Landeskunde*, 27 (1961), 87–106.
Berdahl, R. M. "The *Stände* and the Origins of Conservatism in Prussia," *Eighteenth Century Studies*, 6 (1973), 298–321.

Berge, Otto. "Der Ausbau der hessischen Handels- und Verkehrswege nach dem sieben-jährigen Krieg," *Hessische Heimat*, 14 (1964), 30–2.

"Aus der Entstehungsgeschichte der hessischen Friedrichsdörfer," *Hessische Heimat*, 5, N.F. (1955–6), 6–9.

"Beiträge zur Geschichte des Bildungswesens und der Akademien unter Friedrich II.," *HJLG*, 4 (1954), 229–61.

"Die hessische Forstwirtschaft nach dem 7jährigen Krieg," *Hessische Heimat*, 15 (1965), 11–12.

"Die Innenpolitik des Landgrafen Friedrich II. von Hessen-Kassel," Mainz University diss., 1952.

"Kassel, eine Messestadt. Ein handelspolitischer Versuch vor 2000 Jahren," *Hessische Heimat*, 13 (1963), 21–3.

"Wohlfahrtspflege und Medizinalwesen unter Landgraf Friedrich II.," *ZHG*, 65–6 (1954–5), 120–52.

Bing, Hermann. *Finanzgeschichte Waldeck-Pyrmonts von der Wende des 18. Jahrhunderts bis zum Jahre 1929* (Corbach, 1929).

Birn, Raymond. *Crisis, Absolutism, Revolution: Europe 1648–1789/91* (Hinsdale, Ill., 1977).

Blanning, T. C. W. *The French Revolution in Germany* (Oxford, 1983).

Reform and Revolution in Mainz 1743–1803 (Cambridge, 1974).

Bleek, Wilhelm. *Von der Kameralausbildung zum Juristenprivileg. Studium, Prüfung und Ausbildung der höheren Beamten des allgemeinen Verwaltungsdienstes in Deutschland im 18. und 19. Jahrhundert* (Berlin, 1972).

Bluche, François. *Le Despotisme éclairé* (Saint Amand, 1968).

Bödeker, Hans Erich. "Strukturen der Aufklärungsgesellschaft in der Residenzstadt Kassel," in *Mentalitäten und Lebensverhältnisse: Beispiele aus der Sozialgeschichte der Neuzeit; Rudolf Vierhaus zum 60. Geburtstag* (Göttingen, 1982).

Boehlke, Hans-Kurt. *Simon Louis du Ry* (Kassel, 1981).

Böhme, Hans-Georg. *Die Wehrverfassung in Hessen-Kassel im 18. Jahrhundert bis zum siebenjährigen Kriege* (Cassel, 1954).

Borgeaud, Charles. *Histoire de l'université de Genève* (Geneva, 1900).

Both, Wolf von, and Hans Vogel. *Landgraf Friedrich II. von Hessen-Kassel. Ein Fürst der Zopfzeit* (Munich, 1973).

Landgraf Wilhelm VIII. von Hessen-Kassel. Ein Fürst der Rokokozeit (Munich, 1964).

Brandt, Harm-Heinrich. *Die Industrie- und Handelskammer Kassel und ihre Vorläufer 1763–1963* (Cassel, 1963).

Von der fürstlich hessischen Commerzienkammer zur Industrie- und Handelskammer (Cassel, 1960).

Braubach, Max. *Die Bedeutung der Subsidien für die Politik im spanischen Erbfolgekriege* (Bonn and Leipzig, 1923).

Braun, Hans. "Hessische Medizinalverhältnisse im 18. Jahrhundert," *Hessenland*, 17 (1903), 102–4, 126–8, 144–5.

Braun, Hans-Joachim. "Economic Theory and Policy in Germany 1750–1800," *Journal of European Economic History*, 4 (1975), 301–22.

Brauns, C. *Kurhessische Gewerbepolitik im 17. und 18. Jahrhundert* (Leipzig, 1911).

Brauns, E. "Die Agrarpolitik Landgraf Friedrichs II. von Hessen," *Hessische Heimat*, 17 (1967), 82–6.

Brenner, Hans Georg. *Das Geheimnis des Adolph Freiherrn von Knigge* (Hamburg, 1936).

Brocke, Bernhard vom, "Preussen – Land der Schulen nicht nur Kasernen," in Ulrich Scheuner et al. *Preussen eine Herausforderung* (Karlsruhe, 1981), 54–99.

Brockmeier, Peter, Roland Desné, and Jürgen Voss, eds. *Voltaire und Deutschland* (Stuttgart, 1979).

Brunner, Hugo. *Geschichte der Residenzstadt Cassel* (Cassel, 1913).

Kassel im siebenjährigen Kriege (Cassel, 1884).

"Rittergüter und Gutsbezirke im ehemaligen Kurhessen," *Jahrbücher für Nationalökonomie und Statistik*, 115 (1920), 50–62.

Büsch, Otto. *Militärsystem und Sozialleben im alten Preussen 1713–1807* (Berlin, 1962).

Butterfield, Lyman. "Psychological Warfare in 1776: The Jefferson-Franklin Plan to cause Hessian Desertions," *Proceedings of the American Philosophical Society*, 94 (1950), 233–41.

Carsten, F. L. *Princes and Parliaments in Germany from the Fifteenth to the Eighteenth Century* (Oxford, 1959).

Carswell, John. *The Prospector. Being the Life and Times of Rudolf Erich Raspe* (London, 1950).

Cauer, P. "Das ehemalige Blaufarbenwerk Schwarzenfels," *Unsere Heimat*, 20 (1928), 255–9.

"Zwei heimatliche Glashütten des 18. Jahrhunderts," *Unsere Heimat*, 21 (1929), 2–5.

Chisick, Harvey. *The Limits of Reform in the Enlightenment. Attitudes toward the Education of the Lower Classes in Eighteenth-Century France* (Princeton, 1981).

Christern, H. *Deutscher Ständestaat und englischer Parliamentarismus am Ende des 18. Jahrhunderts* (Munich, 1939).

Cobban, Alfred. *In Search of Humanity* (New York, 1960).

Cohn, Abraham. *Beiträge zur Geschichte der Juden in Hessen-Kassel im 17. und 18. Jahrhundert* (Marburg, 1933).

Connelly, Owen. *Napoleon's Satellite Kingdoms* (New York, 1965).

Craig, Gordon A. "Engagement and Neutrality in Germany: The Case of Georg Forster," *JMH*, 41 (1969), 1–16.

Dambacher, Ilsegret. *Christian Wilhelm von Dohm* (Frankfurt, 1974).

Danckelmann. "Die Einschiffung und Überfahrt der hessischen Brigade von Mirbach nach Nordamerika im Jahre 1776," *Mitt* (1881), 1–2.

Darnton, Robert. "In Search of the Enlightenment: Recent Attempts to Create a Social History of Ideas," *JMH*, 43 (1971), 113–32.

Dascher, Ottfried. "Die hessische Handlungskompagnie zu Karlshafen (1771–1789)," *HJLG*, 22 (1972), 229–53.

Das Textilgewerbe in Hessen-Kassel vom 16. bis 19. Jahrhundert (Marburg, 1968).

Delasselle, Claude. "Abandoned Children in Eighteenth-Century Paris," in Robert Forster and Orest Ranum, eds., *Deviants and the Abandoned in French Society* (Baltimore, 1978).

Demandt, Karl E. *Geschichte des Landes Hessen* (Cassel, 1972).

"Die hessischen Landstände im Zeitalter des Frühabsolutismus," *HJLG*, 15 (1965), 38–108.

"Die hessischen Landstände nach dem 30jährigen Krieg," in Dietrich Gerhard, ed., *Ständische Vertretungen in Europa im 17. und 18. Jahrhundert* (Göttingen, 1974), 162–82.

Dersch, Wilhelm. "Beitrag zur Geschichte der Universität Marburg im Zeitalter der Aufklärung," *ZHG*, 54 (1924), 161–203.

Desel, Jochen, and Walter Mogk. *Hugenotten und Waldenser in Hessen-Kassel* (Cassel, 1978).

Dickoré, Marie. *Hessian Soldiers in the American Revolution* (Cincinnati, 1959).

Dippel, Horst. *Germany and the American Revolution 1770–1800* (Chapel Hill, N.C., 1977).

Dorwart, Reinhold. *The Prussian Welfare State before 1740* (Cambridge, Mass., 1971).

Dott, Friedrich. "Ein Zahlenlotto in Kassel, 1771–1785," *Hessische Heimat*, 14 (1964), 22–4.

Dreier, Franz-Adrian. *Glaskunst in Hessen-Kassel* (Cassel, 1969).

Ducret, Siegfried. *Die landgräfliche Porzellanmanufaktur Kassel 1766–1788* (Brunswick, 1960).

Dülfer, Kurt. "Fürst und Verwaltung. Grundzüge der hessischen Verwaltungsgeschichte im 16.–19. Jahrhundert," *HJLG*, 3 (1953), 150–223.

Die Regierung in Kassel, vornehmlich im 19. und 20. Jahrhundert (Cassel, 1960).

Duncker, Albert. "Drei Briefe Rudolf Erich Raspe's an den Landgrafen Friedrich II. von Hessen," *ZHG*, 20, N. F. 10 (1882), 125–50.

Dutcher, George Matthew. "The Enlightened Despotism," *Annual Report of the AHA for the Year 1920*, 189–98.

"Further Considerations on the Origins and Nature of Enlightened Despotism," in *Persecution and Liberty. Essays in Honor of George Lincoln Burr.*

Ebert, Wilhelm. *Die Geschichte der evangelischen Kirche in Kurhessen* (Cassel, 1860).

Eckel, Martin. "Das kasseler Werkhaus 1782–1823," *ZHG*, 75–6 (1964–5), 431–43.

Eckhardt, Albrecht. "Die Gewerbestruktur der Landgrafschaft Hessen-Kassel um 1740," *HJLG*, 15 (1965), 162–216.

Eelking, Max von. *Die deutschen Hülfstruppen im nordamerikanischen Befreiungskriege 1776 bis 1783* (Cassel, 1976).

Eisentraut, G. "Die Herren von Meysenbug," *Hessenland*, 31 (1917), 102–3.

"Hessen zur Zeit des Regierungsantritts Friedrich II.," *Mitt* (1924–6), 37–40.

"Johann Gottfried Seumes Rekrutenzeit 1781/83," *Hessenland*, 24 (1910), 57–60.

"Spiesruten- oder Gassenlaufen," *Hessenland*, 19 (1905), 74–6.

"Über das Leben Friedrichs II.," *Mitt* (1913–14), 88–91.

Engelhardt, Ulrich. "Zum Begriff der Glückseligkeit in der kameralistischen Staatslehre des 18. Jahrhunderts," *Zeitschrift historischer Forschung*, 8 (1981), 37–79.

Engelschall, Josef Friedrich. *Johann Heinrich Tischbein, ehemaliger fürstlich hessischer Rath und Hofmaler als Mensch und Künstler* (Nuremberg, 1797).

Epstein, Klaus. *The Genesis of German Conservatism* (Princeton, 1966).

Fenske, Hans. "International Migration: Germany in the Eighteenth Century," *Central European History*, 13 (1980), 332–47.

Fischer, Joachim. "Eisern Gespartes 1776 bis 1783 aus Amerika," in Hermann Bannasch and Hans-Peter Lachmann, eds., *Aus Geschichte und ihren Hilfswissenschaften. Festschrift für Walter Heinemeyer zum 65. Geburtstag* (Marburg, 1979), 741–56.

Fischl, O. *Der Einfluss der Aufklärungsphilosophie auf die Entwicklung des Strafrechts in Doktrin, Politik und Gesetzgebung* (Darmstadt, 1973).

Flitner, Andreas. *Die politische Erziehung in Deutschland. Geschichte und Probleme 1750–1880* (Tübingen, 1957).

Forst-Battaglia, Otto. *Eine unbekannte Kandidatur auf dem polnischen Thron. Landgraf Friedrich II. von Hessen-Kassel und die Konföderation von Bar* (Bonn, 1922).

Fox, George Thomas. "Studien zur Agrargeschichte Oberhessens 1650–1830," in Arthur E. Imhof, ed., *Historische Demographie als Sozialgeschichte*. 2 vols. (Darmstadt and Marburg, 1975), 2: 1029–35.

"Studies in the Rural History of Upper Hesse, 1650–1830," Vanderbilt University diss., 1976.

Franz, Günther. *Geschichte des deutschen Bauernstandes vom frühen Mittelalter bis zum 19. Jahrhundert*, 2d ed. (Stuttgart, 1970).

Freschi, Marino. *Dall'occultismo alla politica. L'itinerario illuministico di Knigge (1752–1796)* (Naples, 1979).

Friderici, Robert. "Hugenotten in Hessen," *Merian*, 6 (1953), 66–70.

"'Juchheisa nach Amerika.' Haben die hessischen Landgrafen ihre Truppen verkauft?" *Kasseler Post* 22, 23, 29, 30 December 1951.

Fuckel. "Die Beziehungen des bekannten Schriftstellers A. Freiherrn von Knigge," *Mitt* (1917–18), 24.

Führer, Justus. "Ein zeitgenössisches Urtheil über den 'Soldatenhandel' Landgraf Friedrich's II. und seine Würdigung," *Hessenland*, 14 (1900), 5–8, 21–3, 35–7.

Fulbrook, Mary. *Piety and Politics. Religion and the Rise of Absolutism in England, Württemberg and Prussia* (Cambridge, 1983).

"Religion, Revolution and Absolutist Rule in Germany and England," *European Studies Review*, 12 (1982), 301–21.

Fulda, [Karl], and [Jacob] Hoffmeister. *Hessische Zeiten und Persönlichkeiten von 1751 bis 1831* (Marburg, 1876).

Gagliardo, John. *Enlightened Despotism* (New York, 1967).

From Pariah to Patriot. The Changing Image of the German Peasant 1770–1840 (Lexington, Ky., 1969).

Reich and Nation. The Holy Roman Empire as Ideal and Reality, 1763–1806 (Bloomington, Ind., 1980).

Gagnebin, Bernard. *Burlamaqui et le droit naturel* (Geneva, 1944).

Galéra, Karl Siegmar von. *Die Riedesel zu Eisenbach: Geschichte des Geschlechts der Riedesel Freiherren zu Eisenbach, Erbmarschälle zu Hessen*, 5 (Neustadt an der Aisch, 1961).

Gallinger, H. P. *Die Haltung der deutschen Publizistik zu dem amerikanischen Unabhängigkeitskriege, 1775–1783* (Leipzig, 1900).

Ganssauge, Gottfried. "Bauernsiedlungen des Landgrafen Friedrich II.," *Hessische Heimat*, 5 (1939), 17–24.

Gay, Peter. *The Enlightenment: An Interpretation*, 2 vols. (New York, 1967–9).

Gebauer, C. "Auslieferung von Deserteuren im 18. Jahrhundert," *Archiv für Kulturgeschichte*, 2 (1904), 78–83.

Geisel, Karl. "Invaliden in Carlshafen im 18. Jahrhundert," *Hessische Familienkunde*, 6 (1962).

Gerland, W. "Die Tätigkeit der ... hessischen Gesellschaft für Ackerbau und Kunst," *Landwirtschaftliche Jahrbücher*, 59 (1923–4), 245–89.

Gordon, Joseph S. "Georg Forster und die Juden," *Jahrbuch des Instituts für deutsche Geschichte*, 7 (1978), 215–53.

Gross, Hanns. *Empire and Sovereignty. A History of the Public Law Literature in the Holy Roman Empire, 1599–1804* (Chicago and London, 1973).

Grotefend, W. "Die Ergänzung des hessischen Offizierkorps zur Zeit Landgraf Friedrich's II.," *Hessenland*, 14 (1900), 2–4.

"Ein gefälschter Brief," *Hessenland*, 9 (1895), 70–1.

"Der Soldatenhandel in Hessen," *Hessenland*, 14 (1900), 94–6.

Günther, Kurt. "Aus der Geschichte der hessischen Brandversicherungsanstalt," *Ins dritte Jahrhundert. 200 Jahre hessische Brandversicherungsanstalt* (Cassel, 1967).

"Das Truppentagebuch des hessischen Grenadier-Regiments von Bischhausen 1776–1783," *ZHG*, 86 (1976–7), 109–83.

Gundlach, Franz. "Johannes von Müller am landgräflich hessischen und königlich westfälischen Hofe in Cassel," *Jahrbuch für schweizerische Geschichte*, 18 (1893), 161–227.

Haberling, W. *German Medicine* (New York, 1978).

Hallo, Rudolf. "Kasseler Synagogengeschichte," in Hallo, ed., *Geschichte der jüdischen Gemeinde Kassel* (Cassel, 1931), 9–108.

"Rudolf Erich Raspes kasseller Tätigkeit," *Mitt* (1926-7), 46–9.

Hammerstein, Notker. "Die deutschen Universitäten im Zeitalter der Aufklärung," *Zeitschrift für historische Forschung*, 10 (1983), 73–89.

[Hardenberg]. *Ein kleinstaatlicher Minister des achtzehnten Jahrhunderts. Leben und Wirken Friedrich August's, Freiherrn von Hardenberg* (Leipzig, 1877).

Hartenstein. "Wilhelm Dietrich von Wakenitz," *Mitt* (1933–4), 12.

Hartung, Fritz. *Enlightened Despotism* (London, 1957).

"Die Epochen der absoluten Monarchie in der neueren Geschichte," *HZ*, 145 (1932), 46–52.

Hartwig, Theodor. "Instruktion für die Erziehung des Landgrafen Friedrich II.," *ZHG*, 43 (1909), 75–89.

"Mitteilungen aus der Geschichte des Collegium Carolinum in Cassel," *ZHG*, 41 (1908), 68–96.

Harvey, Ray F. *Jean Jacques Burlamaqui. A Liberal Tradition in American Constitutionalism* (Chapel Hill, N.C., 1937).

Hazard, Paul. *European Thought in the Eighteenth Century* (New York, 1963).

Heidelbach, Paul. "Ein Bauernstreik im Amte Bauna," *Mitt* (1907–8), 46–50.

Die Geschichte der Wilhelmshöhe (Leipzig, 1909).

Kassel (Cassel and Basel, 1957).

Heil, Bernhard. *Die wirtschaftliche Entwicklung der Stadt Hersfeld* (Hersfeld, 1924).

Heinemann, Käthe. "Aus der Blütezeit der Medizin am Collegium illustre Carolinum zu Kassel," *ZHG*, 71 (1960), 85–96.

Henderson, W. O. *Studies in the Economic Policy of Frederick the Great* (London, 1963).

Henking, Karl. *Johannes von Müller 1752–1809*, 2 (Stuttgart and Berlin, 1928).

Henseling, Jakob. *Die hessischen von Münchhausen* (Cassel, 1971).

Hensmann, Folkert. *Staat und Absolutismus im Denken der Physiokraten* (Frankfurt, 1976).

Hentsch, Gerhard. *Gewerbeordnung und Emanzipation der Juden in Kurhessen* (Wiesbaden, 1979).

Heppe, Heinrich. *Kirchengeschichte beider Hessen* (Marburg, 1876).

Hermelink, H., and S. A. Kaehler. *Die Philipps-Universität zu Marburg 1527–1927* (Marburg, 1927).

Herrmann, Fritz. *Die Familie Jungkenn* (Oppenheim, 1931).

Hertner, Peter, and George Thomas Fox. "Lebensmittelpreise in Marburg 1764–1830," in Arthur Imhof, ed., *Historische Demographie als Sozialgeschichte*, 2 vols. (Marburg, 1975), 2: 855–917.

Hertzberg, Arthur. *The French Enlightenment and the Jews* (New York, 1968).

Higginbotham, Don. *The War of American Independence* (New York, 1971).

Hildebrand, Erich. "Trenton 1776 – die Schuldfrage in neuer Sicht," *ZHG*, 87 (1978–9), 297–320.

Hoffer, Peter C., and N. E. H. Hull. *Murdering Mothers: Infanticide in England and New England 1558–1803* (New York and London, 1981).

Hoffman, Elliott. "Black Hessians: American Blacks as German Soldiers," *Negro History Bulletin*, 44 (1981), 81–2, 91.

Hoffmann, Jochen. *Jakob Mauvillon. Ein Offizier und Schriftsteller im Zeitalter der bürgerlichen Emanzipationsbewegung* (Berlin, 1981).

[Hopf, Wilhelm]. *Friedrich II. und die neuere Geschichtsschreibung. Ein Beitrag zur Widerlegung der Märchen über angeblichen Soldatenhandel hessischer Fürsten* (Melsungen, 1879).

Die Landesbibliothek Kassel 1580–1930 (Marburg, 1930).

"Soldatenhandel," review in *ZHG*, 59–60 (1934), 277–8.

Hubatsch, Walther. *Frederick the Great of Prussia. Absolutism and Administration* (London, 1973).

Hufton, Olwen. *Europe: Privilege and Protest, 1730–1789* (Ithaca, N.Y., 1980).

Illgner, P. "Zum Soldatenhandel," *Hessenland*, 26 (1912), 60.

Imhof, Arthur E., and Helmut Schumacher. "Todesursachen," in Imhof, ed., *Historische Demographie als Sozialgeschichte*, 2 vols. (Darmstadt and Marburg, 1975), 1: 559–625.

Ingrao, Charles. "'Barbarous Strangers': Hessian State and Society during the American Revolution," *AHR*, 87 (1982), 954-76.

"Enlightened Absolutism and the German States," *JMH*, 58 (1986).

Israel, Friedrich. "Beiträge zur Geschichte der hessischen Auswanderung nach dem Osten," *Hessenland*, 49 (1938), 70–6.

"Die Kriegs- und Domänenkammer Landgraf Friedrichs II. und ihre Wurzeln," *Mitt* (1925–6), 89–90.

Jacob, Bruno. "Die hessische Ritterschaft," *Deutsches Adelsblatt*, 52 (1934), 352–4.

Johnson, Hubert. *Frederick the Great and His Officials* (New Haven, 1975).

Just, Leo. "Der aufgeklärte Absolutismus," *Handbuch der deutschen Geschichte*, 2 (Stuttgart, 1938), 1–126.

"Die Konversion des Erbprinzen Friedrich in Berichten des mainzer Kanonicus Behlen 1754/55," *Jahrbuch für das Bistum Mainz*, 4 (1951), 187–93.

Justi, Karl Wilhelm. *Grundzüge einer Geschichte der Universität zu Marburg* (Marburg, 1827).

Kaiser, Erich. "Nachschub für die hessischen Regimenter in Amerika. Das Rekrutendepot in der Festung Ziegenhain," *ZHG*, 86 (1976-7), 185–200.

Kallweit, Adolf. *Die Freimaurerei in Hessen-Kassel* (Baden-Baden, 1966).

Kapp, Friedrich. "Friedrich II. von Hessen und die neuere Geschichtsschreibung," review in *HZ*, 42 (1879), 304–30.

Der Soldatenhandel deutscher Fürsten nach Amerika (Berlin, 1874).

Kennett, Lee. *The French Armies in the Seven Years' War* (Durham, N.C., 1967).

Kersten, Kurt. *Der Weltumsegler Johann Georg Adam Forster 1754–1794* (Bern, 1957).

Kimpel, Heinrich Theodor. *Geschichte des hessischen Volksschulwesens* (Kassel, 1906).

King, Henry Safford. *Echoes of the American Revolution in German Literature* (Berkeley, 1929).

Kipping, Ernst. *The Hessian View of America* (Monmouth Beach, N.J., 1971).

Die Truppen von Hessen-Kassel im amerikanischen Unabhängigkeitskrieg 1776–1783 (Darmstadt, 1965).

Kitchen, Martin. *A Military History of Germany from the Eighteenth Century to the Present Day* (Bloomington, Ind., 1975).

Klüssendorf, Niklot. "Das Feldgepäck eines hessischen Offiziers aus dem amerikanischen Unabhängigkeitskrieg," *HJLG*, 30 (1980), 265–82.

Koenig, Heinrich. "Althessische Silhouetten," *HJLG* (1854), 5–56.

Kolbe, Wilhelm. *Zur Geschichte der Freimaurerei in Kassel 1766–1824* (Berlin, 1883).

Marburg und der siebenjährige Krieg (Marburg, 1880).

Koser, Reinhold. "Die Abschaffung der Tortur durch Friedrich den Grossen," *Forschungen zur brandenburgischen und preussischen Geschichte*, 6 (1893), 233–9.

Krieger, Leonard. *An Essay on the Theory of Enlightened Despotism* (Chicago, 1975).

The German Idea of Freedom (Chicago, 1972).

Kings and Philosophers 1689–1789 (New York, 1970).

Krüger, Kersten. "Absolutismus und Stadtentwicklung: Kassel im 18. Jahrhundert," *HJLG*, 28 (1978), 191–212.

Krüger-Löwenstein, Uta. "Hessen im siebenjährigen Krieg: Berichte französischer Offiziere," *ZHG*, 87 (1978–9), 269–75.

Die rotenburger Quart (Marburg, 1979).

Krzymowski, Richard. *Geschichte der deutschen Landwirtschaft*, 3d ed. (Berlin, 1961).

Kürschner, Walter. *Geschichte der Stadt Marburg* (Marburg, 1934).

Das Werden des Landes Hessen (Marburg, 1950).

Lefebvre, Georges. "Enlightened Despotism," in Heinz Lubasz, ed., *The Development of the Modern State* (New York, 1964), 48–64.

Lennhoff, Eugen. *Die Freimaurer* (Vienna, 1909).

Lepel, Burkhard von. "Der hessische Finanzminister . . . Wakenitz," *Mein Heimatland*, 12 (1937), 68–9.

Lerch, Hans. *Hessische Agrargeschichte des 17. und 18. Jahrhunderts, insbesondere des Kreises Hersfeld* (Hersfeld, 1926).

L'Héritier, Michel. "Le rôle historique du despotisme éclairé, particulièrement au 18ᵉ siècle," in *Bulletin of the International Committee of Historical Sciences*, 1 (1928), 601–12.

Lichtner, Adolf. *Landesherr und Stände in Hessen-Cassel 1797–1821* (Göttingen, 1913).

Liebel, Helen P. "The Election of Joseph II and the Challenge of Imperial Unity in Germany, 1763–64," *Canadian Journal of History*, 15 (1980), 371–97.

"Enlightened Despotism and the Crisis of Society in Germany," *Enlightenment Essays*, 1 (1970), 151–68.

Lohse, Hans. *600 Jahre schmalkaldener Eisengewinnung und Eisenverarbeitung* (Meiningen, 1965).

Losch, Philipp. *Kurfürst Wilhelm I., Landgraf von Hessen: Ein Fürstenbild aus der Zopfzeit* (Marburg, 1923).

Soldatenhandel (Kassel, 1974).

"Der Uriasbrief des Grafen von Schaumburg. Zur Geschichte der öffentlichen Meinung über den sogennanten Soldatenhandel," *Hessische Chronik*, 2 (1913), 37–40, 82–88, 99–105.

Loss, Carol Rose. "*Status in Statu*: The Concept of Estate in the Organization of German Political Life 1750–1825," Cornell University diss., 1970.

Lotz, Albert. *Geschichte des deutschen Beamtentums* (Berlin, 1909).

Lotz, W. "Armenwesen und Armengesetzgebung im vormaligen Kurfürstenthum Hessen," in A. Emminghaus, ed., *Das Armenwesen und die Armengesetzgebung in den europäischen Staaten* (Berlin, 1870), 134–40.

Lowell, Edward Jackson. *The Hessians and the Other German Auxiliaries of Great Britain in the Revolutionary War* (New York, 1884).

M., F. W. "Schreiben eines englischen Werbeoffiziers aus dem Jahre 1780," *Hessenland*, 17 (1903), 82–3.

McClelland, Charles E. *State, Society, and University in Germany 1700–1914* (Cambridge, 1980).

Mack, Rüdiger. "Juden an den hessischen Hochschulen im 18. Jahrhundert," in *Neunhundert Jahre Geschichte der Juden in Hessen* (Wiesbaden, 1983) [*Schriften der Kommission für die Geschichte der Juden in Hessen*, 6], 263–302.

Manheim, Ernst. *Aufklärung und öffentliche Meinung* (Stuttgart, 1979).

Martin, James Kirby, and Mark Edward Lender. *A Respectable Army: The Military Origins of the Republic, 1763–1789* (Arlington Heights, Ill., 1982).

Maurer, Wilhelm. *Aufklärung, Idealismus und Restauration. Studien zur Kirchen- und Geistesgeschichte in besonderer Beziehung auf Kurhessen 1780–1850* (Giessen, 1930).

"Kirchliches Leben in Hessen-Kassel zur Zeit der ausgehenden Aufklärung," *Mitt* (1926–7), 53–4.

Melton, James Van Horn. "From Enlightenment to Revolution: Hertzberg, Schlözer, and the Problem of Despotism in the Late Aufklärung," *Central European History*, 12 (1979), 103–23.

Metz, H. "Die Juden in Hessen," *Hessenland*, 10 (1896), 61–3, 73–5, 89–90, 104–6.

Metz, Wolfgang. "Das Eindringen des Bürgertums in die hessischen Zentralverwaltung," Göttingen University diss., 1947.

"Zur Sozialgeschichte des Beamtentums in der Zentralverwaltung der Landgrafschaft Hessen-Kassel bis zum 18. Jahrhundert," *ZHG*, 67 (1956), 138–48.

Möker, Ulrich. *Entwicklungstheorie und geschichtliche Wirtschaft. Makroökonomische Erklärungen wirtschaftlicher Zustände und Entwicklungen der Landgrafschaft Hessen-Kassel vom 16. bis zum 19. Jahrhundert* (Marburg, 1971).

Nordhessen im Zeitalter der Industriellen Revolution (Vienna and Cologne, 1977).

Morazé, Charles. "Finance et despotisme, essai sur les despotes éclairés," *Annales Économies, Sociétés, Civilisations*, 3 (1948), 279–96.

Mousnier, Roland. *Histoire générale des civilisations*, 5: *Le xviiie siècle* (Paris, 1953).

"Quelques problèmes concernant le monarchie absolue," in *Relazioni del x° congresso internazionale di scienze storiche*, 4: *Storia moderna* (Florence, 1955).

Müller, Gerhard. "Theologie in Marburg zwischen Aufklärung und Restauration," *Jahrbuch des hessischen kirchengeschichtlichen Vereins*, 28 (1977), 27–41.

Münscher, Friedrich. *Geschichte von Hessen* (Marburg, 1894).

"Lebensbilder von Marburger Professoren. Karl Wilhelm Robert," *Hessenland*, 3 (1889), 113–4.

Muhlack, Ulrich. "Physiokratie und Absolutismus in Frankreich und Deutschland," *Zeitschrift historischer Forschung*, 9 (1982), 15–46.

Neuber, N. "Über das Landkrankenhaus zu Bettenhausen," *Mitt* (1898), 45–6.

Neuhaus, Wilhelm. *Geschichte von Hersfeld* (Hersfeld, 1927).

Nisbet, H. B. "'Was ist Aufklärung': The Concept of Enlightenment in Eighteenth-Century Germany," *Journal of European Studies*, 12 (1982), 77–95.

Nuhn, Helmut. *Industrie im hessischen Hinterland* (Marburg, 1965).

Oestreich, Gerhard. "Zur Heeresverfassung der deutschen Territorien von 1500 bis 1800," *Forschungen zu Staat und Verfassung. Festgabe für Fritz Hartung* (Berlin, 1958), 419–39.

Oeynhausen, Julius Graf von. *Geschichte des Geschlechts von Oeynhausen* (Paderborn, 1870).

Paetow, Karl. *Klassizismus und Romantik auf Wilhelmshöhe* (Cassel, 1929).

Palmer, Robert R. *The Age of the Democratic Revolution: A Political History of Europe and America, 1760–1800*, 2 vols. (Princeton, 1959–64), 1.

Pappenheim, Gustav Freiherr Rabe von. "Aus der Studienzeit eines hessischen Edelmannes in den Jahren 1767–1770," *Hessenland*, 19 (1905), 267–84.

Payne, Harry C. *The Philosophes and the People* (New Haven and London, 1976).

Pedlow, Gregory Wick. "The Nobility of Hesse-Kassel: Family, Land, and Office, 1770–1870," Johns Hopkins University diss., 1979.

Peitsch, Helmut. *Georg Forsters "Ansichten vom Niederrhein." Zum Problem des Übergangs vom bürgerlichen Humanismus zum revolutionären Demokratismus* (Frankfurt, 1978).

Peter, Marc. *Une Amie de Voltaire. Madame Gallatin* (Lausanne, 1925).

Pfaff, Friedrich. *Geschichte der Stadt Hofgeismar* (Hofgeismar, 1954).

Pfeiffer, D. B. W. *Geschichte der landständischen Verfassung in Kurhessen* (Cassel, 1834).

Pfister, Ferdinand von. "Friedrich II. und die neuere Geschichts-Schreibung," *Mitt* (1898), 29–30.

Landgraf Friedrich II. und sein Hessen (Cassel, 1879).

"Über die Heerverfassung hessischer Soldaten im nordamerikanischen Unabhängigkeits-Kriege," *ZHG*, 10 (1865), 361–73.

Philippi, Hans. *Landgraf Karl von Hessen-Kassel. Ein deutscher Fürst der Barockzeit* (Marburg, 1976).

Landgraf Karl von Hessen-Kassel 1654–1730 (Marburg, 1980).

"Zur diplomatischen Vorgeschichte der Erhebung des Landgrafen von Hessen-Kassel zum Kurfürsten," *ZHG*, 84 (1974), 11–19.

Piderit, Franz. *Denkwürdigkeiten von Hersfeld* (Hersfeld, 1829).

Geschichte der Grafschaft Schaumburg (Rinteln, 1831).

Geschichte der Haupt- und Residenz-stadt Cassel (Cassel, 1882).

Geschichte der hessisch-schaumburgischen Universität Rinteln (Marburg, 1842).

Pistor. "Die hessische Gesellschaft des Ackerbaues und der Künste," *Mitt* (1898), 58.

Plumpe, Gottfried. "Anfänge der deutschen Versicherungswirtschaft. Die hessische Brandversicherungsanstalt 1767–1885," *HJLG*, 31 (1981), 149–84.

Porter, Roy, and Mikulas Teich, eds. *The Enlightenment in National Context* (Cambridge, 1981).

Preser, Carl. *Der Soldatenhandel in Hessen. Versuch einer Abrechnung* (Marburg, 1900).

"Über die angeblich nach Amerika verkauften Hessen," *Hessenland*, 2 (1888), 4–7, 24–7, 36–8, 50–2, 68–70; 3 (1889), 22–5; 11 (1897), 161–3.

Priebatsch, Felix. "Die Judenpolitik des fürstlichen Absolutismus im 17. und 18. Jahrhundert," in *Forschungen und Versuche zur Geschichte des Mittelalters und der Neuzeit* (Jena, 1915), 564–651.

Prince, Carl E. *The Federalists and the Origins of the U.S. Civil Service* (New York, 1977).

Raeff, Marc. *The Well-Ordered Police State. Social and Institutional Change through Law in the Germanies and Russia 1600–1800* (New Haven and London, 1983).

"The Well-Ordered Police State and the Development of Modernity in Seventeenth- and Eighteenth-Century Europe: An Attempt at a Comparative Approach," *AHR*, 80 (1975), 1221–43.

Redlich, Fritz. *The German Military Enterpriser and His Work Force*, 2 vols. [*Vierteljahrschrift für Sozial- und Wirtschaftsgeschichte*, 48 (1965)], 2.

Reininghaus, Wilfried. "Vereinigungen der Handwerksgesellen in Hessen-Kassel vom 16. bis zum frühen 19. Jahrhundert," *HJLG*, 31 (1981), 97–148.

Renouard, C. *Geschichte des Krieges in Hannover, Hessen und Westfalen von 1757 bis 1763*, 3 vols. (Cassel, 1863–4).

Rogge-Ludwig, Wilhelm. "Landgräfin Maria von Hessen," *Hessenland*, 4 (1890), 297–9, 307–9.

Roscher, Wilhelm. *Geschichte der National-Oekonomik in Deutschland* (Munich, 1874).

Rosenfeld, Felix. "Ein Diplomat des 18. Jahrhunderts in hessischen Diensten," *Mitt* (1913–14), 115–17.

"Geheime Kanzleien und Kabinett in Hessen-Kassel," *ZHG*, 51, N. F. 41 (1917), 117–48.

"Landgraf Friedrich II. von Hessen-Cassel und die Herrenhüter," *Mitt* (1912–13), 81.

Rosengarten, Joseph George. "A Defense of the Hessians," *The Pennsylvania Magazine of History and Biography*, 23 (1899), 157–83.

"Die hessischen Gefangenen im nordamerikanischen Freiheitskrieg," *Hessenland*, 5 (1891), 63–6.

Rudloff, Hans L. "Beiträge zur Geschichte der Bauernbefreiung und bäuerlichen Grundentlastung in Kurhessen," *Jahrbücher für Nationalökonomie und Statistik*, 105 (1915), 802–10.

"Die gutsherrlich-bäuerlich Verhältnisse in Kurhessen," *Schmollers Jahrbuch*, 41 (1917), 111–47.

Ruhl, S. L. *Einiges vom Hof Landgraf Friedrich's von Hessen* (Melsungen, 1884).

Sakai, Eihachiro. *Der kurhessische Bauer im 19. Jahrhundert und die Grundlastenablösung* (Melsungen, 1967).

Sauer, Josef. *Finanzgeschäfte der Landgrafen von Hessen-Kassel* (Fulda, 1930).

Savory, Reginald. *His Britannic Majesty's Army in Germany during the Seven Years War* (Oxford, 1966).

Schade, Maria. *Eine Fürstin. Maria von Hessen, geborene Prinzessen von England* (Königsberg, 1926).

Schelenz, Hermann. "Kassel, Goethe, und die Luftschiffahrt," *Hessenland*, 25 (1911), 1–3, 20–2.

"Über das kasseler Collegium Carolinum," *Hessenland*, 18 (1904), 78–80.

Scherer, Carl. "Dietrich Wilhelm von Wakenitz in hessischen Diensten," *Hessenland*, 5 (1891), 247–8.

"Erbprinz Friedrich von Hessen-Kassel und Pfarrer Valentin Fuchs von Rasdorf," *Fuldaer Geschichtsblätter*, 7 (1908), 1–26, 37–57, 71–7.

"Die landgräflichen Menagerien in und um Kassel," *Mitt* (1890), 6–11.

"Martin Ernst von Schlieffen, sein Leben und sein Verhältniss zur Sprachreinigung," *Hessenland*, 5 (1891), 222–3, 238–40, 254–6, 270–1, 282–3.

Schib, Karl. *Johannes von Müller 1752–1809* (Constance, 1967).

Schmidt, Eberhard. *Einführung in die Geschichte der deutschen Strafrechts-Pflege*, 3d ed. (Göttingen, 1965).

Schmidt, H. D., "The Hessian Mercenaries: The Career of a Political Cliché," *History*, 43 (1958), 207–12.

Schmidt, Jürgen. *Melsungen. Die Geschichte einer Stadt* (Melsungen, 1978).

Schmidtmann, Rudolf. "Die Kolonien der Réfugiés in Hessen-Kassel und ihre wirtschaftliche Entwicklung im 17. und 18. Jahrhundert," Marburg University diss., 1928.

Schmincke, Julius L. *Geschichte der Stadt Eschwege* (Eschwege, 1922).

Schmitz, Rudolf. *Die Naturwissenschaften an der Philipps-Universität Marburg 1527–1977* (Marburg, 1978).

Schormann, Gerhard. *Academia Ernestina. Die schaumburgische Universität zu Rinteln an der Weser (1610/21–1810)* (Marburg, 1982).

Schröder, Edward. "Goethes Beziehungen zu Kassel und zu hessischen Persönlichkeiten," *ZHG*, 52 (1919), 21–36.

Schulz, Hermann. *Das System und die Prinzipien der Einkünfte im werdenden Staat der Neuzeit (1600–1835)* (Berlin, 1982).

Scott, Hamish M. "Whatever [*sic*] Happened to the Enlightened Despots?" *History*, 68 (1983), 245–57.

Seier, Hellmut. "Zur Entstehung und Bedeutung der kurhessischen Verfassung von 1831," in Walter Heinemeyer, ed., *Der Verfassungsstaat als Bürge des Rechtsfriedens* (Marburg, 1982), 5–71.

Selle, Götz von. *Die Georg-August-Universität zu Göttingen 1737–1937* (Göttingen, 1937).

Shy, John. *A People Numerous and Armed* (Oxford, 1976).

Sieber, Eduard. *Die Idee des Kleinstaates bei den Denkern des 18. Jahrhunderts in Frankreich und Deutschland* (Freiburg, 1920).

Small, Albion W. *The Cameralists. The Pioneers of German Social Polity* (Chicago and London, 1909).

"Soldatenhandel," *Mitt* (1898), 29.

Soliday, Gerald L. "Städtische Führungsschichten in Marburg, 1560–1800," *Marburger Geschichte* (Marburg, 1980), 345–52.

Speier, Hans. "Militarism in the Eighteenth Century," *Social Research*, 3 (1936), 304–36.

Staatliche Kunstsammlungen Kassel. *Aufklärung & Klassizismus in Hessen-Kassel unter Landgraf Friedrich II. 1760–1785* (Kassel, 1979).

Staehly, Axel. "Der hessische Bauer im 17. und 18. Jahrhundert," *Hessenland*, 41 (1930), 372–3.

Stein, Karl. "Das Waisenhaus in Kassel von seiner Entstehung bis zum Ende der kurhessischen Herrschaft 1690–1866," Frankfurt University diss., 1923.

Stern, Selma. *Preussische Staat und die Juden*, 1 (Tübingen, 1971).

Stoeffler, F. Ernst. *German Pietism during the Eighteenth Century* (Brill, 1973).

Stoff, Leopold M. E. *Die Katholiken in Kassel* (Cassel, 1899).

Strieder, Friedrich Wilhelm, et al. *Grundlage zu einer hessischen Gelehrten, Schriftsteller und Künstler Geschichte vom 16. Jahrhundert bis auf gegenwärtigen Zeiten*, 21 vols. (Cassel, 1781–1863).

Stutzer, D. "Das preussische Heer und seine Finanzierung in zeitgenössischer Darstellung," *Militärgeschichtliche Mitteilungen*, 24 (1978), 23–47.

Taylor, Paul, and Hermann Rebel. "Hessian Peasant Women, Their Families and the Draft: A Social-Historical Interpretation of Four Tales from the Grimm Collection," *Journal of Family History*, 6 (1981), 347–78.

Thielen, Peter Gerret. *Karl August von Hardenberg, 1750–1822* (Cologne and Berlin, 1967).

Thierfelder, Hildegard. "Die rintelner Professoren der Ökonomie Johann Hermann Fürstenau und Philipp Georg Schröder," *Schaumburg-Lippische Mitteilungen*, 24 (1978), 91–104.

Treitschke, Heinrich von. *Das neunzehnte Jahrhundert*, 3 (Leipzig, 1889).

Tribe, Keith. "Cameralism and the Science of Government," *JMH*, 56 (1984), 263–84.

Uhlhorn, G. *Die christliche Liebesthätigkeit*, 3 (Stuttgart, 1890).

Ulbricht, G. "Einige Materialen zur Geschichte der Realschule im Zeitalter der Aufklärung," *Jahrbuch der Erziehungs- und Schulgeschichte*, 13 (1973), 249–65.

Vann, James Allen. *The Making of a State: Württemberg, 1593–1793* (Ithaca, N.Y., 1984).

Vehse, Eduard. *Badische und hessische Hofgeschichten* (Munich, 1922). *Geschichte der deutschen Höfe*, 27 (Hamburg, 1853).

Vesper, Willi. "Die Gründung von Friedrichsthal," *Heimatsjahrbilder für den Kreis Hofgeismar* (1962), 77–81.

Vierhaus, Rudolf. "Deutschland im 18. Jahrhundert," in Franklin Kopitsch, ed., *Aufklärung, Absolutismus, und Bürgertum in Deutschland* (Munich, 1976), 173–91. "Die Landstände in Nordwestdeutschland im späten 18. Jahrhundert," in Dietrich Gerhard, ed., *Ständische Vertretungen in Europa im 17. und 18. Jahrhundert* (Göttingen, 1974). "Montesquieu in Deutschland. Zur Geschichte seiner Wirkung als politischer Schriftsteller im 18. Jahrhundert," *Collegium philosophicum. Studien Joachim Ritter zum 60. Geburtstag* (Basel and Stuttgart, 1965), 403–37.

Volm, Matthew M. *The Hessian Prisoners in the American War of Independence and Their Life in Captivity* (Charlottesville, Va., 1937).

Volz, Gustav Berthold. "Prinzessin Philippine von Schwedt," *Hohenzollern-Jahrbuch*, 15 (1911), 287–90.

W——, von. "Rekrutierung and Werbung unter Landgraf Friedrich II.," *Hessenland*, 13 (1899), 315–18. "Vom höheren Unterrichtswesen in Hessen unter Landgraf Friedrich II. (1760–1785)," *Hessenland*, 13 (1899), 202–4.

Wagner, Walter. *Hessen-Kassel und der Fürstenbund vom Jahr 1785* (Darmstadt, 1932).

Walder, Ernst. "Zwei Studien über den aufgeklärten Absolutismus," *Schweizer Beiträge zur allgemeinen Geschichte*, 15 (1957), 134–71.

Walker, Mack. *German Home Towns: Community, State, and General Estate, 1648–1871* (Ithaca, N.Y., 1971).

Johann Jakob Moser and the Holy Roman Empire of the German Nation (Chapel Hill, N.C. 1981).

"Rights and Functions: The Social Categories of Eighteenth-Century German Jurists and Cameralists," *JMH*, 50 (1978), 234–51.

Wangermann, Ernst. *From Joseph II to the Jacobin Trials* (Oxford, 1969).

Warren, Mercy Otis. *History of the Rise, Progress and Termination of the American Revolution*, 1 (Boston, 1805).

Wegert, Karl H. "Patrimonial Rule, Popular Self-Interest, and Jacobinism, 1763–1800," *JMH*, 53 (1981), 440–67.

Wegner, Karl-Hermann. "Gründung und Einrichtung des Museums Fridericianum in Kassel. Seine Bedeutung für die Kulturgeschichte der Aufklärung," *Hessische Heimat*, 27 (1977), 154–64.

Weis, Eberhard. "Absolute Monarchie und Reform im Deutschland des späten 18. und des frühen 19. Jahrhunderts," in *Geschichte in der Gesellschaft. Festschrift für Karl Bosl* (Stuttgart, 1974), 436–61.

Montgelas 1759–1799. Zwischen Reform und Revolution (Munich, 1971).

Weisser, Michael R. *Crime and Punishment in Early Modern Europe* (Atlantic Highlands, N.J., 1979).

Wepler, Emilie. "Zum hundertjährigen Todestage des Landgrafen Friedrich II. von Hessen-Kassel," *Hessische Blätter*, 17 (31 Oct. 1885).

Whaley, Joachim. "The Protestant Enlightenment in Germany," in Roy Porter and Mikulas Teich, eds., *The Enlightenment in National Context* (Cambridge, 1981), 106–17.

Wiesloch, Friedrich Henkel zu. "Die von Donop in hessischen Diensten," *Hessenland*, 6 (1892), 247–50.

Woelfel, Margaret. "Memoir's [*sic*] of a Hessian Conscript: J. G. Seumes [*sic*] Reluctant Voyage to America," *William & Mary Quarterly*, 5 (1948), 553–70.

Wolff, Fritz. "Absolutismus und Aufklärung in Hessen-Kassel 1730–1806," in Uwe Schulz, ed., *Die Geschichte Hessens* (Stuttgart, 1983).

Wolff, Wilhelm. *Die Entwicklung des Unterrichtwesens in Hessen-Kassel vom 8. bis zum 19. Jahrhundert* (Cassel, 1911).

Wolff-Cassel, Louis. *Entstehung und Anfänge der Kolonie Friedrichsfeld in Hessen (1775)* (Cassel, 1912).

Woloch, Isser. *Eighteenth-Century Europe. Tradition and Progress, 1715–1789* (New York, 1982).

Woringer, August. "Das kasseler Lotto 1771–1785," *ZHG*, 47 (1914), 17–47; 48 (1915), 215; 54 (1924), 231–3.

"Martin Ernst von Schlieffen und Windhausen," *Hessenland*, 35 (1921), 145–7.

"Zoll und Schmuggel in Hessen im 18. und 19. Jahrhundert," *Hessenland*, 20 (1906), 46–8, 62–5, 80–3, 90–3.

Zedler, Gottfried. *Geschichte der Universitäts-Bibliothek Marburg* (Marburg, 1896).

Zögner, Lothar. *Hugenottendörfer in Nordhessen* (Marburg, 1966).

Zwenger, F. "Hessische Städte und hessisches Land vor 100 Jahren," *Hessenland*, 8 (1894), 60–1, 104–6.

Index